THE WORM FORGIVES THE PLOUGH

John Stewart Collis was born in 1900 of an Irish
family. He was educated at Rugby School and
Balliol College, Oxford. Among his publications
are *Shaw* (1925), *The Sounding Cataract* (1936),
Down to Earth (1947), which won the Heinemann
Foundation Award, *The Life of Tolstoy* (1969),
The Vision of Glory (1973), *Christopher Columbus*
(1976) and *Living with a Stranger: A discourse on
the human body* (1976). He also contributed to
The Genius of Bernard Shaw (1976: ed Holroyd).
John Stewart Collis died in 1984.

JOHN STEWART COLLIS

THE WORM FORGIVES
THE PLOUGH

The cut worm forgives the plough
– William Blake, *Proverbs of Hell*

PENGUIN BOOKS

Penguin Books Ltd, Harmondsworth, Middlesex, England
Viking Penguin Inc., 40 West 23rd Street, New York, New York 10010, U.S.A.
Penguin Books Australia Ltd, Ringwood, Victoria, Australia
Penguin Books Canada Limited, 2801 John Street, Markham, Ontario, Canada L3R 1B4
Penguin Books (N.Z.) Ltd, 182–190 Wairau Road, Auckland 10, New Zealand

—

First published by Charles Knight 1973
Published in Penguin Books 1975
Reprinted 1976, 1982, 1986

—

—

Set, printed and bound in Great Britain by
Cox & Wyman Ltd, Reading
Set in Intertype Times

CONTENTS

BOOK I: WHILE FOLLOWING
THE PLOUGH

CONTENTS

CONTENTS

BOOK II: DOWN TO EARTH

PART ONE: DOWN TO EARTH

PART TWO: THE WOOD

CONTENTS

BOOK I
WHILE FOLLOWING THE PLOUGH

PREFACE

'What made you go and work on the land?' I have so frequently
been asked the question that perhaps an answer should be attempted. When a reason is completely obvious to oneself it is
often difficult to explain it. Since 'because I very much wanted
to' will not serve, I must be more explicit. While not refusing
the term 'an intellectual' as applied to myself, since I believe
in the Mind more than in anything else, I had hitherto regarded
the world too much from the outside, and I wished to become
more involved in it. The war gave me the opportunity. The
previous war had left me as an Honorary Lieutenant in the
Irish Guards, for it had stopped when I was at an Officer Cadet
Battalion, and in 1940 I was offered an Army post. Since it was
clear to me that I would be given some home job for which
I should be entirely unfitted, I asked to be excused in favour
of agriculture. This granted, I gained the opportunity of becoming thoroughly implicated in the fields instead of being
merely a spectator of them.

I worked at this for nearly six years, a period which included
much forestry, though I have not written of that experience in
this volume. For the sake of unity I have restricted my narrative within given periods of time. My approach is one of
genuine ignorance, and I have described many operations and
implements as if the reader were as fresh to them as I was.
Hence there is no instruction in this book; and I fear that my
views tend to be as inconsistent as my moods, for my chief aim
has been to present my physical and mental reactions regardless
of their consistency, and to give a truthful picture of what I
found in the agricultural world.

JOHN STEWART COLLIS

This book was written just before both the corn-rick and the

11

hay-rick were deemed unnecessary by modern methods. The change of scene followed rather swiftly. Thus this book is about the last of its kind that can now be written in England.

J.S.C., 1973

PART ONE
A FARM IN SOUTH-EAST ENGLAND

1. My First Job

It was 16 April 1940. I could find no lodging close to the farm, but a friend did me the great service of putting me up at her cottage which was about thirty-five minutes' bicycle-ride distance. This meant rising in time to shave, breakfast, sandwich food for the day, and be ready to start out by six-thirty. I had always wanted something to force me up at this hour, this unsmirched hour of promise and of hope; and now I stepped out into a clear morning, with frost laid across the whole land, the air biting, and the hollows clouded. I arrived at the farm punctually, trying not to feel nervous and like a new boy at school. I gave up shyness some time ago when I realized that it was a form of self-consciousness and conceit, as well as being, like bad manners, a sign of ignorance of human nature; but to turn up into a completely new milieu – and not looking the part in person or clothes – to meet employers and employees and do something I had never done before, certainly made me apprehensive.

The foreman came out and shook hands and we walked across the farm towards some job that had been arranged for me. He was about thirty, non-rustic in appearance, quiet, accentless, pleasant, and exceedingly grave. We walked past some acres of fruit trees, for it was more than half a fruit farm, till we arrived at some ranks of apple trees. Their branches had been cut off and a new kind had evidently been grafted. My job consisted of dragging away and piling up the branches that lay on the ground.

The foreman went off and I was left alone at this my first job on the land. It was not very inspiring, but it was at least foolproof. I worked on for what I felt to be a very long time – nine hours to be exact, with one break, before the day was done. Already I began to ask at intervals what I discovered later is quite a famous question amongst agricultural labourers – *what is the time?* And after a few hours I began to feel lonely. This was a new experience and foreign to me; for complete isolation with a book is Solitude, a blessed state; but isolation with physical labour can be Loneliness, a very different thing. In the distance I could hear the chug of a machine (it was the spraying engine), a most welcome and important noise. I should have liked to get closer to it. Funny, I thought, that in the first few hours of labour on the land I should welcome the sound and long for the sight of a piece of machinery!

I had plenty of time to examine the grafting. Attached to the stumps where the branches had been cut off, were twigs about the size of a short pencil. Each was attached in a highly skilled manner, as if glued on by some black substance, and tied round with thread. The foreman told me that these apple trees were cookers and would require too much sugar to sell at a profit, so they were putting a sweeter apple on to the trees. I knew nothing whatever about grafting, and it surprised me that this could be done, now that I saw it in front of me.

When I had made some big piles of branches I was instructed to burn them, which I did. A pleasant task – for to reduce bulk to practically nothing, to make a hard thing soft, to cause substance to become insubstantial, is as interesting as making something out of nothing.

2. Broadcasting Artificial Manure

After a few days my next job conducted me nearer the centre of the agricultural world: the spreading of artificial manure. Taking a horse and cart from the stable, Morgan (that was the name of the foreman) and I went across the farm to a far field which had been reserved for potatoes. It was a beautiful morning, and as we jogged along in the early sunshine with a wide view of the countryside and passed by a field of corn just coming up and looking more like a green light than a green object, I thought how pleasant it was to be here and to be doing this *as my job* – no longer to be looking at a horse and cart jogging through a field, but to be part of it now, to be *on the field* instead of a spectator of it. And I also reflected that if the countryman receives less pay than the townsman, he should not mind, since the latter ought to be compensated for his self-sacrificing denial of essentials.

We filled up with artificial at an old oast-house that served as a lower stable and barn. I had heard of artificial manure but that's about all, never seen it nor even considered what it looked like. Anyway, here was the stuff in front of me, neatly parcelled up in sacks of hundredweights and half-hundredweights. There were two kinds here, one a substance like very fine sand which I gathered was superphosphate, the other like salt which was potash. We loaded the superphosphate on the cart and brought it to the field, dropping the sacks at fixed intervals along the edge. This done we proceeded to broadcast it. The method was simple. We each filled a bucket, slung its rope over head and shoulder, and then holding the bucket steady with one hand, scattered the manure with the other at the rate of one handful to every second step as we advanced across the field. From a distance it would look the same as sowing grain.

A rather strong wind blew and the powder flew up into our eyes so frequently and so painfully that we had to give up and sow potash instead – which being much heavier and moister is not blown about by the wind. Thus we sowed the potash walking forward and backward across the field, filling up our buckets at each end, for the rest of the morning and the whole afternoon. The ground of course was extremely uneven and I stumbled over the clods as I walked. I now remembered the word *clod-hopper,* the term of reproach reserved by townsmen for those who produce food, and I was interested to touch the reality. On account of my very early breakfast, with only a snatched bite since, I began to wonder if I could really last out till dinner. At length the great moment came when we knocked off, and then I experienced a pleasure in just *sitting down*, and in eating cheese, such as I have never known before.

After this I did a lot more manuring on my own for several days. One afternoon I sowed potash up and down twenty-five long rows of blackcurrant trees and plums. Up and down, filling my bucket at each end until eight sacks were empty, five hours had passed and it was five-thirty. It struck me as qualifying for the term 'grinding toil'. I found these long afternoons something of an endurance test. Owing to laziness I possess a secret reserve of strength, and was not afraid that I wouldn't be equal to anything that turned up with regard to physical labour; but that afternoon's expedition, and subsequent work, seemed to me long drawn out. This opinion of mine, soon formed, never abandoned, I found held good for all labourers on the land not doing the more interesting jobs.

However, this particular job evidently left something to show for it, and to my amazement it made an impression on the foreman who remarked on it favourably the next day.

Continuing further at this I began to feel that it could now fairly be said that I was familiar with artificial manure – commercially spoken of as fertilizer. But at this stage I can put forward no opinion on the great Artificial *v.* Pure Compost problem. I have watched the waging of this war with some care, but consider myself as yet too much a provincial in truth concerning this matter even to state a preference. Yet talking of schools of thought on the subject, it seems that should you live in the U.S.S.R. it would be wise to watch your step about this. Arthur Koestler in his *Darkness At Noon* says: 'A short time ago, our leading agriculturalist, B, was shot with thirty of his collaborators because he maintained the opinion that nitrate artificial manure was superior to potash. Number 1 is all for potash; therefore B and the thirty had to be liquidated as saboteurs.' Now in England if anyone disagrees with anyone else he doesn't get angry, he just says: 'That's a point of view anyway, old man.' This may not promote progress. Yet some of the thirty-one nitrate-supporters may have secretly wished that Number 1 – i.e. Stalin – was less un-English.

Without airing views on this subject I may add that one day, having been instructed to spread some artificial and to get the sacks, and not remembering whether it was potash or superphosphate that was to be used, I asked by a slip of the tongue: 'Which sort of *superficial manure* am I to use?' This was greeted with laughter by the boss who was not totally devoid of a sense of humour, and though a great supporter of these fertilizers, seemed to discern some slight element of justice or irony in this strange nomenclature.

3. My Furrow

Presently I found myself back on the potato field broadcasting a final portion with 'super', while Morgan harrowed with a tractor, and the carter, a genial young Dane, ploughed open furrows for potato planting.

When the coast was clear later on I asked the carter if I might try my hand at ploughing a few furrows. I knew that he would be far from pleased at the request, but putting my pride in my pocket (a thing I do all my life at intervals with deliberation), and going on the principle that 'nothing dare, nothing do' I approached the ploughman. And as it is harder to refuse than to acquiesce in such things, he let me try. He said he would lead the horse (only one was being used) the first time, while I managed the plough. This was an easy way of starting. Even so I immediately felt in need of four hands, two for reins and two for plough. However, imitating this man's method, I put the reins over my head till they were held taut round the right shoulder and under the left arm. And since the horse was started and led by my companion I reached the bottom of the field leaving behind a moderately straight furrow. It would be hard to make a complete bosh of this under the above condition. We returned to the other end again without marked mishap. Then I took over the whole thing. Now I would plough a furrow. It was a psychological necessity for me to plough a furrow – at last about to be fulfilled. I took up my position, and it only remained for me to proceed.

The horse refused to move.

I urged it forward, but it then moved sideways, upsetting the plough. And I spent some time in putting it into position again.

It then moved over the other side with the same result. I had not yet advanced a step. My psychological furrow still remained in the realm of the imagination.

Once more I got into position. This time we did really start, we did really move forward. But after ten yards the horse swerved badly left. Using one hand for the reins, thus leaving only one on the plough, I pulled him round too much. Nevertheless we proceeded, but again owing to lack of rein control the horse went sideways and my furrow, after a few yards of near straightness, went west. Still, when I had reached the bottom the thing had been done. I had ploughed a furrow. It could hardly have been less straight, but a weight was lifted from my mind, for whatever geometrical terms might be necessary to describe my line, to me it was an Event – I had at any rate ploughed a furrow.

4. Potato Planting: Broadcasting Seed

A wet day now drew us indoors – into an old house, at a far corner of the farm, unoccupied and with no road to it. It was serving as a general store-house for artificial and potatoes and tools. We made use of the wet day to prepare the potatoes for planting. From a pile on the floor we sorted out the medium ones for planting, putting those that were too small on one side, and splitting the large ones to serve as two. So the Potato now came into my field of vision as a definite object on its own. Not being a garden or allotment man I had hitherto never looked at a potato save with my mouth, as it were. Now I decided to fix my eye on it and follow its act.

Early in May we assembled for planting. The personnel included all who worked on the farm: the boss (who, though frequently called away on another job at this period, was present at most of the important occasions), Morgan, the Dane, a general labourer called Arthur Miles and his wife, a land girl, and myself. We each took a row, filled buckets from sacks placed at intervals down the field, and planted the potatoes in the furrows at one foot distance from each other – which seemed to me a lot of room for them to play in. I was glad to put them in and let them get on with it. They have no beauty to recommend them, it is their performance we admire, and now they could start moving. But I soon lost interest in them and became much more concerned with my back. Since it is necessary to carry a bucket and to place each potato right down in the furrow as you advance, the back-strain is unexampled – in fact there is no other agricultural job so hard on the back. A machine-planter has been invented of course, and is much in use. And a good job too, thought I, many thanks and salaams to the benefacting inventor. 'So you are a believer in thorough agricultural mechanization, are you?' 'Pardon me, but I'm in no fit state to think it out – my back's aching too much. Empirically, as seen here regarding *this*, a machine seems excellent.' And I fear that machines come into the world, not following a principle, nor with an eye to future developments, nor in relation to the whole, but by fits and starts, one by one, each seeming splendid to those concerned. I have to admit that whatever views I might hold in the study concerning mechanization, on the field, from this labouring angle, I would cast a highly favourable eye upon any man who appeared with a potato-planter.

'What did you do today?' my friends often asked when I got home. 'Spread potash round the foot of fruit trees was about all I sometimes could reply. Thus an accurate day-to-day account of life on a farm would be almost laughably dull – though I wish someone would do it if only for the benefit of the romanticists. But spreading potash at the foot of fruit trees was in no way an irksome job. You simply filled your bucket and circled round each tree in the line, throwing down handfuls of the manure in a circle well away from the foot of the stem – for the roots which it is designed to reach are spread several feet outwards. There was thick grass round most of the trees which I dressed thus, and I wondered how much good I was really doing. I did not care, for I was not responsible. I was most happy and at ease in my non-responsibility. No farmer can be at ease hanging daily upon the response of nature to his decisions.

While on this manuring job one day I noticed that a certain attractively situated field with a long view was being sown with corn by Arthur Miles. This farm (a little less than a hundred acres) had not gone in for much arable work, the concentration being on fruit, hence it was not fitted out with much equipment for the former. The old method of broadcasting seed was adopted. I saw that Arthur Miles, who seemed to do anything and everything, was engaged at this. And just as I had longed to put my hand on a plough, so again I felt the strongest desire to broadcast a field, or some of it, in creative contrast with broadcasting artificial. When the boss came round I asked him if I might take a turn. He was an understanding man and did not make fun of the awkward request. In fact he brought me up to the field and left me with Arthur Miles – though not going so far as to say anything to him about it. He just left me there. This made it a bit awkward. But again I overcame the resistance and he showed me how it was done. It is extremely concentrated work. You must walk straight and you must throw out the seed so as never to leave a patch uncovered. Thus, fixing your eye steadily upon an object at the end of the field, you start out, throwing the grain forward at every step. This means that the hand must work very quickly in seizing the grain from the bag or bucket slung by a strap over the shoulder, and the arm must go out evenly and rhythmically with the legs – otherwise there will be gaps and patches when the corn grows.

It was exactly this steady synchronization that I found most difficult and I did a portion of the field none too well, and made Miles none too pleased. But I did do that portion and never in my life felt better employed. I was doing the oldest and most necessary work known to man. When you do it by hand there is the further attraction that not only are you doing something necessary for the life of mankind, but you are outside the Machine Age, so that even if the machines went up in smoke you would remain untouched and could continue to work across the field. And if we are moved by the poetry of tradition and the procession of time, remembering that a two-thousand-years-old Parable held up the image of the Sower at the self-same task, we shall be glad indeed, if only for a brief period in our lives, if only once, to do likewise and cast abroad these envelopes of life.

5. The Old House

Another wet day followed and I was sent to the old house to crunch potash. This chemical, lying up all winter, gets damper and damper, forming into hard lumps in the sacks. My job was to open the sacks, throw the potash on the floor, crunch it up into a fine powder and then re-pack it.

I carried on alone throughout the day at this, in the large old, empty house. Enormous beams, many doors, three stairways, attics, cellars – the whole empty save for the sacks of artificial, some broken chairs, one wash-basin, tools and potatoes, and in an upper room an enormous bedstead fitted with mattress.

At lunch-time – or, more properly, dinner-time – I went into this upper room. The bed certainly was formidable – one of those old Victorian 'beds like battlefields', as George Moore described them. There I had my meal, using the mattress as table and chair. This house was tucked away in a lost corner, far from any other house, with no road or even pathway to it. A lonely mansion at the best of times; on that day, that desolate room, one window stuffed up, one broken, one filled with cardboard, the wind whistling, the rain without and the damp within, I felt discouraged and inclined towards melancholy. I lay down on the bed, using my haversack as pillow, and, curling up, placed my overcoat over my body and head. The wind rattled the panes and various doors banged, but I felt secure now and remote from the world, as if I had buried myself.

In spite of this I rose conscientiously after an hour and returned to the potash, and while crunching the strange white substance tried to grapple with the mystery of its action against the potatoes that I had put in the ground – and was irritated beyond measure by my ignorance.

The afternoon seemed remarkably long – longer than the usual longness. And no wonder, for my watch had stopped and I had worked two hours' overtime – for continuing to hear the distant chug-chug of the spraying-machine, I thought it could not yet be five-thirty; but there had evidently been a pause for tea, and then on again. So that day my hours were from 5.30 a.m. when I rose, till 8 p.m. when I got back. Going home I remembered that I had to get some eggs (you could still get eggs at this time). After some searching up a hill I found the place and bought the eggs. The woman who gave them to me also gave me three small cakes gratis, for I had impressed her with 'a tired look'. This was encouraging. I seldom succeed in working either long enough or hard enough to look properly tired, and this was the first time in my life that a kind woman had taken pity on me as a worn-out man and given me three cakes.

If you have a fair distance to cycle to your work, then the question as to whether it is uphill going or coming back is of some moment – freshly considered every day. Is it better to have it downhill on the way to work? Yes, for as you always start out late you can arrive on time. But the return home! A slow push up a long slant is no pleasing prospect to the labourer who has achieved his 5.30 p.m. That was to be my experience later. Here, going home I started with a long swoop down, lovely in the evening but imperfect in the morning. However, I now asked the boss whether instead of doing this long bicycle journey every day I could live in the old house, putting into it the furniture which soon had to be taken out of a house in Kent, my wife having to go in another direction. This was agreed to. There was no road to the house, as I have said – only a railway line! No doubt it once had a fine approach to it: some of it dated back to the Elizabethan era, I believe. But any such approach had long since been abandoned, and the house itself forgotten and finally lost. Only in England, with its forty-seven million inhabitants, could you actually lose a house.

However, during certain months of the year there was a sufficiency of dry ground and even a track to make approach by lorry possible, even to the doorway. But of course in the eyes of furniture removers and tradesmen it was 'out in the wilds'. This latter phrase is frequently heard in twentieth-century England. 'You *are* out in the wilds!' people will say to anyone in the Home Counties living somewhere not on or very near a bus route, and perhaps two and a half miles from a railway station. Such is the imbecility to which industrialism can reduce a nation whose sons have travelled to the ends of the earth, pioneering and colonizing into the unknown and ruling millions of waves just for the fun of the thing.

Nevertheless I managed to persuade a firm to undertake this tremendous task. Unluckily, when the driver got near the house he left the hard track at one point and the van sank into swampy ground and had to be dug out. But in the end the furniture was carried into the house with amused condescension by the men.

I decided to occupy two rooms of the seven or eight – a large one upstairs, and the one underneath it, both supported by col-ossal beams. Thus beamed and buttressed by earlier centuries, I felt myself in a strong position. The ground floor of my bed-sitting room upstairs was uneven with age, as roughly wrinkled as the waves of the sea. Twelve beams crossed the ceiling from east to west, while a really fine one, besieged in vain by insects, crossed from north to south. The ancient cupboards, knotched and dented by the artillery of Time, might well have concealed alarming skeletons. The fireplace was so wide that you could have put a child's bed into it. The long latticed window looked across at the old oast-house, which in the declension of the sharp evening light had a wood-cut perfection about it. And the evening, after-tea sun came into the room – one of the most soothing of all Nature's effects. It was an ideal room, and all the time I was there I thought how I would hate to leave it when the time came. But there was a curious draught near the door.

When you approached it, it became quite windy, almost hat-blowing-off, even when it was calm outside. The cause was obscurely connected with the peculiar exit. It opened on to two doors, one trap-door, and two stairways, and whichever one was opened at this junction was banged by a cold tempest, the gale not coming from any certain direction but rather occupying a central typhoonish position. To complete this survey – the trap-door led to two separate attics which, like all attics, were utterly abandoned to despair. One door led to a bathroom, itself leading into a small room and it into another up two steps. The other door opened on to a commodious staircase and four big front rooms. While if you opened no door you could go down a steep back staircase leading to a scullery and one-time kitchen, now filled with sacks of potash. And then, should you wish to continue your odyssey, you could open a door in the corner of that and go down some stone steps to a cellar, damp and dungeoned as the Cells of Chillon. Many of these rooms, I sometimes felt, when in no lofty mood, would have been less lonely with a few ghosts.

Having installed myself here, it was suggested that I should have a meal per day with the boss and family. 'Our chief meal of the day,' he said, 'is tea, at 5.30. What about coming in to that?' I gratefully accepted, at the same time wondering how that meal could be the chief one on a farm. Next day he told me that his wife preferred to make it dinner. The truth was of course that the midday meal was a real square one, and the other just tea; but he couldn't bear the thought of letting me have the dinner. His charming wife, however, wasn't standing for that. I have often noticed farmers' wives, before giving anyone anything, glance nervously to see if the husband is looking.

I had heard it said over and over again that 'Mother Earth' keeps men sane. This is so. But I have found from my own limited experience, and from a certain amount of note-comparing with others, that she makes all farmers, with few exceptions, go slightly off their heads. The above instance would easily find its counterpart, and shows to what a pass these men are brought by their unique struggle. I must add, if only to make the psychology of the thing more difficult, that this man did not charge me a penny rent for the house nor a penny for potatoes. He may have had ulterior motives, but I don't know what they were; and there it is, he charged me nothing, while at the same time he really could not bear serving a double-helping at table.

6. The Spraying Operation

My services were soon called for at a new job – as assistant at the spraying of fruit trees. What we performed in this line was something wholly outside any previous experience of mine. Once or twice in my life I had sprayed; that is, I had taken a hand-syringe in the garden at home in childhood, put it in water, filled it, and squirted rose trees. But here was something colossal.

It might be thought that an apple or plum tree would bear fruit as satisfactorily as a gooseberry or black-currant bush, if left alone to a certain extent. This is too optimistic, it appears. The pear, the plum, but especially the apple, it seems, are open to the attack of hosts of enemies. First to the fungi: a fungus being a plant which does not prepare its own food but feeds on other plants. The apple tree lends itself as such food better than most, so it has to be protected against the Leaf Blight which is capable of despoiling all the leaves of whole orchards; against the Bitter Rut, Black Rut, and the Brown Rut which devour their way into the fruit: against Rust which yellows the leaves and eats into the growing apple; against Scab which forms dark circular spots on the fruit and leaves. It must also be protected against a host of insect enemies; against the Aphis, an insect which, gathering in massed battalions, sucks the juices from leaf and blossom; against the Bud Moth which chooses the tree as good hatching ground in the crevices of the twigs so that the larvae can feed upon the foliage; against the Canker Worm, a caterpillar which, after feeding upon the tree, lowers itself to the ground by means of its self-produced thread; and against seven other kinds of moth and worm.

Such is the story, at any rate. How the unattended apple tree in your back garden manages to survive and produce fruit in considerable quantities would therefore seem something of a mystery. But it is not for me to question or even raise an eyebrow. My place is beside the spraying-machine. It consisted of a motor-pumping engine attached to a tank – the whole being mobile. A large tubular sucker (glorified hose-end) entered the tank which was filled with the spraying liquid, and a long coiling hose conveyed the spray to the place desired. I must say I took a fancy to this machine, partly because of its important noise while it chugged away pumping out the stuff; partly because it often went wrong, thus creating diversion and relaxation; partly because of its dramatic filth and habit of leaking and spitting out green slime.

Its accompanying tank was filled with water, sulphur, and lime, a combination of such a poisonous complexion that even to look at it was mentally disturbing. Nor was I always in a position to keep my distance; for when the tank began to get empty and it became necessary to deal with the tubular sucker, it was like grappling with a vicious inhabitant of the first swamp. I have rarely handled an inanimate object that was more animated. It seemed bent on spraying me personally with its unspeakable juices.

My main task was to lug round the immense length of hose after Morgan who thus could hold a free lance with which to spray the trees when he went down the aisles. This was the most exhausting job I have ever had to do. It was like a solo tug-of-war of interminable duration. As the morning wore on and wore me down, dinner and its, as yet, appalling distance from realization, became too often and too painfully my sovereign thought. Morgan seemed entirely indifferent either to time or hunger – he never carried a watch and never appeared to be hungry. Luckily this endurance test was occasionally broken by the hose bursting at some point and sending up a high fountain of spray like a whale's jet, or the machine would go wrong, or the tank need refilling. And sometimes I sprayed also, both of us pulling the hose after us as best we could. It was anything but easy to spray effectively. No use just squirting a tree and passing on: the tree must be wet all over, on all the branches, and on both sides of every leaf; for an insect or fungus is not killed until the poison gets it – and does not accommodate a farmer by committing suicide. The direction of the wind was an important matter: it was necessary to see that it was blowing away from you, otherwise the lotion blew back upon your face . . . not itself in need of protection against fungus, scab, or blight.

Thus it goes on at this time of the year in all the big orchards of the country, hour after hour and day after day, an unceasing offensive against these enemies of table-fruit.

The refilling of the tank provided a species of light entertainment. The spraying-engine and the tank were mounted on the chassis of a Morris Oxford. When refilling time came we attached a tractor to the chassis and proceeded towards a pond, the engine of the spraying-machine still chugging away. Morgan drove the tractor while I guided the platform, since the steering-wheel of the old car was still attached. We reached the pond and filled the tank with water, and then poured out two bucketfuls of the sulphur-lime liquid from a barrel, and added that to the tank. We were now ready to return to the scene of operation. The jolts and jerks caused by the exceedingly uneven ground made the liquid in the (now very full) tank splash about, shoot up, and pour down the back of my neck – the steering-wheel being between the tank and the tractor. Meanwhile the open radiator of the spraying-machine full of hot water splashed in a similar manner, going down the back of Morgan's neck and into my face. Thus we would proceed, the roar of both the engines and the double splashing of the waters providing a spectacle sufficiently disquieting in itself, you might fancy, to frighten away any enemies of the fruit.

'Will you have an apple, Mr Brown?'

'Thanks very much.'

'Oh dear, Bridget hasn't put any on the table! She must have forgotten to bring them up. I'll ring.'

'Please don't bother, it doesn't matter a bit.'

'But I particularly told her to put them on the table!'

Yet, before Bridget can bring them up, I, for one, am glad to realize what a lot must be done by God and man before she is even in a position to forget to 'put them on the table'.

7. Morgan and Miles

In spite of Morgan's extreme neglect of clock and absence of hunger, it was a pleasure to work with him. I thought at the time, and have frequently thought since, how impossible it would have been to have had a nicer foreman to start with. He was not in the least like the usual kind of foreman. He never lost his temper, never even raised his voice – it was quite phenomenal. He was a 'working man' but with no accent one way or the other. Almost totally lacking in class-consciousness. Very grave, respectable, correct, and ungossipy, but also with a sense of humour that lit up a peculiarly pleasant smile. There are so many classes within classes and grades upon grades in England that I am hard put to it to describe the social position of Morgan. His complete absence of accent or dialect was rather baffling. He had been the clever boy at school and could have taken scholarships and risen 'higher in the world', as it is called, but he had not liked schooling and had gone to Canada at first to farm – hence his wider horizon. He liked his work (not so common with land workers, I was to find). He was also fond of reading. This generally means, quite simply, reading novels. For many readers it is hardly known that there are any other books. And so it was with Morgan – a book was a novel. As he liked to mention books sometimes, I found it a bit awkward. Indeed I know few things more psychologically harassing than this kind of literary conversation, when one has seldom read any of the books mentioned and cannot name others that will convey anything. However, we managed somehow, and often he asked for a book. He never turned down a good one. I lent him a Hardy. He approved and said it was 'quite good'. He listened to book-talks by the B.B.C. and heard of *War and Peace*. I lent him my copy and he was not to be daunted. But he did not enjoy it. He confessed at intervals that he was 'wading through it'. (I wondered how many would have taken it on at all.) His paper was the *Daily Express* – and he quoted its opinions. Arthur Miles read *Picture Post* – 'very good value' he said. The boss read the *New Statesman* – and quoted its opinions.

Arthur Miles was a rough diamond. At many farms, it seems, there is one man who is 'always right', who 'knows everything', who puts everyone right and shouts loudly. An ordinary man might say 'You will find it in the shed' or 'You've got it the wrong way round', without undue emphasis or excitement. Arthur would yell the information in apparent fury. He was a tremendous blusterer. But an efficient blusterer, the regular handy man always called upon in difficulties for masterly improvisation.

In the agricultural world, I soon discovered, all sorts of problems must be solved on the spot, the difficulty must be got round somehow, there is no question of getting someone from outside to do it. Thus endless improvisation in the mending of breakages and the construction of suddenly essential gadgets. It is an agricultural habit of mind – foreign to the townsman. Wrestling with nuts and screws is an almost daily thing. Hence the agricultural labourer is an amateur mechanic (who afterwards went into the town and specialized). He is the first mechanic, the first man to 'conquer nature' just as he was the first man to get fed up with nature and to wall himself off from her by building the town. All things start on the land – not least the townsman, and most surely the mechanic. The idea that the engineer is a special kind of town-bred person was dispelled for me after a very short acquaintance with agricultural workers. Arthur always got round the difficulty somehow, provided he had a piece of wire. Your agriculturalist can do anything with a piece of wire – not a day passes but he saves some crisis with it.

Arthur, with hands the size of spades, could twist the stuff about like twine.

He was a great master of language, though his mastery was confined to one word, beginning with b. It is a famous word, yet never reaching the status that would allow it to appear on the page, though it has long since lost its etymological significance. It is used equally as a noun, an adjective, or a verb. Dr Johnson, I think, described it in his *Dictionary* as '*a term of endearment amongst sailors*'. That is when used as a noun, one sailor calling another a b. On land it is used less as a sign of affection than in terms of music-while-you-work – an accompaniment. Swearing came as naturally to Arthur as leaves to a tree, and having command over all the possible variations in which the word could be used it came from his lips almost in terms of song – 'It's a b,' 'well I'm b'd', 'he's a b', 'you can b off' ... Once, when I heard him preserve silence for a few minutes on account of the proximity of the boss's wife, it seemed unnatural and disquieting, and I felt anxious for him until he started up again.

He roared out his council to everyone, including Morgan, *his* way being the right one, never allowing for two schools of thought even about potato planting. Morgan was careful to keep his temper, thus avoiding a pig-headed hold-up. Arthur's roaring at me was more extensive and violent – sometimes I thought he overdid it. But he possessed what is called 'a good heart at bottom' – which is by no means true of all men with rough tongues. He had another mood, perhaps later in the day, in strange contrast. He would be doing something in the lower stable, say; he would swing the door open slightly (it slowly went back on its hinges without needing any push) and would say as it swung back – 'Open Sesame'. I do not know what he thought the words meant, but with a gentle humorous expression he would give the door a little kick with his toe, saying – 'Open Sesame'.

Arthur's wife also worked on the farm. Like a number of women she was made of iron and capable of endless work. It was said of her also that at bottom she had a good heart. I think this geographical description was true enough. But I felt that she belonged to the category of those who would gain in amiability what they lost in virtue by having a bad heart at bottom and a hypocritical one on top. All women are more self-conscious than men, and many far more class-conscious. It blows from them like a wind. Arthur Miles 'didn't give a damn' for anyone or anything: 'I don't mind 'ow 'e is or wot 'e is' he'd say – and one liked him for it. Mrs Miles went on the same principle, but in a less engaging way. One of her minor pleasures was to work with some new land girl or amateur assistant. She would work at a pace impossible for the others to keep up, and shout at intervals (she never spoke, always shouted as if there was a gale on), 'How do you like wurking? This is *wurk*, you know!' All remarks addressed to her, whether in terms of the weather, the joke, the grouse, were answered by one sovereign rejoinder – 'You're telling me!'

8. The Third Day of Creation

A fortnight to three weeks having elapsed since I had broadcast seed with Arthur, I decided to have a look at that field. Hitherto I had always been too much of a Wordsworthian (not that I can ever bring myself to denigrate in any way the greatest of the nineteenth-century poets) and was content to see things only in the round, feeling that the scientific approach *is* to peep and botanize upon your mother's grave. But my chance had come to *see the particular*, now that I was personally implicated in it.

It was certainly true that in this instance I had little real idea of what precisely I should see. On approaching the field I saw a low green mist clinging to it, which turned out to be substance in the nature of grass, now covering what had been the brown surface of the field. I dug up a spadeful. We had sown a mixture of oats and peas. Those handfuls of round and oblong caskets that I had helped to broadcast had performed a peculiar act after leaving the hand and reaching the soil. Quite dead in the sack, it had seemed; but on touching the soil they had become animated, alive, and full of surprising moves. It were as if that little oat-seed, a tiny and inferior-looking piece of matter such as one might chip off a log, had been galvanized on being touched by Earth – making me think of gunpowder when touched by Fire. The envelopes had exploded. The pea seeds, those hard little balls like dented miniature ping-pong balls, had softened and shot downwards white webs and claws as long as my fingers, and shot upwards into the air a complicated system of green tubing and frills. The oat seeds, the shape of tiny fish, had performed a similar feat below and had sent up into the air long thin pieces of material like green ribbons. No matter how they had fallen on the ground or how they lay when they had fallen, they had all exploded in two directions only – down and straight up. None slanted, all preserved the perpendicular.

We glorify the present only when it has become the past. This is a recognized tendency in terms of history. It is equally true in terms of metaphysics. We imagine that Creation took place in the remote past. No doubt it did; but the same thing takes place today. The third Day of Creation, as fabled in the book of Genesis, happens once every year no less certainly than the Sixth Day happens all the time. If this were not so the world would speedily dissolve. As I stand beside the rising corn I feel no need to have been present on the Third Day of the First Week, since I am witnessing the same thing. The same Force is at work, the same Voice obeyed. That which I would have seen then, I see now – sheer miracle, pure purpose. He who tries to dispose of this, uttering some mumbo-jumbo about 'chance' or 'mechanism' is the only real heretic, the only real atheist. All other denial, all other unbelief is mere speculation, and of no consequence. But this denial of clear witness is not speculation, and reveals the denier, not as a clever casuist, but as a stupid ass.

I have spent some time in the company of the philosophers and the priests, and have undertaken long journeys with them in search of the Absolute. It was all necessary. For only then could I understand that it was not necessary, and that if we will but look out of the window the answer is there. It is clear to me now that if we take the trouble to regard phenomena, with the eye, *not* of a child, but of an adult who weds intelligence with wonder, we shall soon find ourselves at ease with the Problem of Purpose and all the rest of it.

9. Some Fallacies

The orchards were now beginning to bloom. The Coxes, the James Grieves, the Beauty of Baths all appearing much more real to me than in the old days, already an ancient time left far behind, when an apple was 'only' a fruit which you bought for sixpence a pound, and an orchard just a pretty sight. Having opened the gate of labour I had suddenly stepped inside the world, and could see the objects with fresh eyes.

The spraying-machine had been put aside, of course, and my new job for a time was hoeing. The hoe, unlike the spade, having its knife-edge turned at right angles to the handle, allows you to thump it down into the ground while at the same time pulling it towards you – with the result that you can remove one or more weeds at each stroke. Still, it is not an inspiring job. I have met one or two people who liked it. But on the whole it is far from popular. Indeed, faced with many hours of it, there is a general agreement that it breaks the back and the mind. There is only one way by which it can be conquered – namely by good company. Absorbing conversation alone can overcome hoeing. And one can hardly expect to find that on the land.

Actually, the hoeing I did on this farm was the easiest and the least boring I have ever done. I had a good hoe, sharp and heavy (I never handled its like again). And the ground was soft. Hence one swoop easily removed the thistles and docks. Moreover, I worked not in an open field but between fruit trees. I have never since had a combination of similar qualities for softening the blows of monotony. At first I vastly preferred it to my recent tug-of-war with the hose. Nevertheless I soon began to wish I was doing something else.

This job, and the previous ones, brought me up against one of the fallacies concerning agricultural work held by the citizen of our mean cities. It is supposed that 'on the land' you have 'time to think', and that conditions are such that the mind can indulge quietly in wise expansive meditations in the open air. Certainly the place in which to think is the open air. But not during work. To be able to think *consecutively* about anything you must concentrate; and there are few jobs on the land that you can do so automatically as to be free to really think. Perhaps hoeing should be one of these. For a short time it is. Then the body interferes with the mind. The back begins to ache. You become physically preoccupied. You become tired. And then the mind, instead of being able to concentrate upon something consecutively, indulges either in fatuous daydreams or nurses petty grievances or dwells upon the worst traits of one's least pleasant friends. At such times I have often been appalled at my mind and wondered if others could have such rotten ones. And if a Great Idea does descend, well, I stop working to take it in, and rest on my hoe, and look across the land (as a matter of fact I don't: I carefully gaze on the ground in case anyone is looking – for he who gazes towards the earth presents a less agriculturally reprehensible spectacle than he who looks towards heaven).

There is another fallacy, closely related. People say to me – 'It must be wonderful to feel perfectly fit, working on the land as you do.' I am fit enough, I suppose; but there is a misapprehension here. The best way to feel really fit is through games. A good game of tennis for two hours or a run for half an hour will give you a better feeling of physical well-being than a whole day's agricultural labour (with about three exceptions concerning the latter). In the former case you perspire and feel fine – and the mind often then moves with remarkable freedom. In agriculture you seldom perspire; you merely keep on keeping on, and at the end of the day do not feel amiably tired but somewhat exhausted – and the mind sticks fast. Neither hoeing nor other agricultural work is really conducive towards the formation of what is called 'a good figure'. Arnold Bennett went so far as to say that veteran countrymen resembled 'starved bus-conductors twisted out of shape by lightning'. (Did he mean *train-drivers*?) Still, I think they match their surroundings better that way than if they stood up with the straightness of a soldier.

He who seeks happiness can find it in two ways. He can find it when the mind is absorbed and the body pleasantly active. This happens during certain games and during one or two agricultural activities. This pleasure is very great. He can find it also when the mind is absorbed and the body forgotten. This happens when reading a great book: on such occasions we as good as leave our bodies and go a journey without them. Few if any pleasures excel this. And the secret is that in both cases the ego is disposed of – quite forgotten. Conscious or not, that is the goal of everyone, to forget his ego, and to subdue the ego's two servile and obsequious slaves – the restless body and the wandering, lunatic mind.

Such are one or two of my reflections recollected in tranquillity after hoeing. But I would not like it to be thought that I have any grouse against hoeing, against any job that has to be done. I was not seeking pleasure. And I got a good deal of satisfaction from a disciplinarian point of view. Self-discipline is splendid. I am all for it. But I cannot apply it without external pressure. It was now applied for me. I was forced to do what I could not force myself to do. And this was one of the things I wanted to do, which I needed to do if ever I were to understand and know the world instead of only 'knowing about' it.

10. My Difficulties as Carter

The carter or horseman (the former term being the most usual but not so satisfactory) had to leave, and I took on the job. I was not wholly unfamiliar with horses from a riding point of view – and at one period could even jump without stirrups or reins and with a sword in my hand. All forgotten – along with horselore. And of cart-horses and harness I knew nothing whatever.

It was now a welcome change to start the morning rounding

up the horses that grazed in the field adjoining the old house, and to bring them into the oast-house which served as the lower stable, where I groomed and harnessed them. One was easy to catch and hard to work with – Prince. The other was hard to catch and easy to work with – Beauty, a mare. Any moral? I found, however, that provided I brought out oats I could get hold of Beauty by her excellent forelock all right. It was no good simply going up with a bridle held behind the back, she was too wary. I never tried it that way, but always took a tray of oats which she always fell for, and then I could catch that substantial forelock and lead her into the stable easily enough with Prince following at her heels like a lamb. They were great friends, these horses, grazing together cheek beside cheek, nose by nose, mouth by mouth as they ate the grass – a sight so affecting that I couldn't bear to think of the day when one would be taken and the other left.

Incidentally, this method of catching Beauty was considered too elaborate. When others went to fetch her they only fell back on the bag of oats trick as a last resort, or did it one time and not the next. I remember reading how a man, having occasionally brought out oats to a difficult horse, and then only pretending to do so for several days on end, was suddenly kicked and killed, my sympathies being with the horse. Arthur was not good at catching Beauty. His blustering methods didn't work and the mare gave him a clean pair of heels. One day when I wasn't using the horses Arthur had to fetch in Beauty for some purpose. As usual he went out, holding the bridle behind his back, and consequently couldn't get hold of her at all. As I happened to be in that direction I said I would get her, which I did (by a lucky stroke really, for I didn't take out any oats). Whereat he thanked me. This made me smile on the right side of my face for I was secretly both amused and gratified at the resourceful, efficient, always-right Arthur actually thanking *me* for doing something that he couldn't do himself.

He seemed to think that horses have horse sense. It is the custom to give your horse food while you harness and groom it. But Arthur on this occasion just chucked the harness on and gave her nothing – in order 'to teach the sod a lesson'. This seemed to me an inadequate psychological approach to a horse who can read little about crime and punishment, and in any case didn't learn the lesson.

When I came to deal with harnessing for the first time I was surprised at the weight of the harness. I found that the breeching and attendant straps were as heavy as a saddle. When I tried putting the collar on I found I had put the bridle on first. Having taken off the bridle, the collar still wouldn't go on – for the simple reason that you must *reverse* it while negotiating the head, which I had not done, thus following the example of Wordsworth who also failed in this matter. I was no more successful with the hames; I got them the wrong way round, and when at last I got them the right way round, I failed to pin them under the collar in a sufficiently tight notch. This done, I was now ready to put the horse into the cart. But I was not prepared for the difficulty of backing it straight between the shafts, nor for the weight of the cart when lifted up by one of the shafts, nor for the difficulties now confronting me in continuing the good work. For, having thrown over the long chain that rests on the breeching, and dodged under the horse's neck to catch it on the other side. I missed it and it rolled back so that I had to throw it over again, all the time holding up the shaft with one hand while I went to the other side. And after this came the fixing of the remaining chains, all of which I put into the wrong notches.

I hadn't realized that so 'simple' a matter as harnessing a horse and putting it in a cart entailed so many moves. I found that the same held true regarding what must seem to the man on the road to be the elementary performance of going through a gate. Yet it is quite remarkably more easy to gatecrash than to make a smooth passage. The thing must be done skilfully if you don't want to knock into one of the posts. On the whole I wasn't too much a post-knocker, but this was due to the absence of many gates. There was something else more difficult than a gate. The track from the house-end of the farm went down an incline and up another. At the bottom was a stream with a bridge over it. This bridge was narrow, breaking down, and with huge ruts near the edges. When it rained the mud was very thick on this clayey soil, and going over the bridge with a heavy load was extremely precarious. One wheel always fell into the rut at the very edge of the fenceless bridge, and in pulling the cart across the horse would generally lurch and slip. This bridge was in direct view of the house, and the boss often watched this part of my journey with some anxiety – lest we fall over and the horse be injured, he explained.

My next difficulty was the negotiation of sacks. The horseman has a great deal to do with sacks. All sorts of sacks, varying from half a hundredweight to two hundredweight, the potatoes or corn or artificial, must be continuously loaded up and carted somewhere. The loading of sacks is an easy job for two if done in the right way (hand linked with hand behind the sack), but not so simple for one. No use hauling the bag about in one's arms – you must get it on the back and high on the back. Once in that position the weight doesn't matter much. This is all right when you are taking them from the top layer of a well-built pile; but how about those on the ground? How about the stragglers, the sacks of superphosphate which when moved generally break and pour out the stuff? It was a job to elevate them ... I was glad to learn that a loaded cart seen going quietly along has to be loaded first.

I never really became a good sack-lifter by myself. Beware of the phrase – 'It is all a question of knack.' It isn't. A certain kind of brute strength is just as much part of it, and although I am reasonably strong I was often surprised at the strength of others. One more thing about sacks, and I've done – namely unloading. I'll never forget how once I had to cart ten loads of potatoes from one end of the farm to the other and unload them in the barn in readiness for collection by a merchant. Believe it or not I just took the sacks out of the cart and *dumped them.* I was in a hurry, for the merchant was supposed to be arriving at a stated time, but it was ignorance of the first principle in all such operations – tidiness. It is as easy to unload and place the sacks in neat layers as to dump them in an unregulated heap, or nearly as easy, and much more satisfactory. But I didn't do so. '*Must* you put them down like that?' asked Morgan, when he saw them later. Until he said that, I hadn't noticed what the uncorrelated heap looked like. But he was so mild about it, though annoyed, that it made an impression on me never forgotten.

11. New Vision of the Field

Often, then, my day now started with getting a horse harnessed into a cart and then jogging across the farm to load up something. The morning young, the sun slanting, mist clinging to the ground, the bird in the tree, hope in the heart – the eternal, million-times repeated promise of the dawn. While jogging along at such times I often reflected upon some of the strange phrases in common use, so lightly spoke, so obsequiously swallowed by the multitude. We speak of the *cost of living*, without discomfort. It means that we must pay *money* to be alive, a definite fee for being in the world, with a heavy Entrance Fee. Everyone must *make a living* rather than make a Life. What is he going to *be*? it is asked of boys, for it is understood that it is not sufficient that he shall be *himself* – only a girl is permitted to say that she already *is*. I was not making a living at all well by jogging along here, but I could not help feeling Alive, the freedom of the fields, the freedom of the sky, the freedom of movement gratuitously bestowed upon me – far more substantial than if I had been given the Freedom of the City of Birmingham, or had had pressed into my hands huge Atlantic Charters and other paper monuments to the perfidy of Man.

I had only been working on the land a question of weeks, but one morning as I went past the potato field I realized with what fresh eyes I now could see a field, this field. It was no longer just a bit of earth the beauty of which I perceived from the outside. I saw it a hundred times more clearly, it was a hundred times more real. For I had sown it with potash and superphosphate, I had walked up and down it endlessly, I had counted the minutes nearer the midday meal, I had tried to plough it, I had put down potatoes in the furrows. Already I was no longer an onlooker, a spectator, excluded as if by excommunication from its factual and actual existence. I no longer hung in the void, but had entered in at the door of labour and become part of the world's work in its humblest and yet proudest place.

12. Harrowing

I soon began to use harrows. Formerly, when I had walked across the farm I had continually come across strange-looking instruments at odd corners. Useless things thrown away, they seemed, old rusty chains and spikes with grass growing over them. They reminded me, somehow, of those awful crocodile-teeth traps that used to lie concealed in woods against poachers in the nineteenth century. But I found that these creatures were by no means dead. They were harrows – that is horse- or trac-tor-drawn rakes for breaking up the soil. There were the three main kinds here: the chain harrow or drudge, the spiked harrow or drag, and the spring tines harrow. Thus now I would go up to one of these rusty abandoned instruments, connect it with the horse-traces and bring it to life. A surprising transformation.

'Only a man harrowing clods ...' Like many others I had read and loved that famous poem by Thomas Hardy called 'In Time of "The Breaking of Nations" '. To me just a picture in the mind, no knowledge of what harrowing entailed. Now actualized and made an absolute reality for me – my own job. And does the poem gain thereby? Mr Adrian Bell tells us that he had only been harrowing for a very short time before he began to find fault with the poem. *Only* a ploughman harrowing; that seemed to him all wrong (that deadly realm of 'only') while *half asleep as they stalk* seemed absurd. I find it difficult ever to say anything against Hardy (except with regard to *Tess*), but though the message of the poem perhaps requires that 'only', there seems to me now no excuse for the 'half asleep'. From the road a number of agricultural jobs look remarkably quiet, serene, slow, and easy; but if you stand beside the man in question you may find that he is putting out all his strength, is moving quite fast, and is in anything but a serene state of mind. So with harrowing. I didn't find anything sleepy or serene about it. Not only is it impossible to walk with ease behind the harrow, since you are stumbling the whole time over the clods, but you can't *see* your work properly. You try to go straight across the field exactly beside your previous line, but you cannot see it without close inspection, and even when you do see it the horse is always standing you away from it, and in checking this you come back too much. Consequently you have the uncomfortable feeling most of the time that either you are going over ground already done or are missing out considerable areas. In short, it is exasperating. Certainly not something you can do half-asleep.

However, at first it did not matter to me in the least whether it was exasperating or not. Each thing I did was a new experience, equally interesting to me whether it turned out exciting or dull. And harrowing, above all, gave me great satisfaction. There is a special pleasure in doing something that brings one into line with all ages. While using this instrument I might just as well have been a contemporary of Virgil.

> Nor is the profit small the peasant makes
> Who smooths with harrows, or who pounds with rakes,
> The crumbling clods; nor Ceres from on high
> Regards his labour with a grudging eye;
> Nor his, who ploughs across the furrowed grounds,
> And on the back of earth inflicts new wounds,
> For he, with frequent exercise, commands
> The unwilling soil, and tames the stubborn lands.

Above, I have been thinking of harrowing the open fields. On this farm I also did a good deal, in fact a lot of harrowing and cultivating between fruit trees – using the horse-hoe (that is several reversed hoes or shoes attached to a tray), the spring tines, the chain harrow, and the leverage cultivator. With this last you can lever the instrument in such a way as to plough into the earth at the very foot of the trees without the horse being stopped by the outspreading branches. This was harder work than using the others, much strength being required to keep it in position; but since skill was also called for, it was most interesting.

The difficulty with the chain harrow was that in endeavouring to get it as near as possible to the foot of the trees as you went up and down the aisles, the pole of the harrow often caught on them if you were not careful, and barked the barks. This was highly reprehensible. A hideous gash was presented, clearly seen by the inspecting eye. On more than one occasion, having thus gashed a bark, I gathered some grass and then built it round the scar, thus hiding it!

I generally used two horses for this kind of harrowing – one in front of the other. There was often little enough space to turn them at the ends, but I managed somehow and was proud of the achievement. But on one occasion, when far away in a corner field, one of the horses backed on to the tines, the other became excited, and then both began to pull and kick. They stepped back over the traces which, together with the reins, became an involved mess.

The horses stopped their stamping. They became quite still. They might have been statues.

They were simply unable to move. The reins had got into such an extraordinary arrangement that, taut to breaking-point, they were held in opposite directions so that neither horse could move its head. The bit in Prince's mouth was pressing with an extremity of tightness against the rubbered lower lip. They made no sound – for the most striking thing about horses is their almost total dumbness.

It was a job to extract them. Not performed without some of the harness breaking. I was tying the several parts together with string when Morgan appeared. 'I'm afraid you haven't got a knack with horses, Collis,' was his comment. A beginner, I reflected, should not make an outstanding mistake or have an emphatic mishap; for the mistakes he has *not* made, and the mishaps he has *not* had, will make no impression, while the emphatic error will loom hideously over his head.

13. Absent-mindedness

The field that I most enjoyed dealing with was the potato field.
First I harrowed away the lines and knocked the soil into small
pieces; and when the potato-stems rose above ground, thus re-
establishing the lines, I horse-hoed between them. A great deal
of attention was given to potatoes on this farm – far more than
I have seen anywhere else. Often enough, after a few hoeings,
nothing more is done until late in the season when they are
earthed up. Much more trouble was taken here. I did much
horse-hoeing and a considerable amount of preliminary earth-
ing up – the term used here was 'shinning'. For this I used the
plough that turns a furrow on each side of it – ploughing the
earth exactly as a ship ploughs the main. This was a grand job
and I never tired of it, nor did it tire me since it made me sweat.
It was not ploughing proper, but a close relation to it; and with
the plough-handles to grasp and to guide, and the two horses,
and a field to myself in a corner of old England, I felt the
freedom of having extricated myself from the fetters of modern
civilization – a civilization which, for the literary man, is a good
working definition of hell.

Various land girls came and went on this farm. One of them
was sent to assist me. She had been working with Mrs Miles
and had been worn down by the effort to keep up with her. So
she was given a change, and led my leading horse. She confessed
that she was 'mad about poetry'. This was very cheering; for as
we progress it becomes more common to meet a person who
writes bad books than who reads good ones. So we talked
poetry, and I told her how I always hoped that in the course of
my ploughing I would come upon a mouse, and thus be able to
join with Burns who in November 1785 turned up the mouse
that became immortal:

> I'm truly sorry man's dominion
> Has broken Nature's social union,
> And justifies the ill opinion
>   Which makes thee startle

> At me, thy poor earth-born companion
> An' fellow mortal.

Before leaving the farm, my friend expressed the hope that I would meet my mouse. But I didn't.

During some conversation with her she said – 'You're so absent-minded they say.' I was surprised at this. The last thing I had ever allowed myself to acknowledge was anything in the nature of the 'absent-minded professor'. Later, I faced the matter and thought it out. Evidently I had been the subject of laughing commentary at the tea-table. Was it true after all? Come to think of it, it was true! In ordinary life I had always forgotten things and mislaid them to an astonishing extent. Carelessness shows up badly on a farm. I used to drop things. I would load so many sacks on the cart, and on arriving at the other end would find that two had simply dropped off. Looking round for them I would see, a long way off, a lump on the track! Or I would hang a coat on the hames, and again, at journey's end, would miss it. I had forgotten all about it and had quite failed to realize that nothing stands jerking about unless it is tightly tied on. But the worst instance of forgetting things was when one day, after the midday meal, I went right across to a field which I had to harrow – *without my horse*. This was recounted to me by the girl, who added that when I realized that I hadn't got the horse, I was seen running back madly. Now, no agricultural labourer is ever seen to run – except after rabbits at harvest. The spectacle of me (*a*) minus the horse and (*b*) running back to get it, had provided a sufficiently comic picture to raise a considerable degree of mirth.

I had another habit – one which particularly distressed the boss. When I went from one portion of the farm to another sitting upon the cart, I let the horse go its own pace and did not urge and hurry it on. This gave the impression of absent-minded lolling. Actually, my mind was present to a certain extent while I looked round and took the scene in. But you never know what may make a bad impression. One of the things that makes a bad impression, incidentally, is turning up late in the morning. I mean just a little late – you incur the odium of the other workmen, even more than of the boss. They can't stand anyone turning up late if they themselves are punctual. I was fairly punctual during all the time that I worked anywhere on the land, though I was always a good distance from the meeting place. At this farm I had a twenty-minute walk before reaching the upper part where we assembled. I shall never forget the Norwegian News (preceding 7 a.m.), the clock, as it were, against which I fought to get ready and be gone! But at one period, owing to an unfortunate remark made by Morgan about it not mattering if I got to the stable before 7.15 as the horses would be eating, I turned up at that time regularly. During this period Arthur Miles always seemed in a black, enraged mood towards me, I couldn't make out why. It was not for a long time that I realized that it was due to my arriving at 7.15. He just couldn't bear it.

But to get back to my method of driving the horse and cart, I am not sure that Arthur's method had really anything more to recommend it. He was a great urger-on of horses. Yet his technique struck me as curious. As he drove Beauty along (a lazy mare) he would swear at her ceaselessly . . . 'What the hell are you doing? All right *go* into the ditch, I don't care, it's you that'll have to take the blank cart out not me, come on you blank sod or I'll be blank well blanked', and so on. These solicitations may have sounded as sweet nothings in the ear of Beauty for all I know (and certainly his tone was wholly lacking in either malice or cruelty), and it is fair to say that the mare responded to a perceptible degree. And it made a good show, suggesting the zeal and urgency that appeals enormously to any boss.

Sometimes a whole morning was spent in carting something to the station, and I fear it was wrong of me to have found this a delightful break. It took a good long time to get there, and one was paid just the same as for hard work. Human nature being what it is, the agricultural labourer loves earning easy money when occasion offers, such as going along to a station on a cart or when rain sends him indoors to a cushy job; while, human nature being what it is, the employer is intensely irri-

tated by the same – for few employers give themselves psychological ease of mind by looking at the thing in the lump and
regarding their wage payment as so much a year, instead of
seeing it in pieces and feeling when a man is doing such and
such a thing, *it's not worth the money*.

There was a pub along the road to the station, and on one
occasion I stopped and had a drink. It struck me afterwards that
this would have been regarded as incredibly reprehensible had it
been known. I say it struck me afterwards for I was not ac-
climatized to my new milieu. The freedom of the more
favoured professions, doctor, lawyer, writer, B.B.C. man, etc., is
scarcely realized by their members: the weekly wage-earner
who sells so many hours of his time is *owned* during those hours.
Somehow I didn't get this clearly into my head at first. But
before I was finished with the agricultural world as a labourer, I
was keenly aware of a tense atmosphere if I stopped work for a
few minutes to hold a conversation or even to pat my dog.

14. Indignation of Mrs Miles

As carter, it was often my job to collect sacks of apples and
centralize them. One day I was engaged in collecting a number
of earlies from a certain portion of the apple orchards where
Mrs Miles was working with a number of land girls and temporary assistants. The sacks were not always properly filled.
Feeling full of beans that morning, I said to Mrs Miles in a
jolly kind of way, and with what I imagined was an obvious
acknowledgement of her as the overseer of the company – 'Mrs
Miles, would you see that they fill up the sacks properly.' I had
hardly finished the sentence when she flew into a rage. 'I don't
take no orders from nobody!' she shouted very, very loudly.
'I'm not taking no orders from you, I only take orders from the
boss,' she screamed seven times, as if I had said something
mortally insulting to her. This silenced me properly, and I did not
even attempt to start replies beginning with 'I only said ...'
knowing that it would be useless, and I went on my way without

rejoicing. While she, I was later informed, continued to rail against me during the entire afternoon. In future I steered clear of any possible repetition of such behaviour, handling her with the respect one pays to a time-bomb which may explode at any minute.

All the same, she had one more shot at me, as it were, at a later date. I was engaged with a bill-hook on a hedge near a field where hoeing was in progress. Some friends of the boss, or rather neighbouring gentry, had come out to do 'a spot of work' for the afternoon – a pretty girl and a somewhat la-di-da young man. After about half an hour of hoeing they began to weary of well-doing, and resting on their hoes looked round the farm. Catching sight of me, a short distance away, I heard one of them ask idly – 'Who is that?' Mrs Miles, being present, answered, in even louder tones than usual so as to make sure that I could hear – *'Oh that's nobody. He's only a workman here.'*

I could not help wishing that Mrs Miles could realize how completely she had failed to offend me. There is a certain type of intellectual, of which I am one, who suspects that his observations on life lack something vital, feeling uncertain as to the validity of reflections that owe nothing to experience of everyday work. So with me. Hence I had eagerly grasped at the opportunity of entering the manual working world. A man may do this and still feel an outsider and not accepted as a proper worker by the others. Thus it was with a real sense of satisfaction that I heard the tribute of Mrs Miles, and I was sorry that the irony of this was lost on her.

But it was easy to say the wrong thing to Mrs Miles. A young lady of the neighbourhood came in and worked quite regularly in the afternoons, knocking off at about four. Being a middle-class girl of pre-war days she was brought up to be permanently out of work (though not receiving any dole). She came along now and hoed with Mrs Miles, going home at four. The afternoons always seem long and she was glad to knock off then. Being a very amiable person, I heard her say once to Mrs Miles when she was about to leave – 'I'm so sorry you have to go on till five-thirty, Mrs Miles.' This was, of course, a fearful psychological mistake. *'I don't mind!'* said Mrs Miles in tones which combined intense indignation at the presumed commiseration, with amused contempt.

Anyway she was certainly a wonderful worker, worth her weight in gold to any employer – she belonged to the old-time type of woman who has always worked on the land, putting in an amount of work seldom witnessed nowadays. She had also another contribution which endeared her to the boss. She had an observant eye, and if anything seemed to have been pinched, say some plums, she would report the same. The boss had carried the technique of 'being in a hurry' almost as far as it would go; but, curiously, he forgot his urgency and would stand quite still and pleasantly absorbed if 'the tale' was being told, or if someone had a complaint to make about someone else.

15. The Judes the Obscure

Most of the ends and sayings, saws and clichés, have their origin in agriculture, and it amused me to find them coming to life. Ploughing a lonely furrow. Putting your back into it. Doing the spade-work. Putting the cart before the horse. Separating the chaff from the wheat, the sheep from the goats. Spilling the beans. Stepping over the traces. Nipped in the bud. Getting the lie of the land. Having a harrowing experience. Barking up the wrong tree. Jogging along. A mere drudge.

The last-named is really another term for the chain harrow, which I often used on the grass between the fruit trees. The verb which rhymes with it so well, trudge, was certainly born on the land, and fitly describes the job of harrowing. After the interest of novelty had worn off I never took kindly to harrowing, it was too much of a trudge, too drawn out a clod-stumbling amble. The horse gave me the impression of hating it – though I may be wrong. It struck me forcibly, and to my surprise, that here was the job of jobs for a machine, a tractor. I think violent exercise suits me better than steady work, and on these harrowing occasions a certain weariness sometimes overtook me, and going home I often murmured to myself Gray's lines 'the weary ploughman homeward plods his way', wondering how exactly the line went, was it as above or 'the ploughman homeward plods his weary way'? but never having the energy to look it up.

On cheerless days I sometimes fell into a low mood and wondered what on earth I was doing there, and began to feel that by doing it I was not pulling my full weight for myself. Such moods gave me insight into the Judes the Obscure of the world. Of all the fundamentally necessary professions, the pursuit of agriculture is the most manly and the most worthwhile – about this there can hardly be two opinions. But it is not the job for Young Ambition, nor for a person potentially gifted at something else, nor for the very intellectually inclined. Luckily most people are not ambitious in a big way, nor specially gifted. Yet there are the Judes. One day when I was covering-over by harrow a freshly sown field, I recalled how in the old days the job of keeping the birds off was done by boys rattling a clacker for sixpence a day, and I remembered how Hardy's Jude, in the hour of his greatest obscurity, standing in the ploughed field, clacker in hand, looked round and murmured – 'How ugly it is here!' It is a fine piece of realism. That field must indeed have seemed hateful in the eye of the small beholder, a torment of desolation, the veritable image of the awful monster that devours children – boredom. He must, he would escape it! He did. Thus in fiction. Not in life. I fell into conversation with a neighbouring labourer, a man exceptionally skilled with a team of horses that he could make follow him while he walked in front. I expected this man to say that he enjoyed his work and to sing the praises of horses versus machines. But no, he hated the life. He had been started on it very young, he told me. 'I didn't like it then,' he said, 'and I don't like it now.' He could have been a musician or singer. He played and sang in the village church and sometimes in the pub. But his talents had not been pronounced enough to allow him to make good his escape. The Judes of real life, the truly obscure Judes, are found at the end as at the beginning, in the field, by the side of the hill, not having achieved the exalted calamity of tragic failure.

16. A View of Literary Production

The most exhilarating sight I saw this May, or for that matter during any May anywhere, was a big beanfield in bloom. It was a lovely sight for it was a superb crop, but perhaps I should write *smell*. I was ignorant that the bean-flower had such a magnificent scent. We sing the rose, we sing the honeysuckle; but a whiff from such a beanfield carries us further.

This field belonged to a neighbouring farm, and there was a right of way through it to the station. The farmer was an extremely friendly man and I often had a meal with him and his kind and generous wife. I do not know what he was like as an employer, but he was very human, and he resembled in person and ways my preconceived idea of the old-time farmer. He groused of course, and he 'made no money'; but he was not in a state of nervous tension; he was not in a hurry; he liked to stop and chat; a land girl who walked through his premises in a two-piece bathing-dress set him up for a week; and he enjoyed going to the Hippodrome on a Saturday.

One evening there was some talk of books and I happened to mention the existence of certain novelists who produced two books a year, regularly. I spoke as one shocked at this. He also was shocked, but for the opposite reason. 'Is that *all?*' he kept repeating. 'Surely with all that imagination they could turn out more than that!' This broadened my mind a bit. Life is incredibly departmentalized, and we deceive ourselves if we think that others outside our department see us in the smallest degree as we see ourselves. The above remark of the farmer gave me the angle from which literary production is seen by many agriculturalists, no doubt. A farmer accustomed to produce vast quantities of corn, eggs, milk, roots, and bacon, which at given periods is all sold, eaten, and never seen again, assumes that literature is produced in similar perishable quantities, and that the author will turn out, say, ten books a month.

I said that I appreciated his point of view. The more so, I added, since there are far too many writers who accept the food that appears on the table without a conception of the skill, the ardours, and the devotion that makes its appearance possible. This was well received. But I could not help wondering what he would have thought if I had told him how Oscar Wilde, on being asked what he had done on a certain day, had replied – 'I spent the morning putting in a comma, and the afternoon in taking it out again.' We must hold that Wilde, in displaying such devotion over punctuation (it takes a great man to handle the comma: see Cobbett at one extreme, Shaw at the other, and Macaulay in the middle) thereby advanced the cause of Culture. But if I had spent the morning in putting down one seed-potato and the afternoon in taking it up again, it could scarcely be claimed that I had thereby advanced the cause of Agriculture. I went away that evening reflecting sadly upon the magnitude of the gulf that in this matter separated me from the farmer. I could understand his art, he could not understand mine, nor have a glimmering of what T. E. Lawrence meant by saying that he would rather write a great sentence than win a battle, nor appreciate why Churchill declared after an illness that though he was now strong enough to fight the Germans he was still too weak to paint a picture.

17. The Farm in Late May

When I came to the farm there was little to see in the way of colour save various shades of wood and grass. How it had changed near the end of May! The old story – that which was brown turning green, that which was black seen as white: an old story, differing from all other tales, from all art, from all tricks, in that though repeated every year, it still surprises us, still calls for applause and praise.

The Grenadiers were just coming out, the Beauty of Bath in blossom, the Coxes in blossom – then over the hedge another field with James Grieves and Worcesters in blossom, while the trees which had submitted to the grafting were budding on those branches. The dark hedges had become green. The corn was steadily rising. In a four-acre field into which were crowded black-currants, plums, gooseberries, blackberries, strawberries, and tomatoes, the bushes that began to change their appearance first were the black-currants. For some weeks in the midst of a general greyness their parallel green rows shone out with arresting distinctness. But at length the plum trees were in full bloom, and when I took the leverage cultivator up and down between the rows, the white petals fell upon the back of the perspiring horse and stuck there – a most decorative sight. Later, I spent some hours rescuing the miserable strawberry plants from under thistles and docks. Never did a poorer-looking plant produce so ostentatious a fruit as the strawberry. It looks well on a plate, but on the ground it looks absurd – the cultivated one, not the wild strawberry. The huge fruit, far too heavy for its frail stem, lies helpless on the soil, and it is necessary to put straw under the berry to keep it from rotting – hence *strawberry*, I suppose.

Thus this field, which when the owner took it over eight years previously was barren, now was bursting with life. As I passed alongside of it on the cart, getting a good view of it as a whole, I often thought of the *latent power* that lay there till released and channelled by man. Nothing to see on that former dry and barren field, save tangled yellowish grass: yet holding within it the force to throw upward what I now beheld. A farmer is a liberator of the energy in the earth, ceaselessly creating what is good, and adding on a vast scale to the beauty of the world.

The boss here had built up all these orchards from scratch, and had battled successfully in the end through the lean years. It was a truly creative achievement. The struggle had left its mark upon him. Melancholy by nature, he was now, I think, inclined to detest the world. I did not hear him say anything good of it or anyone in it. But he was obviously a man who held, or thought he held, ideas. He could be affable, if not courteous. Having had a bit of education, he rather enjoyed sometimes making me feel small in front of others over practical matters; but I could hardly blame him for that, and I marvelled at his patience with me during these green days of mine.

18. Scene on the Meadow

June is generally the great hay-making month. But as this was not a mixed farm, and it was only under the pressure of war that arable was being extended, our hay-making did not amount to much. In fact there was only one field to cut. As Prince was often extremely difficult to manage with any unaccustomed instrument behind him, Morgan and Arthur Miles took over the horses with the idea of getting things going before I carried on. This turned out just as well. For Prince refused to move. He just would not pull the machine. 'I'll make the b move all right!' shouted Arthur, and laid on to his hindquarters with a stick. This did not make the slightest impression on the horse. 'You'll get what's coming to you, you sod!' bellowed Arthur again, this time attacking from the side. But the horse only stepped back on to the machine. Then Arthur, thundering at Morgan to get on to the seat and use the reins, made a frontal attack on Prince, striking his head and nose, until some blood began to trickle from the nostrils. Yet it had no effect, and I looked on at this quiet rural scene in the nice June morning with some interest, wondering who would win the battle of will-power. Of course the man did, and eventually the horse moved forward, and after a certain amount of preliminary unsteady going, he went quietly and I was ready to take over without mishap.

It was a rather miserable meadow, so I cannot pretend that I got much of a kick out of this new experience. Indeed the whole thing was hardly hay-making proper. Nor did we rick it. We carried it into the barn – one portion of the old oast-house.

During the loading-up I heard Arthur expand on the subject of modern wages and prices. 'The higher wages don't make no difference,' he said. 'We're worse off today, I reckon. Take baccy: twopence an ounce in the old days – now eightpence. Take boots: a fine pair for six shillings before – look at the price now. Take a suit: nice suit for twenty-five shillings in the old days. Now you can't get nothing for that.'

And so on through a list. To which Morgan replied – 'Yes,

but consider the laws and regulations these days. The wages are constant. A boss can't stand his men off. In the old days there was a well-paid foreman to keep the others down. On a wet day he would say to a man, "You can go home, *and play with the cat*". Or take piece-work. Think of the rates there. It depended upon the boss. I knew a man who used to say to a hedger, "Let me see now, perhaps I can manage a halfpenny per five yards", and then would add, "I dunno. *It's too much for a halfpenny, and too little for three-farthings*".'

I have since often heard variations on Arthur's reckoning on wages as good or better in the old days. It is quite a favourite theme amongst the older men. But I have never been able to swallow it. It is often downright contrariness – one might almost say it is nonsense. And if taken up on it, many are inclined to agree that it is nonsense – for though the agricultural labourer tends to be a very pig-headed person with regard to views and practices, he is incredibly inconsistent in his thought and argument, often unsaying what he has just said in the most surprising way. The point is that though prices are so different today they are *not* commensurate with the rise in wages. And though in the old days labourers received a great deal of pay in kind, there was no definiteness about it, no absolute constancy, it depended upon the place (with regard to wood, for instance), and upon the boss, who always had you to that extent in his pocket. Finally, if you discount both the above considerations, the present wage puts the labourer into a far more dignified position than when he received a question of shillings as opposed to the pounds received by town workers. It is a psychological point of some importance. Not that I have any axe to grind on this or any other agricultural matter, and I should add that Mr Fred Kitchin, the author of that great book *Brother To The Ox,* opens his memoirs by saying that in his youth 'seventeen shillings went as far as two pounds in these days'. Also I have seen some formidable statistics on this subject produced by Mr H. J. Massingham which tell against my view.

But I am quite certain that if any of the present-day labourers were given the sudden option of going back to the old days, they would change their tune in a flash. I would be interested to meet the piece-working hedger who would like to go back to the boss who thought that while five yards' worth of work was too much for a halfpenny, it was 'too little for three-farthings', or to meet any labourer who would consider the old days as rose-coloured under foremen who could at any moment stand you off and say 'go home and play with the cat'.

19. While Thinning, Picking, Pruning

The farmer who deals in corn can leave the situation in the hands of Nature for some months before harvest. The farmer who deals in fruit has to *thin out* his crop before it gets ripe and full. This was an eye-opener to me. When, for instance, the plum trees had become heavily weighted with rows of already large plums, it became necessary to do away with a large number of them. That is to say, you picked and threw down what seemed to be about two-thirds of the trees' fruit. It felt like appalling wastefulness, and went much against the grain to do it. Here was a branch hanging with dozens of excellent plums, all about the same size: and it was your business to snip away all that were closer together than two inches. Those remaining would grow, it appeared, into such fine plums that they would equalize the quantity of fruit that had been thrown away. Perhaps this was true; but it was impossible to believe it at this stage, and while engaged on the job, one felt – everyone new at it felt – a scandalous waster of nature's abundance. Yet custom stales. And I remember how a voluntary helper – a girl from the university – once became so doped and dazed by the work that I saw her thin *every plum* off one branch. An agonizing sight.

This thinning was a lengthy proceeding and went on for some weeks. To get it done at all many helpers were needed – another difficulty confronting the fruit-grower. For temporary labour is neither the easiest to get hold of, nor the most satisfactory. However, the boss was fairly strong on land girls. He was able to get some university students who came just for the thinning and the picking. Also he had one Land Army girl for milking (but there was only one cow) and other jobs; while he also employed another girl who was the daughter of a farmer, and who in liveliness, guts and knowledge of literature was worth all the university students put together. She was strong but not hefty. In fact her figure left so little to be desired that she turned out in a two-piece bathing-dress, thus creating more sensation than the place could carry.

The university girls sometimes created a problem for Morgan. Not being afraid of getting the sack, they did not always keep the work going with that earnestness which is proper to agricultural proceedings. There were a number of pools on this farm surrounded by trees – very tempting places for a swim. One afternoon during working hours the girls decided to jump into one of these pools. Leaving their clothes on the bank, they began to enjoy a swim. Soon Morgan became aware of their disappearance, and at length, approaching the pond, spotted their clothes and then the swimmers. They were delighted. But he did not seem to appreciate the sylvan poetry and classic simplicity of the scene. Should he remove their clothes? he asked himself indignantly. It was clear that if he removed their clothes to a distance, or out of sight altogether, it would advance the cause of discipline. But would it advance the cause of morals? And was a diversion of this sort agriculturally advisable at this busy time? Being a very discreet man, he thought better of it – greatly to the disappointment of the multitude, amongst whom I must number Mrs Miles as well as myself.

If extra workers were needed for thinning the fruit, a great many more were necessary for the final operation of harvesting it in August. Seeing them all – perennial, professional fruit-pickers – I wondered how the owner could possibly make a profit after he had paid them all. This department of agriculture calls for a farmer of stout heart. He who deals with arable land can count upon a certain degree of harvest in the worst of seasons. He sows his seed and according to his skill in husbandry he will reap his reward. Luck, sheer luck may elevate or destroy the fruit-grower. The beauty of Spring, the whole parade of bloom and blossom, can change overnight into the whiteness of the flowers of frost. The spectacle of promise and bounty turns into a picture of blasted hope. This sometimes happens three years in succession. He can do nothing about it – no tarpaulin being large enough to spread over his farm at night.

First came the black-currant harvest. Enter crowds of women from round about, some of them pushing prams. They went at it hard all day, being paid so much a pound. They belonged to a very low-class stratum – a depressing crew, pale-faced, unhealthy-looking, truculent, their minds bent simply and solely upon l.s.d.; seeing nothing else in the fruit, absolutely nothing but so much l.s.d. There seemed no progress here from the similar kind of scene that Jack London used to write about in years gone by. However picturesque this sort of thing can be made to appear by a painter, the thing itself is pitiful, so charged with the harshness, not of life which all round is smiling and warm and beautiful with abundant increase, but of man's life, of man's narrowing down of life till there is nothing before his eyes but a few pieces of silver – which he can only get into his hands by doing work from which he robs all the enjoyment.

It was not a good black-currant crop this year, and the more truculent women demanded more money per pound since they couldn't pick the poor crop fast enough to make the turnover they expected. Since the boss was going to make less, he must pay them more – a good example, I thought, of the fraternal link between employer and employee in our democracy.

These outside fruit-pickers were all the more conspicuous since they were accompanied in their work by other strata of society. There were Arthur and Mrs Miles lording it after their fashion. There was the boss at the receipt of custom, and Morgan filling up the van. There were the various girls in bathing attire contrasting forcibly with the heavily clothed pickers who, of course, regarded such dress as scandalous, since Nature herself is not seen by them, the human body when seen is a sore.

And there were several other people who came in from round about to give a hand, including two who looked in for an hour, symbol of carefree leisure. All spoke, all behaved according to upbringing and chance in life. Marx was not wholly right. Everything is not caused by environment. But it is more than a half-truth. It is a three-quarter truth. And the more I see of people the more I see that they are for the most part what circumstances have made them, and the less I feel inclined to scoff or condemn, however little I seem to gild. Certainly this spectacle here was a neatly framed object lesson in the inequality of life. Also, I may add, a lesson in the equality of man – under the law of battle. At not infrequent intervals we all assembled in the ditch. For while we assisted at these old tasks upon the earth, a singular job was being performed in the sky by others. History was going on up there. England had again been challenged by the Hun, and her answer was being made above our heads. We witnessed an air battle twice daily. We enormously enjoyed the show. When the fall of metal became dangerous it was our *duty* to seek the ditch. These diversions considerably lightened our humble toil.

When the pickers had reached the plum harvest, my job was to prune the black-currant bushes. This means cutting away all the branches that had borne fruit, leaving the fresh shoots that had already grown up. For this purpose I used a long pincer-like shears with which I could reach down and cut right on the stool. As I went along I often came upon currants that had been left over by the pickers, a certain number of which I brought home every day, during which time I was freer, more completely free, from constipation, pardon my mentioning it, than I have been in the course of my life.

It was a lengthy but stimulating job. I made huge piles of the discarded branches, leaving behind the already renewed bushes which should repeat the work of the others next year. I find such well-known physical facts to be metaphysically most exhilarating. The ordinary is rather more extraordinary than the extraordinary just as the material is rather more immaterial than the immaterial, and it is surely the mark of an inferior mind to be moved to wonder by the exception instead of the rule. The rule beats the exception at its own game. It is not the rabbit out of the hat but the rabbit out of the rabbit that is so surprising. No phrase such as 'Nature's fecundity' is able to dismiss it. I confess it still stirs me at intervals, this the most conspicuous of all phenomena, the recurrent increase, the ever-lasting something out of nothing. Contrary to what one might expect. Granted, it is not quite something out of nothing: I'm surrounded by plums, apples, currants, hard and concrete sub-stances miraculously appearing, but they are made out of earth, they are made out of air, they are the earth, they are the air – granted, but the circle is continued eternally, the washing is always taken in all round, yet no bankruptcy, no waste. The mind, made rotten by political economy, expects otherwise, fears waste. I still feel nervous when I throw away a piece of bread. But in Nature nothing can be lost, nothing wasted, nothing thrown away, there is no such thing as rubbish. It might be good for us if we threw things away a bit more, so that we might grasp that they cannot be destroyed – this, the first of the miracles of God.

As a matter of fact I see there is a tendency in some quarters to take this uneconomic and metaphysical view of the matter. There is the famous case of the coffee growers in Brazil who in 1938 threw away six hundred thousand bags of coffee every month. That's the spirit.

About this time, several tons of Shoddy were delivered and deposited on the track beside the fruit trees. Previously shoddy had been merely an adjective as far as I was concerned. I had heard of shoddy goods or a shoddy person. I was interested to come upon the noun. It consisted of huge bundles of woolly material. It was the gleanings from cloth factories, fibres that had been thrown away, rubbish from the industrial angle. We proceeded to spread the stuff out, covering the ground between the trees with it as a species of manure. It was pleasant to see this 'rubbish' thus enter into a new mode of activity, and in obedience to the rule of eternal return, dedicate its action to the cause of Agriculture.

20. Threshing Scene

The small corn harvest was gathered simultaneously with the fruit, and as I did not take part in this to any complete extent, I shall say nothing about that operation in this place. But in early September I took part in my first threshing experience.

Since there was only one rick to do, it was not very elaborate. The old-time affair was used – the hired thresher with steam engine. We got going by about eight o'clock – and a few extra men came from outside to give a hand. The owner of the engine, having set the thing going, walked round looking on with a somewhat superior air. Indeed I was surprised to see how nearly he conformed to Hardy's description in *Tess* of the owner of the tackle who came to the farm that employed Tess. It was none of his business to lend a hand or in any way to take part in proceedings once he had started his engine. Occasionally he went to one of the bags and took a sample of the grain in hand and looked at it knowingly, then moved round rubbing the forefinger and thumb of his right hand in a thoughtful manner in order to cancel his absence of thought. It was clear that for him also 'the long strap which ran from the driving wheel of his engine to the red thresher under the rick was the sole tie-line between agriculture and him'.

There was no elevator and my place was at the shaft where the straw came out from the thresher, my job being to serve it to the rick-makers, Morgan and Arthur Miles. Quite enough of it came out to keep me engaged, and quite enough shreds went down my neck and back, since I had not grasped the necessity of a tightly buttoned shirt for this affair. There was no let-up for hours, and owing to the prickling discomfort I began to feel it as an endurance test, for as the rick grew my handing up became increasingly harder; but I had no intention of giving any hint of fatigue, and in any case always rather enjoy that kind of thing. But I was quite blind to the scene as a whole, seeing nothing in fact but my own ever-falling straw.

In the interval for a morning meal, Mrs Miles, feeling the

need for self-expansion, shouted (as usual as if against a high wind) – 'How do you like this *wurk*, Mr Collis, this is *wurk*,' etc., rather embarrassing everyone else as well as myself, I thought.

Before we knocked off, the remainder of the rick had to be covered with an old tarpaulin which we dragged out of the stable close-by. We unfolded it gradually, and as we did so more than one nest of mice came to light, mice large and small and tiny. They began to try and scuttle away, the baby ones running round helplessly. Arthur grabbed at them with his enormous hands, catching two or three at a time. He squeezed them to death and stuck them in his waistcoat pocket. He disposed of a large number of them in this manner. He took a mouse, squeezed it between his forefinger and mighty thumb, stuck it in his pocket, then grabbed another, squeezed it and likewise stuck it into his coat or waistcoat until he was bulging with mice. At first I couldn't imagine the object of this collection. It turned out that they were for his cat at home. On returning he would call the cat to him and steadily produce mice from his person. Not so much for love of the cat, I gathered, as in order to encourage further research in this direction.

Before finishing for the day I made a typical beginner's *faux pas*. I left a prong lying on the ground. Arthur nearly stepped on it. And did he swear! Certainly he had every cause to do so. Failing to stick a prong upright and leaving it on the ground, is the sort of crazy thing beginners do, being blind to the extreme danger of such a thing.

21. While Potato-lifting

Time marched on. Each day seemed long, each week short. It was already autumn. What is the salient characteristic of autumn? The spiders' threads in the early morning frost. I am not thinking so much of the circular networks, marvellous as these are, hung along the gate; but rather the threads that are strung across everything, so that if you bend down till your eye is level with the field you can see a white veil over the whole expanse. They are everywhere, on everything. 'Do they drape the cannons in France?' asked Mr Ralph Wightman, true poet, in a striking image, the other day. To look down at these things is like looking up at the stars – we are baffled by quantity.

The time had come for potato-lifting. I was particularly interested in the potato field. I had been on it from the start, manuring, planting, harrowing, hoeing, shinning. At intervals I had examined the growth of the potatoes, minutely, from the appearance of the shoots that look like white worms coming out of the original potato, till down under, that one thing had produced many things, and sent up whole bushes which then flowered very prettily indeed in August – a lovely sight, strangely unsung. By which time the original potato, the cause of it all, having rendered up its virtue, had become a squashy bag of pulp.

A great deal of agriculture is simply common sense modified by experience. Thus, even if I assumed ignorance in the reader about potato-lifting, I know that without my help he could say in advance almost exactly what is done: first, the potatoes ploughed out; then the pickers with buckets each go up a row filling sacks already spread out at given distances along the lines; while at the same time a horse and a cart or tractor and cart take the filled sacks away. That is how one would imagine it is done: and that is how it is done. We did one thing here though, which I never did anywhere else since. The soil was very damp and the potatoes were clung with clay. Before we bagged them we went up the rows with a specially designed hand-fork which we used to dig the potatoes out of their clay covering, leaving them in heaps to dry.

This potato harvest calls for really dry weather. And one seldom gets it. We got plenty of rain. It was very clayey soil. Clay is not always called clay in the agricultural world; it is often called sand. A sandy soil means earth that is not very thick and cloggy. Clayey soil means thick stuff, with much mud in winter. It was the latter here. The mud was terrific. It clung to one like glue. I soon qualified not only as a clod-hopper but also as a clod-lifter. With such a soil potato-lifting in rain provides considerable discomfort. It was so extreme in sheer wetness, slipperiness and muddiness that I enjoyed it.

Some extra hands came along for this job, also, casual labour sent out from the local labour exchange (foul official words all, 'hands', 'casual', 'labour exchange', containing the maximum of dehumanization). One was an actor. I worked beside him as we went up our respective parallel rows. There is nothing like conversation for making this kind of job go well. We talked about all sorts of things. We got on to psychologists for some reason. 'I hate their style and their outlook,' I said. 'I hate their motives,' he said. We soon turned to the theatre. 'What is the point in T. S. Eliot's *Murder in the Cathedral*?' I asked. 'Is it that egotism is always the real reason for our actions?' 'I believe the point is,' said he, 'that men do the right things for the wrong reasons.' At this point unfortunately our respective lines came to an end, and circumstances were such that we would not work together up two fresh rows, and so we parted. His name was Stanley Messenger, and I hope he is still posted somewhere in this world.

When he had gone I reflected upon how companionship depends upon what we have in our heads and not on what we have in our pockets. If one of us had been very rich and the other very poor it would have made no difference. The gulf between people is not one of money, it is one of mind. If I am working with a man who has nothing in his mind, with whom one can exchange no idea, no knowledge, no opinion, no witticism, then there is a real cleft between us far greater than anything that could be caused by class or money. All very obvious, perhaps. But I mention it because I continually have day-dreams of a time when lots of people would come out into the fields and love working with their hands, and also love working with the mind, their manly heritage, and make such jobs as these go quickly and delightfully. It will be a sad criticism of life if we have to say that such a dream is futile.

Anyway I wouldn't ask much more than this of my Utopia – easier to come by, more worth coming by, than the honey-sweet Nowheres of the pseudo-poets.

22. Hedging and Ditching

After this I took on a new job for the rest of the winter. There was much hedging and ditching to be done, and it was delegated to me. This opened up another field of labour for me. Hitherto, hedging and ditching were merely terms residing in the top floor of my head. Now I could take them down and look at them. The hedges on a farm, or anywhere else, do not stay quietly dividing the fields. If left to themselves too long they invade the fields. During the agricultural slump nearly all the hedges on farms became neglected and out of hand. I have seen farms where shoots from hedges were advancing out into the fields in columns of fours. We are accustomed nowadays to statistics such as 'if everyone saved one lump of coal per day, this means a national saving of twenty thousand tons a year' or 'one old kettle given to salvage by every housewife means a squadron of Spitfires' or some such nonsense (if it is nonsense). In the same way the number of acres lost through neglected hedging might amuse a statistician's mind.

Whatever the national loss by such neglect, it is clear that hedges on any given farm soon get out of hand, growing far too high, straggling all over the place, and clogging the ditches. It is the job of the hedger to cut them down to about the height of his waist, to foster growth where there are holes, to 'lay' them where they are too thin, and to clear the ditches beside them.

After due instruction I approached the hedges of this farm with the necessary implements –a bill-hook, a hook, and a slasher. I soon made an impression on them. No job has more to show for it. I would come to a great straggling growth with an accompanying ditch quite concealed under grass and hedge shoots, and presently I would have reduced a number of yards of it so that it was unrecognizable. A complete transformation of the scene. The whole character of the place changed, and beside the hedge, a neat ditch. As I went on at this, week after week, I felt I was making my mark on the farm. Especially at one place where a field sloped down to a river-bed. The hedge at the bottom came out several yards into the field, and my progress was almost like changing the landscape.

Incidentally, that river-bed was an eerie place. There was a sort of little glen running along at the bottom of two converging slopes. Indeed, except for its smallness it was a perfectly genuine glen, with trees and steep rocky clefts, at the bottom of which was a river-bed. But one thing was outrageously lacking. There was no river. During most of the year one could walk along the smooth, cliffed waterway. It was like going along a road where no traffic ever passed, where no man trod – a ghostly place, a haunted, silent, deadly lane.

At this job I was paid by the rod – that is, I did it as piece-work. I found that if I kept at it I was able to make about the same as being paid by the week in the ordinary way. But this was because Morgan gave me a generous cash measurement, not exactly on a par with the 'too little for three-farthings' man.

Doing work by the piece opened my eyes to the difference between Space and Time. Philosophers are pleased to inform us that we live in a Space–Time Continuum and that both are the same thing. I do not question it. But I am free to say that in the agricultural world they are mighty opposites. When you are working by the hour, time drags. When you are working by the space, time flies. Doing piece-work you want to cover so much ground, so much space – and so time moves fast. If you have no Space to conquer but only Time – then time stands still.

Apart from this, hedging is certainly not a monotonous job, because each hedge is different and there is so much to show for the work. But even so one can have enough of a good thing, and not for worlds would I take on a roadman's life. I began to weary of hedges after I had done only a few; but to see nothing but hedges all your life, to hang perpetually on the periphery of agriculture, never in it, hedged off from it, and do the same thing every day, must be the devil of a business, especially in winter. I shall never again dash along the roads in a motor car without knowing just why the ditches and banks are so trim and neat.

There was plenty of firewood to be got out of these hedges, which came in very useful, for every week I could empty a cartful at my house, the boss not having the least objection to my doing so. The well from which I drew water was some distance from the house, a journey through two fields and over two fences. So I became 'a hewer of wood and a drawer of water'. That popular phrase, with the adjective 'mere' in front of it, suggests that here is the bottom rung in the ladder of life. Well, it may be. But if so, I cannot say that I want to climb the ladder much. I have no objection to these simplicities.

Still, I could have done with a bit of coal. But it was too much 'out in the wilds' for a delivery. So I had to cut down some trees also in order to get through the winter. Luckily the fireplace was so big that I could put in long logs and thus save much cutting up. When they were too long to fit, I let them come out into the room. When I was behindhand in my cutting I sometimes sawed them in the fireplace in the evening while the fire was going. There were some very cold spells, and I became more than a hewer of wood, I became a hewer of water. I often didn't go to the well, and when the rain-water froze in the tub I had to axe it . . . However, space forbids further trivialities of this kind, for I am eager to get on to Part Two of this book, and offer the reader a change of scene.

PART TWO
A FARM IN SOUTH-WEST ENGLAND

1. First Day

On the evening before the day I was due at the farm – the time being March 1942 – I unfortunately took something that disagreed with me, and felt ill at intervals throughout the night and no better at six o'clock the next morning. But feeling that I should stick to the engagement, I got up and cycled down (a twenty minutes' ride) to the farm, arriving punctually at seven.

I found no one in the farmyard. But soon the boss's son, a boy of fifteen, came out of the dairy and told me that I would find his father at the other dairy where there had been some mishap that morning. This meant a ride to a far portion of the farm, which was about a thousand acres. Very welcome, indeed a godsend, this ride, for in my present state I knew I would be actually sick if I did any work. So I took my time and in due course arrived at this other dairy where I found the boss. He instructed me to go and help the carter who was getting a load of hay from a certain rick. I didn't follow the geography of the instructions, but I gathered that it was necessary to go back the way I had come and then pass further on. But when I reached the farmyard again, I decided quite definitely to fail to find the carter, still feeling certain of sickness if I bent my body about in the slightest degree – which would be a maddening way of starting work at this new place.

So I went into the barn and sat down. It was a large barn, full of sacks of all sorts and for all purposes, some on the floor, some filled with artificial and others with corn. I saw more than one grain-grinder, and there was an engine with an extremely high funnel. One of the grinders had a good traditional air about it, for imprinted on it were the words – 'Patronized by Her Gracious Majesty the Queen, the late Prince Consort, and His

Serene Highness the Viceroy of Egypt'. I sat down on one of the sacks, feeling very low, wondering what on earth I was doing here. I gazed round at the sacks, at the engine, at His Serene Highness, and out through the door into the paddock in the middle of which was a pool of water, to the left the stable, and straight ahead to a long shed in which were two wagons, a tractor, a drill, a binder, and some miscellanea. It was cold and raw, a drizzle coming down from the unbroken grey.

Here I remained for nearly an hour. Though not an inspiring hour, it saved my situation, for I was recovering and no longer felt that movement would undo me. So when the boss arrived and I had explained that I had missed the carter, I was ready for a job. There was a wagon waiting to go out and I was told to get a load of hay. Did I know how to use a hay knife? I was asked, and had to reply in the negative – an annoying start. I joined the boy whom I had met earlier and we went along up a track, past several large fields, and across a down till we reached the hayrick. We did not use the hay knife but took the hay from the top. My experience had been solely with a cart and I had never loaded a wagon, and I was surprised at the amount of stuff that one could put on to it. And when it came to fastening a rope round it I did not go about the fixing of it in the right way, and it was accomplished deftly by the boy who seemed very amiable. We brought the load down then and deposited it in the dairy.

The afternoon was spent in getting more loads and putting them in the stable-loft. This time I had a new companion, a young man called Dick, about twenty. He was very pleasant and friendly – an opinion I was never to change. We used the hay knife this time, an instrument which I found needed a greater physical effort than any other I am familiar with. One of these days they will introduce a hay knife like a bread knife with teeth, let us hope. A haystack is simply a huge loaf for feeding cattle, and is cut just as one cuts an ordinary loaf, in slices. Not hacked away in bits and pieces. A half-cut stack should present a nice perpendicular wall on the cut side – then the rain won't hurt it.

Dick said that he had found hay very difficult at first, and still didn't like dealing with it (I have yet to find the labourer who finds it easy). He didn't make the slightest attempt now or at any other time to show off or to show me how to do a thing, or get a rise out of me, or put me right. That was his nature. It was also due to the fact that he did not like agricultural work and took no pride in it. He had been forced into agriculture – as so many cases – simply for the convenience of his parents. There were many other jobs he would have preferred, perhaps an engineering one of some sort. In the reaction caused today by the insolence, the folly, and the greed of many townsmen, there is a tendency for writers on country themes to assume that the countryman alone is splendid, the townsman a poor specimen. This view can be overdone. A man may loathe agriculture, have no love for the earth and no reverence for it, and yet be a superior human being to an ordinary countryman. In the same way it is superficial to suppose that the man who has dealings with animals, with sheep or cows or horses, is thereby more human or humanized than the man dealing solely with machines. The latter may be and often is more fully a human being than the former, who may be and often is most inhuman, callous, violent, and cruel.

2. Unromantic View of Agriculture

I continued on this sort of job for some days, either loading and unloading hay or spreading straw for the heifers. But my companion now was not Dick. It was the carter. He was a small man with a peculiar kind of stumping walk as if his legs were in some degree mechanical. His lower lip either hung down or closed over his upper lip. His tiny pale blue eyes glinted out from a red face. He spoke no word. He said neither good morning nor good evening. He answered no questions. He never said where we were going nor what we were about to do. I found this trying, as I did not then know that he was nearly as uncommunicative with everyone else. I thought that he harboured a special detestation for myself. And as a matter of fact, he did.

But I did not realize to what extent this was true till one day when we were hitching a horse to a wagon and I was being slow with the chains on my side, he dashed round, fuming and hissing in a remarkable manner, snatched the chains out of my hand, connected them himself, and said that he would rather work by himself than with a blank like me. Again, we were fetching harrows one day from a field. I handed one up to him the wrong way round. He took it and flung it on the ground, muttering – 'I don't know why my old man keeps me!' I never knew when this sort of thing might happen, especially as it was never very clear what we were about to do next, and I am slow in the uptake in practical matters. Thus at any moment he might break out and wonder why his old man kept him (in view of the fact that the old man, i.e. the boss, thought fit to employ me).

Thus these early days were no picnic.

This carter was a man whose bite was worse than his bark. In fact he didn't bark at all, he only bit – suddenly. It was not long before I met the man on this farm whose bark was worse than his bite – the shouter, 'the man with the iron bellows' as Dick called him, the man everyone had to treat with circumspection. This was Robert, the shepherd.

Having loaded up a wagon of hay we went over to a field one day in which the sheep were being folded. Here we deposited it for the benefit of the sheep (I did not previously know that sheep ate hay). My dog was accompanying me as usual, but as we arrived in the field a great shout went up, for the shepherd's dog and mine had collided, and so I heard for the first time this man's famous voice. At the time I didn't know it was famous, and that his shouting at his dog *all* the time, whatever it was doing and wherever he went, was accepted by everyone as a normal and recognized phenomenon. But hearing it for the first time under these circumstances, I thought a crisis had occurred. However, this didn't last long, and I was soon standing beside the shepherd who was ready for a quiet chat as he weighed me up.

He was an elderly man. In his youth he must have been uncommonly handsome. He was still very good-looking, strikingly so; completely rustic, his features, nose, cheekbones, set of eyes were yet at the same time aristocratically fine-shaped. Nor was this a passing fancy of mine; it struck me later whenever I caught him in profile on a rick. His eyes also, a pale-washed blue, were beautiful, except when they flared up in some outburst. And as I have already observed, his voice left nothing to be desired.

We chatted a little. We talked sheep. He said that there was a lack of milk in some of the ewes for no good reason, even when there were twins, and that when a lamb had to be put to a ewe that had lost one of its own lambs it was necessary sometimes to put the skin of the dead lamb over the former. Trying to figure this out, I went on with the carter to the next item on the agenda which consisted of loading up some straw from a very tight rick. I couldn't get the stuff out easily, but the carter could! He dug his prong in and hauled out absolutely huge bundles – indeed, never before or since have I seen a more skilled or more powerful loader than this man.

I did not always work with him. There were five horses in the stable, and I frequently took out a horse and cart or wagon alone, either to distribute straw on the fields for the heifers, or to fill up from a dunghill and distribute it. It had not occurred to me before that so much work is done on a farm which is merely a question of preserving the *status quo*. Work going ahead which is not in terms of tillage or planting or harvesting, but just keeping things going. Yet of course a dairy farm's work consists chiefly in simply preserving the *status quo*.

April came in very coldly, and remained so for some time with a strong east wind blowing. The peaceless, ceaseless wind – how I hate it! If one were to give feelings to Nature, one would say that when the sun comes out she breaks into a smile, and that when the wind blows she is in a temper. Certainly I always feel the wind as a bad-tempered thing, especially a cold one, and my mind contracts in resisting it, and I can enjoy no pleasant, expansive thoughts when ruffled by its peaceless, ceaseless wave. And during the long afternoons in it on this job I would sometimes fall again into low moods, again wondering whether I had lost my way. 'Thin, thin the pleasant human noises grow, And faint the city gleams ...' I would long for that city and a clean warm room. I will arise and go now, I would say to myself most unpoetically, and build me a town, far, far away from Nature and all her winds, where everything shall be artificial and where no man shall be comfortless nor cold for evermore!

I have no objection whatever to standing on a dunghill. There is no place where I am more content to stand. But for how long? That's the question. The dunghill today is rightly celebrated by poet, by prophet, and by priest. It is numbered amongst the highest riches of a land. I never feel better employed than when dealing with one. Thus engaged I can qualify for the approval of Sir Albert Howard and the tributes of statesmen, while also providing a perfect subject for a wood-cut. True. But consider the reality. It is 2 p.m. There are three and a half hours to go. There is an icy wind. Also a drizzle. There is no one to talk to, and if anyone does turn up there will be nothing to talk about. Though I am 'close to the earth' the dunghill soon ceased to be anything but an object, heavy and clogging. One wonders 'what is the time?' Alas – only 3.15!

3. 'E

A farmer is called by his men either 'the boss' or 'the guvnor' or 'the master' (now out of date), or 'the old man' (regard-less of age), or more often simply 'he'. He is never called 'the chief'.

At this farm he was sometimes called 'the boss', often enough 'the old man', generally 'He', or, more properly, ' 'E', and some-times merely 'the Van'. He used a second-hand butcher's van for getting about the premises and carrying oil and what not from one scene of operation to another. So one would hear –

'Look out, there's the van!' or 'I didn't see no van' when his whereabouts was doubtful. But on the whole he was designated simply as ' 'E' – ' 'E's coming!' It is as 'E that I think of him, and as 'E that I shall refer to him.

He was a man somewhere in the fifties. His eyes were impressive in their mildness, but his mouth was large and ugly, partly concealed by a stumpy moustache. You could recognize him a long way off by his walk. He took huge strides, head bent slightly down, like a man measuring a cricket pitch. That walk was very characteristic. There was no dawdling nor diddling about with him: he never strolled; he never looked round quietly at the scene; he never took out a pipe nor smoked a cigarette, any more than he would be likely to drink a glass of beer, pat a dog, or say good night, good morning, or thank you. He was on the go the whole time, as if his life depended on it. When he was at all excited, or indeed when giving instructions, he waved his hands about almost like a man catching invisible balls. Though sturdy to a degree, he was obviously a man of nervous temperament.

He came of a farming family for generations back. He had climbed that famous 'farming ladder' by the only way it can be climbed – by ceaseless energy, relentless toil, and knowledge of the job. Starting with nothing, he now ran this large farm with full equipment. Men who rose by their own efforts in farming between 1900 and 1940, and did not fail during the agricultural depression, had to be unusual men. Whatever else 'E was he was not usual, and not small.

Having adopted a certain pace – a terrific pace – he meant to keep it up. He neither would nor could slow down a bit. ' 'E'll break up one of these days' they would say at intervals. He did not intend to lose a minute if he could help it – for time was money to him as certainly as to any business man. An atmosphere of hurry and almost of crisis prevailed whenever he was around; and he generally was around, for he was his own foreman. He was also one of his own labourers, so to speak, for he joined in anything and everything, no job was beneath him. In this way he got a tremendous amount of work out of his men, as he set the pace, and each person felt that he had his eye on him – and he had.

We assembled in the yard in the morning at 7 a.m. There was no question of a good morning any more than of a good evening at the end of the day, nor any degree of cheerfulness. Life was too earnest for that. Orders would be given, and all dispersed in their several directions as quickly as possible out of his sight.

4. Full-scale Threshing

We did not always disperse in different directions, of course. There were combined operations even at this time of year. Quite a lot of threshing still remained to be done. (I used to imagine that threshing was an after-harvest affair, but bits of it are sometimes still waiting to be done in the following May!)

A corn rick is a bank in which the farmer has lodged about a hundred pounds. He draws the money when he feels inclined. But to get the cash out, as everyone knows, is a rather elaborate affair. I was to learn all about threshing at this farm.

The thresher is a machine which certainly holds the attention. Like a clear thought or a solved riddle, it looks perfectly obvious. And of course every invention is a clear Thought: every hard, concrete thing – chair, table, engine – was once as insubstantial as an idea. The threshing machine is informed with one comprehensive principle, namely to *shake* a series of trays with holes in them, which are cunningly placed one above the other. And the outfit does shake to such purpose that each sheaf falls into six separate pieces; three kinds of grain – good, less good, and poor – flow out of exits at the rear; straw straggles out of a line of cradles in perpetual bobbing motion at the front; chaff pours out of a hole at the side; and at the bottom there is excreted the remaining bits and pieces from ear and stalk which are grouped under the term cavings. Such is the outline. As for the number of belts, I have never been able to count them without getting muddled. It is sufficient to say that here is a useful machine. Here is the right thing in the right place. Anyone 'against machines' should be invited to look at a thresher until it occurs to him that what he is against is simply the wrong thing in the wrong place. He will find few such things on the land, however many he may find in the town.

Plenty of time was spent in assembling the tackle – 'the menagerie' as they called it. Much pulling and shoving about. First the thresher itself goes between two ricks – and when at last it is in the right spot it must be exactly level. A tractor (with special wheel for the purpose) is belted to it at the rear, while an elevator for depositing the straw is placed in front, with its own engine at its side.

Nine of us assembled to deal with this process of separation. The carter and Dick stood on it, on its deck, by the side of its hatchway or mouth into which the sheaves were let down, the carter performing that office, while Dick cut the string that held the sheaf together. Robert, the shepherd, stood under the elevator to make a rick with the straw deposited at his feet. 'E and myself got on to the now unthatched corn rick to deal out the sheaves. Harold, normally the tractor-driver, stood at the rear to deal with the sacks for grain placed under the exit pipemouths of the thresher. Jimmy, the lorry-driver and mechanic, presently appeared for loading up. In the centre on the ground was a land girl to sweep up the cavings. That is generally considered too few for the job, since three or even four people are useful on the corn rick, and two or even three are helpful on the straw rick. Nine was all we could muster. A small staff for a farm of this size. The explanation is that the unit of work had greatly increased owing to the war, two hundred extra acres of downland having been ploughed up, while the housing accommodation did not increase in proportion.

The tractor was started up and we got going. My job was to feed 'E, who passed on the sheaves to Dick. This was my first experience of unpacking this tight parcel. I thrust my prong in to take out a sheaf, but nothing came. I couldn't move it. 'Let's have 'em!' said 'E. But at first I found great difficulty in letting him have them. With the beginner's instinct for starting by

75

doing the wrong thing, I tried to take them out in an haphazard kind of manner, and found myself attempting to move the one I was half-standing on. A rick has been built in layers, and unless you unbuild in layers also you are lost, and so I had to improvise a technique for this immediately, and kept improvising techniques all day (as a matter of fact I have still no rule of thumb for this).

It was a windy day, the wind coming against us on the rick, so that the prickly dust flew into our faces, our eyes, and down our necks. By the middle of the afternoon I could hardly see out of either eye, while the stuff that had got down my neck, again owing to faulty buttoning, made me feel as if I were wearing an ascetic's hair-shirt. As the hours passed I occasionally glanced blurringly round to find a continually changing scene. Away to the left a yellow cliff had grown up, the straw stack, with a yellow mound beside it, the cavings; and over there at the other end bulging sacks now existed, filled with grain. And as other things rose, so I sank. At first high above the show, I was steadily sinking as I shovelled away my pedestal. But there was still a lot to be picked out and I couldn't believe I would ever get it all up this day – though it was known that 'E wanted to finish it. Another two hours passed and there was still some to deal with. Everyone by this time had turned chimney-sweep black, while the carter, not having shaved, and standing in the dustiest of all positions, offered an appearance that recalled earlier periods in the world's history. At length we had sunk to the very ground.

Having reduced the rick to its foundation, we stood on its bedding of straw. Under this were a number of rats. A ring was formed and everyone stood armed with a prong or shovel. Every second someone poked up a rat and slashed at it. Rats began to fly in the air like balls, one actually alighting on 'E's hat. Soon about twenty were disposed of. Then a large one escaped behind a horse-rake and ran under the straw rick. This did not ensure its escape. The carter dived down on his hands and knees beside the hole where it had gone, thrust in his arm, and in a second drew forth the rat in his ungloved hand.

Waving it in the air by its tail, he smashed it down triumphantly on the horse-rake.

In the course of the next two weeks we finished off the remaining ricks. And we were joined by 'E's two sons, who though officially still at school, did a great deal on the farm. They were twins. In build they were not in the least like their father, being extremely slight and thin. Yet both, even in their teens, could do very nearly a man's work. They worked with the same rush and zeal as their father. One of them, Reggie, was gay spirited, the other, John, was earnest to a degree probably never surpassed. There are cases when farmers' sons are in the same position as boys without literary leanings who are forced to appreciate Shakespeare, thereby acquiring a distaste for all things cultural. When farmers' sons have no leanings towards agriculture, I can conceive nothing more calculated to put them off it for ever than being forced to do it as soon as they can be of use, and forced to hear nothing but talk about it. However, by the nature of things this is rare. Certainly these boys had a decided liking and aptitude for agriculture and an equal abhorrence of anything cultural. They stayed away from school as much as possible to be on the farm. And that was very sensible. They had the one skill they were interested in, and they knew that miscellaneous knowledge, quickly forgotten, was absolutely useless to them. There was only one thing necessary to teach them to make them finally efficient at their coming profession, and that was not taught at their grammar school – namely manners. Very necessary when the time came to deal with men in their employment. But they had no exams in this, unfortunately. Thus their popularity with the staff was not marked.

Anyway the fact that they now turned up for threshing meant that I changed my position from being on the corn rick to that of Robert's assistant on the straw rick. This was a great improvement. There was much less dust and the job was easier. The golden river of straw flowed up the hill of the elevator and fell at my feet, needing only distribution. And now I rose while others sank. I could get a calm view of the general proceedings,

77

the fat grain-sacks steadily multiplying, the sheaves dim-inishing, the straw increasing. The vastness of the mystery was so actual before the eye. That field there, sown less than a year ago, with only a few sacks of seed: now all this straw coming up, all that grain flowing out. How well the cinema could show this sort of thing on a big fascinating scale, I reflected. It could show in quick succession, first the sowing, then the appearance of the light green shoots, darkening, browning, yellowing: then the carrying and ricking and threshing. To do it properly would no doubt be expensive, but hardly more so than the expense of some elaborate pictures evidently produced by infants.

My place on the straw rick also gave me a clear view of the well-known peculiarity about threshing. As soon as the tractor has been started up and the belts begin moving a curious change takes place in the situation. Up to now the human beings have had the matter well in hand, taking their time, fixing belts, and getting things ready. But as soon as the machines get going the atmosphere is changed. One gets the impression that the thresher is now more important than those who minister to it. It has evidently become alive. The first consideration of a living thing is food. To get food most creatures have to strain after it. Not so the thresher. It needs bread, certainly one rick a day, which is a fair-sized loaf: but all it has to do is to stand there while men feed it. And they mustn't let up for a minute. If the ever-open mouth doesn't get its sheaf in good time such a hollow roar comes up from the depths of the animal that its menials nervously hasten to hand up the food at double-quick time. Seen from the moon, as it were, the spectacle would look disquieting. If, quite ignorant of the existence of any machines, we turned a corner and suddenly came upon such a scene, it would be sufficiently surprising. There is nothing quite like it, this weird monster of man's conceiving, which, hour after hour, does really chew, digest, and pass out the very bread we eat.

5. Drilling

The next operation in our sequence was the sowing of a hundred-acre field with barley. Hence I became familiar with the drill for the first time – the big Canadian double affair that drops artificial at the same time as grain. Mounted on two wheels, two separate long thin boxes are drawn across the field by a tractor. You open the lid of each box, pouring artificial into one and grain into the other. As the drill moves forward the two things trickle down through pipes to the earth, or rather, right into the soil. Thus you can sow with a drill in a strong wind and yet be sure of an equal distribution of seed throughout the field in parallel lines. Two men are necessary: one to drive the tractor, and the other to stand on the platform of the drill and keep an eye on the supply in the boxes and see that all is falling down according to plan.

Early in the morning we went out with wagon-loads of barley-seed and artificial on to the hundred-acre field. We had our own drill and also a hired one. These drills are nine feet wide; so that two going hard at it can cover plenty of ground in a few days.

We hung about at first in the cold wind, waiting for 'E who had not arrived; for though instructions had been given with regard to the end we were to start from, and which portion to do first, no one was clear about this, and no one would take the responsibility; nor was the extra man in charge of the hired drill fertile in suggestion, simply saying – ' 'E didn't tell me nothing about it.' No initiative was taken; nor did I ever find it taken even in the simplest matters at any time; it was always – 'Better wait for 'E.' Thus we stood about in the wind for some time.

At length the Van arrived and operations were set in motion at once. Taking it by portions, the two drills went round and round the given portion, stopping as they passed me for refilling with seed and manure – for I was the feeder. The carter stood on the platform of the hired drill, while 'E stood behind Harold, our tractor-driver. Since the circle round which the drills raced was a big one I had time enough to get the corn and the manure poured out into the bucket before they appeared, one closely following the other.

Just before dinner I was told to take a wagon and fill up with a dozen two-hundredweight bags of barley which were on another wagon beside a rick in a further field. This was the first occasion when I had to handle two horses (one in front of the other) drawing a wagon, thus when it came to backing the wagon so as to go neatly alongside the other wagon with the sacks on it, I found it anything but easy. A wagon is not at all like a cart; having four wheels, the first pair being on a swivel, backing becomes an art in itself — for if you do not go back straight you will go mighty crooked! And if one horse does not behave properly and shies every time an aeroplane overhead fires at a target (our constant accompaniment), things are thus made no easier. Hence, by the time I had got my wagon alongside the other and had loaded up, it was well into dinner-time, and well past it when I was back on the drilling field. Being the sole feeder of the drills I couldn't very well stop for my food, and had to eat it as opportunity arose. We did not stop at five-thirty, and as no one had taken out any tea we did not stop for tea, but went on till seven-thirty. On this particular day — this has often happened with me — I had taken out far too little for dinner. Thus by five-thirty it became a real question of belt-tightening. I reached home by eight-thirty. Then did I enjoy *sitting down*! And did I enjoy my food! Pleasures normally denied me. Two simple and extreme joys missed by millions of men for no better reason than that they can sit down and eat when they like.

The next day the same thing happened during dinner-hour. I had to go right down to the farmyard to load up twenty sacks of artificial. Having arrived there, the question rose, how elevate them? It was simply solved. This farm was not lacking in equipment, and there was a sack-lifter in the barn. It is like a short ladder with one rung. You put it against your wagon, wheel a sack to it (there was also a sack-wheeler, for which many thanks) and let it slip on to that one rung which is on the ground; and then you turn a handle and force the rung upwards and tip your sack into the wagon.

So far so good. It only remained to go back with the load. Unfortunately I did not make a clean exit. I knocked down a gate-post. The reason for this was simple: in leading the front horse round out of the yard I walked on the right-hand side of the horse instead of the left, which is a mistake as elementary as walking too close to a horse – for which there is often excruciating punishment from the hoof. I thought it advisable to make a general confession of this on my arrival on the field. 'E took it well, as he always took all such things. Harold thought it a great joke, saying that the carter would have to stand up there all night instead of the post. And even the carter himself only said – 'Christ!'

On we went again, my expedition having cost me the whole dinner-hour. I continued getting the buckets full with seed and artificial. In a current number of the *Farmers' Weekly*, artificial had been called 'little pills of comfort'. I quoted this to 'E who handed it on as a great joke – for he was far from being a surly man when things were going well.

As the circle grew smaller and smaller the tractors came round sooner and sooner. I did not now have to feed them each time, but all the same I was not always ready for them. Though much of the equipment had cost over four hundred pounds per item, there had been economy over buckets. They were too small for the job, it was the devil filling from a full sack. Also, the I.C.I. sacks were tied in a peculiar way and could only be opened in a trick manner – which sometimes failed and caused ill-spared delay. Rain loomed ahead and the pace was quickened.

From the road, I have no doubt, our scene looked leisurely and quiet. How different the reality, I reflected, now that I was in it. Everything in a hurry. Anxiety, hustle, nervous tension – anything but the serene rural atmosphere we hear of in books: more in the nature of a battle which by inadvertence may at any moment be lost. And from the field, how far away seemed the outside world that passed by on the road! We did not belong to it, and it knew nothing of us, cared nothing. Yet all its ways and all its tramping depended upon us; by us upheld in its trance and dream; by us made insolent and by us given power. I had come from that outside world, and many a time reflected here upon what now seemed the slack and sloping ease of city people whom I knew. But on this day, while here on this field anyway, I felt no desire to join them. Rather did I feel that I had escaped from the company of dream-walkers into the company of people who were awake and putting out all their strength, without which effort things can never be kept going. Here in the middle of this big field I at last began to feel really inside the agricultural world, part of it, one with it, and was well content to let the distant prancing devil's dance of nonsense, farce and folly fare without me.

The drills began to close in now, my patch becoming smaller at every round, until at last I was driven off it, and had to take up my position in a portion already sown, so that myself and my gear would not get in the way of the vehicles. Once when I had left a sack in the line of an approaching non-stop tractor, the carter leapt from the platform, rushed ahead, threw back the sack, and leapt on again – all for the benefit of his old man who could see the exhibition from close behind. At length the job was finished late in the evening of the third day, and we withdrew, leaving Nature now to get on with it.

6. Sheep

While putting a sack of cake into the shepherd's hut – which resembled a bathing-box on wheels – I looked round inside. In certain respects it suggested a cloakroom. A line of lambskin coats hung from pegs. Wondering who wore these coats, I remembered how the shepherd had told me that he used them for disguising lambs who couldn't milk from their own mothers. Thus, if a ewe lost a lamb and another ewe wasn't giving milk, he put the latter's lamb to the ewe that had lost hers – first dressing it up in the dead lamb's skin. I wish I could have had an opportunity to watch this impersonation of a lamb in lamb's clothing.

My own liking for sheep is limited. As a flock they may fairly be said to be more pitiful than human beings. Their deplorable lack of self-possession and confidence, their perpetual hurrying and scurrying, their weak faces, their ceaseless maa-ing and baa-ing make one feel somehow they have got lost in evolution and are in a frightful state of anxiety about it.

Yet it is no wonder they feel bewildered and lost. Like so many creatures, they are now half created by Nature and half by man. The result is that they are now dependent upon us for everything – while we, of course, have to wait upon them hand and foot as we do on cows, the sheep-waiters being called shepherds and the cow-waiters being called cow-men. They have now so little control over their bodies that a slight hollow in the ground may make them fall over while grazing, and if they do fall over they cannot get up, and often die in twenty minutes. And we may be sure that it is not due to Nature but to us that they become the prey of worms.

There is very little that is romantic about sheep, though for some reason they enter both literature and painting in an idyllic manner not bestowed to an equal extent upon other stock, while it will be some time before the shepherd loses his poetic place. The 'milkmaid', now called a Land Army girl, is ceasing to make any strong appeal to the muse; but the shepherd is still conceived of a haze, for few people know what he actually does. They would be surprised if they knew how heavy a single hurdle is, and that a shepherd needs to be a particularly strong man since he has to move them continually, and carries from two to four at once (I know one who could carry eight). And he is seldom seen searching for a dear lost sheep and rejoicing over it when found more than over the ninety-nine others that did not go astray; he is more often discovered searching their bodies for maggots and finding plenty, whole rings of them worming their way through the wool, through the skin, through the flesh into the very bones – an invasion which, if unchecked, will lead to hideous sores, huge patches of desolated flesh and red clefts in which are clearly seen the reeking ribs.

I write with some feeling about this, for though I had nothing to do with sheep at this farm, it is proper to mention here that I have since had occasion to lend a hand with them in the administration of pills, and also at dipping. It was a question of giving a hundred sheep four pills each (or rather four to the ewes and two to the lambs) against worms. Actually I failed to give a single pill to a single ewe by myself. It was all I could do to sit one up on its haunches, let alone open its mouth. We had them penned in a short space, so it was not difficult to catch hold of the lambs. But it was a game getting a several-hundredweight ewe into a sitting posture, and in my efforts to do so I frequently assumed that position myself, covered with the slobbering saliva of the sheep beside me whose agitated countenance betrayed ill-concealed dislike. The dipping was dirtier but slightly more easy. After penning up the flock beside the dip, it was only a question of catching hold of the sheep, lifting them over the step, and lowering them in. Several of the ewes were so bulky that I failed to lift them up the necessary distance. The splashings and general excitement relieved their bowels, and soon the floor became very slippery and their wool discoloured. What with that and the splashes from the yellow fluid, it was a job calling for very old clothes and a bath afterwards. All the same, contact with sheep, my mate assured me, is good for the health. He said that breathing sheep odour is the healthiest odour, and cures anyone in a low state. His wife's father was thus cured, and he went down again when he left sheep. His brother had to go to hospital after dealing with cows, then went to sheep and became strikingly well ... So it seems doctors should not say – Go to the Riviera, but simply Go to sheep.

I allude to these operations since they served to clarify my mind with regard to sheep, and to take them out of the haze of half-perception. It was no doubt theoretically possible for Mary to have kept that small lamb; and when she went places it could possibly have accompanied her. But I wish we could have been told more about that phenomenal child's dealings with the lamb, for it seems to me now that her choice in pets must have been attended with grave disadvantages. Not that I question her existence. In 1938 my wife and I were in Germany, and had been journeying for a long time without meeting anyone or coming to any village: but at least we came upon a lonely house by the wayside. There was no sign of life anywhere. Then we saw, sitting on the steps and leaning against the closed front door of the house, a little girl about Mary's age as we imagine it. Beside her, with its head on her lap, was a sheep. It should have been a lamb, but it was an adult, quiet, unbleating sheep with an exceedingly amiable countenance. It gazed up towards Monica, and Monica gazed down towards it with her arms round its neck – a most peaceful, unhistoric scene. I say Monica, for my wife took a photograph of this companionship, and the girl gave her name as Monica and the sheep's name as Hans. She accepted a piece of chocolate; and as I left Monica and Hans, much appreciating their ideological position in the Third Reich, a deep voice, proceeding, it seemed from Hans, said – '*Danke schön, auf wiedersehn.*'

7. *The Machine-milker*

My contact with stock here was confined to spreading straw for the heifers and dumping hay in the shed beside one of the dairies, which adjoined the pig run. Pigs are very attractive animals. When a body of them are all together, all snorting and making a general row, and you suddenly appear, silence will immediately fall on the assembly. Indeed, the attention is so encouraging that I have sometimes been tempted to emulate St Francis and preach them a sermon. Next to their intelligence I would place their cleanliness: they don't mind a bit of mud and appear even to eat it, but they are very clean in essentials. As for the sows – there we come upon great personalities, though often rather supercilious in countenance. The only thing about swine is that they scream when being hurt. We don't like this, so we call it squealing.

My journeys sometimes took me past the poultry. Took me

past is right, for I don't stop to look at hens. 'The cold, greedy, completely egoistic eye of the hen,' as Ralph Wightman puts it, is enough to make anyone turn aside – not to mention that smell which suffocates the heart. Nor does the nosiness, the sniffing inquisitiveness of heifers appeal to me. Lie down for half an hour or leave a bicycle in a field with heifers at the far end, and sure enough in a short time the whole lot will come nosing round, and when driven off will presently come again exactly as if you were a magnet. Whereas cows will often regard you with indifference. There were some excellent cows in the dairies here, and there are few animals more comforting to stand beside than a sleek well-fed cow – or more mysterious and baffling. As for their cash value, I was surprised to learn that a really good one can fetch a thousand pounds. The truculent urban motorist who hoots his way through cows on the road would change his tune if he knew their money measure. It now amuses me to think how his jaundiced eye would moisten with greed if he found a thousand-pound cow blocking the path of his car (itself likely to fetch about thirty pounds). Probably he would raise his hat to it.

Both the dairies here were run on the basis of machine-milking. One was an ordinary cow-shed converted, the other a modern building constructed precisely for the purpose of machine-milking. These strawless, woodless, regimented stalls have a sad unhomeliness about them. To look at them when empty does really chill the heart. Nor is it possible to warm up when the work is in progress, and amidst the loud noise of the engine, you witness the red rubber fingers, the milk-pipes, and the truly mechanical nature of the proceedings.

Of course this way is no more illegitimate than the other. Cows were never made originally to be milked by hand, or to be milked by man at all. All that milk was not required. We have created it. We have put those big bags of milk on the cow. Originally a cow, presumably, had about as much milk as a mare, and the teats were violently jerked by the calf. The hand is obviously an unnatural appliance here and, curiously enough, the machine appliance gets nearer to the original jerking of the calf's mouth – a machine, the ugliest of all, actually getting closer to nature! Of course this is a mere accident, a fluke, which is balanced by the heartlessness of the whole thing. Not necessarily heartless perhaps, for at bottom everything depends upon our attitude of mind; but it promotes the tendency to treat animals as if they were machines. 'I always tell my students,' said Professor McGregor to Mr Rolf Gardiner before an approving audience, 'treat a cow exactly as you would treat a tractor.'

As to whether the new method is better or worse than the old from a utilitarian point of view, I express no opinion. But if I go into a hall to hear a subject of this kind discussed by the knowledgeable, I know exactly what to expect. Two schools of thought will be advanced, each giving a convinced opinion backed by experience and particular instance. The argument will swing to and fro, and all to no purpose, for a new invention, when it satisfies an immediate need without obviously doing harm, always goes on its way without reference to ultimate aims.

Why is it so useful? Because it is an immense saver of time and labour – being able to milk twenty-five cows in an hour. A detached mind might contemplate the humour of this answer with some slight degree of amusement. Two things are saved: labour and time. So our question is – What is done with the saved labour? Either nothing at all, since labour-saving devices are coming in every day, or those relieved from hand-milking can theoretically (very theoretically) go now and make machine-milkers. Well, what is done with the time that is saved? Nothing whatever at the moment. We are quite unprepared to deal with this new uneconomic problem. The saved time is chucked away like a dirty piece of paper into the fire. The length of working hours remains exactly the same for the labourers as before. There are fewer labourers, but their hours are the same amount; while the displaced workers (unless they *do* go and make machine-milkers) are paid a fee to keep away, called Unemployment Benefit or the Dole. These are the lucky ones, you may say, who have stolen a march on us and have entered the

Leisure State in advance. The trouble is they don't seem to appreciate their good fortune.

But, it will be urged, since this saving of labour and time is all so unreal, what then is the reality? Quite simple – it saves *money*. The employer's money. There are few employers, many workers. But since power is always in the hands of the few, they can safely embark upon every new money-saving device.

We need not lose heart. It is all paving the way towards the Leisure State of the future. Always an optimist, I feel sure that we shall be economically ready and mentally fit for it in less than three hundred years.

8. *Tractor* v. *Horse*

I cannot regard myself as a tremendous animal lover. I find them too baffling. I have sometimes looked searchingly into the eyes of a cow or a horse wondering what on earth it saw through its own dim windows, what it thought if it did think – hoping it didn't. I am a socialist at heart (also an aristocrat), and am inclined to extend my socialism to animals. So much so that I have to check myself sometimes from apologizing to one or other of them for my behaviour. It seems to me that they also should qualify for the ideal of Rights (there are no natural Rights). For this reason when I see a row of cows strung along the tubes of a machine-milker I feel that there is something deplorable about it – as if the cow itself were our invention.

For the same reason I welcome the tractor. Today horses get a thin time of it on the land. This is not always so, but it is so now in this transition period. There is no emphasis on the *care* of horses, and the young men (soon to be the old men) have no feeling for them. The emphasis is upon the tractor. It is a real machine-horse, and much more powerful, and can go anywhere and do anything that a horse can do. Horses could now be released from their slavery. This view will not meet with the approval of those who dislike machines and love the spectacle of horses in the field. I occasionally meet people who imagine that they are being poetical when they are only being sentimental. They know nothing of the hardness of that rock from which the spark of poetry is struck. They cannot *see*. Hence the proverbial cruelty of your sentimentalist. He does not see a horse for what it is, a living creature in its own right, but only a picture of a horse; and is enchanted by the idea of that most pitiless of all victimizations – *cavalry*. And in this lesser matter of the horse versus the tractor he never dreams of taking into consideration the feelings of the horse.

My own view of machinery is not notable for consistency; but I welcome a machine which is in the right place, when it is full of use, *useful*; and not when we should use much less of it, when it is *useless*. It is unnecessary to go to extremes. Not long ago I saw the photograph of an interesting gentleman called Captain Roberts who had invented a motor car which came to him when he whistled for it, and of a man who had invented the means by which he could drive a tractor while he stood at the corner of the field simply pressing a button. Such men have their place in our comedy and add to the gaiety of nations. But in practice they go too far.

Since the second tractor on the farm was not used by any definite worker, I seized the opportunity to use it myself, I am no engineer and not at all mechanically minded. Further, I lack a natural ingenuity and capacity for improvisation, both of which are called for constantly when dealing with agricultural equipment, mechanical or otherwise – though I now realize that ingenuity and improvisation are largely a matter of habit and experience. And though I had driven motor cars for some years, I had not bothered to form a mechanical sense, considering myself as a person who either knows or doesn't know a thing, and who therefore should not waste time in going into matters which can be dealt with by others. But I did not and do not regard machines and their workings as terribly mysterious or unknowable. A mechanic is only an unglorified botanist. The chemical explosions that occur in the cyclinders of an engine cannot be more difficult to deal with than the chemical explosions that occur in the parenchyma of a plant, and there is surely nothing more complicated about a piston than a pistil.

9. Mishaps with Tractor

One must force the pace if one is ever to do anything, so when a favourable opportunity offered, I suggested to 'E that I should use the spare tractor. He agreed, and said that a given field needed rolling. He took me to the tractor, started it up, told me to drive off, while he stood on the step beside me. By a lucky chance I found the right gear and we went up to the roller. It was a three-piece roller, and not at the moment connected together, the two small rollers that are attached one on each side of the large one having been left beside it. Thus a good deal of turning and backing was necessary in order to couple them up and assemble the whole. I was lucky in my first backing and brought the coupling-pins exactly in line, but got it all wrong on the second occasion, having to go forward and back several times while 'E waited in irritation. Since the three pieces had been left haphazard and since I did not see at a glance where they should go and what moves I should make, and since I could not follow 'E's instructions, it took some time before I did what was required. But at length it was done and I was left to get on with the job.

After a very short time one roller came off. The coupling-pin had been loose and had jerked out. But I managed to find another pin in the box and assembled the roller-piece again, and continued without further mishap. It was a nice afternoon and seagulls swirled about like a species of day-fireworks. Time passed quickly. So far so good.

I was instructed to go when this field was done to a further one, a root field which had been folded by sheep, and needed knocking up with a cultivator. In due course I went there, found the cultivator, coupled it with the tractor without any query arising, and struck out. Since the method of cultivating is obvious and follows a simple rule of thumb, still so far so good.

Then near the end of the day the tractor stopped. All that was wrong was that it had run out of paraffin oil. But as I had put in what I thought was a lot and had no idea how much it ate, I did not realize the cause of the stoppage, and kept urging it on. Then I tested the tank. There seemed to be a certain amount in it, and so I urged it on again for some jerky distance until at last I decided to get some fuel and fill up. Even then it still went jerkily and I had to keep adjusting the choke (about which I understood little). When I left it in the evening I wondered how it would go next day.

I had cause enough to be apprehensive about this. For next day though it started up all right it would not pull the cultivator. It stalled each time at the strain. I was hopelessly held up. It was not firing properly; but – no one not knowing me will believe this – I did not examine the plugs! There was no rule of thumb for me, and I had no mechanical imagination, I could see no line of research for following out. At length the Van came rushing up, 'E leapt out in a flurry of annoyance, and Jimmy the mechanic who accompanied him whipped out a spanner and plug-twister from the box, and in a moment had taken out the plugs, held the dirty one up before us, cleaned it, put it back, and the tractor started up now and pulled properly – and the Van went off.

The tractor was a good type, an International, but it badly needed overhauling, having been looked after very badly and used now by one person then another. Thus it needed tender treatment. A slight pushing out of the choke at the wrong time would be sufficient to smudge the plugs. I did not know this. My rough treatment of the choke on the first day had done harm, and though the tractor now went again it did not pull well as the day proceeded. Next morning it was as bad.as the previous one, and I broke a plug while screwing it out, and there wasn't a spare one. Hence more crisis. 'E's sons came out, saying 'Christ!' The Van appeared, saying 'Handy man! And look where you left the tractor last night – pointing *uphill*!' Learning thus at the cannon's mouth, as it were, it can be guessed that I picked up the tricks pretty fast!

Unfortunately there was always a new thing to pick up regarding this tractor. For the next thing was that it refused to start in the morning. I would leave it in the evening after it had been going all right, but next day it would not start. Even when I took out all the plugs and cleaned them, it wouldn't. One starts-up these tractors on petrol, then switching over to paraffin. It was not easy to lay one's hands on petrol here, and I was always in danger of running out of the small quantity I had in the little petrol tank before I could get started-up – in which case I would be floored again and have to face Van and boys saying 'Christ!' It was necessary to take the plugs to pieces and clean their insides (that was the secret) and I hadn't convenient tools for this at first. Thus you can imagine I had fun and games during these early days. My only merit in matters of this kind is that I don't make the same mistake twice – not on my life! Time certainly never dragged at all now. Indeed I hardly stopped for the morning meal of 'lunch', being too anxious to get on and make a show before something held me up, and in case the tractor wouldn't start again if I stopped it and let it get cold.

I was extricated from many of my early problems and mishaps by Harold, the chief tractor-driver. He was a leisurely chap who took things pretty calmly, though like everyone else, on catching sight of the Van approaching, would display an uncommon earnestness of demeanour and concentration of effort. Now in his late twenties he was already an old hand, having started very young and ploughed with horses long before he took on tractor work. It was clear that he had a good life on this farm and enjoyed it. But the most I ever heard him say was that he 'didn't mind the binder' and I think he 'didn't mind' ploughing. He never took any holidays. He was always about to do so, but never did. He could be very agreeable or very rough, as the mood took him. Robert, always ready to get a rise out of anyone or suddenly shout at anyone who seemed fair game, never tried anything on with Harold. I knew it would not be wise to count on him helping me, but all the same he often did.

When I got a roller stuck in a gateway, for instance, he would come and help me through before the Van appeared. It was instructive to contrast his traditional and leisurely movements – still more those of Robert – with the movements of 'E. For example, the Van would rush up while I was using the cultivator, say; it was perhaps necessary to put on some new tines or shoes to the cultivator. 'E would stride across the ground, head bent forward as he made straight for his objective; then down on his knees beside the implement, and with fast, strong, hurried, furious wrenching, knocking and twisting with pliers and hammer, do the job, assisted by me doing one item of the affair with another pliers, and accompanied by the boys who, imitating him in every way, would push and pull with immense earnestness. Then, having said what I was doing *wrong*, would dash off towards some other portion of the farm, where the signal would go up – ' 'E's coming!'

On two occasions a shaft of the roller broke. Curiously enough this was not held against me as these shafts had several times been to the blacksmith for mendings. But actually on the second occasion it was my fault. I had allowed a certain screw to get loose. Harold discovered this and made it clear in no uncertain terms, but did not tell 'E. I had not yet grasped the cardinal fact that a tractor-driver must keep his eye constantly upon all screws. Any one screw out of half a dozen on an agricultural implement is of supreme importance. A screw with its nut at one end looks rather like a spiral-fluted miniature Doric column such as upholds the Parthenon; and if it falls out it may do damage proportionate to the fall of a column. This is what I had to get into my head. All screws must be *tight*, and when you have tightened them then tighten them some more. I have often thought to myself – well that's tight enough, anyway. But no, tug at it and you can improve it. It doesn't seem necessary but it is; for the shaking of the instrument that it is holding together is equal to your strength in tightening the screw. Hence the tractor-driver must not content himself with looking ahead and watching his implement behind, but must keep his eye on all screws. He need not, as far as I can see, keep bobbing his head backwards and forwards *all* the time as some men do, but he must at intervals really test his joints. Thus then I write down this rule and nail and screw it into my head – though many people think that my head itself has a screw loose.

10. 'Use Your Brains'

At the best of times it was not easy to follow the orders given by 'E in the morning. I often had to get him to repeat them or would ask someone else who happened to have heard – preferably Dick. The latter experienced a certain difficulty himself in taking his orders and said to me that he simply seized upon 'the main outline' of what had been said and carried on from there. Dick's manner while receiving orders was a perpetually repeated comedy. He regarded 'E as his mortal enemy, and when near him lost all his natural gaiety and good humour, becoming at once glum and silent. In the morning he would arrive and make for the stable without glancing his head towards 'E. While going towards it or coming from it, he would receive instructions, but he never took the slightest notice. Had he heard? I used to wonder at first. He had heard all right but merely refused to look in the direction from which the instructions proceeded. Or, out on the field, I would see him being told to do something. He would start off before 'E had finished speaking, his head bent very slightly in one direction which showed that he was really hearing the words that were now addressed to the back of his head.

As I say, I did not always find my orders easy to follow. Sometimes I did not understand what 'E had actually said, and sometimes when I did I still wasn't sure of the moves referred to. For instance one morning it was – 'Take the cultivator back to the centre field, then drag the field you cultivated yesterday. The drags are in the field next to the house. Put one each on they ones that have slides, then take 'ee up to the field. You'll find a pole by the straw rick in the beanfield. When you've finished there get the roller and do the wheat field.' Straightforward enough perhaps, provided I remembered all the geographical designations and the tactics involved. Seizing the main outline, I went along hoping things would clear up as I went on and saw the objects that had been mentioned. I reached the field where he said the drags were. But *slides*? Ah yes, I saw that two of the four drags if turned over became *sledges* so that you could pull them along across roads and so on. So I turned them over and put the other ones on top. This entailed removing the long pole connecting the four, which enlightened me as to the necessity of that other pole he had alluded to, a smaller one for present use, to be found in the beanfield. There it was; I got it and coupled up and went to the far field to be dragged.

That done the next thing was to get the roller and do the winter-wheat field. I found the roller, but how couple-up without assistance? While backing the tractor you cannot hold up the shaft of the roller, and one's arm isn't long enough to reach the ground when you get into positon. Such elementary improvisation as was here needed flummoxed me – again there was no obvious rule of thumb. But come! I said to myself, use your ingenuity! So I looked in the box and found that the hammer was long enough to serve as a prop. And it did do perfectly well in this capacity. But while coupling-up, that is to say while keeping one foot gently on the clutch, the left hand on the steering-wheel, and the trunk bent backwards so that the right arm can reach right down to the roller-shaft, I wondered why some armchair agricultural strategists imagine that tractor-driving is just a question of sitting down all day.

Having then taken the roller to the winter-wheat field I carried on there for some time. This field was beside the track running up through the centre of the farm, and suddenly the Van appeared coming down it. From the Van an arm, 'E's arm, was outstretched – pointing. What was it pointing at? I looked down at the roller. One piece had disappeared! Then I saw that piece at the far end of the field, sitting there quietly by itself. I had been star-gazing. A minute later and on turning a corner I would have seen it; but 'E, with his pointing arm, always appeared at the psychological moment.

His eye would discern one's smallest wrong-doing from some way off. A few days later I was chain-harrowing a pasture when the Van appeared. It looked as if it were passing on but it swerved and came towards me and the Arm pointed at my chain-harrow. A link had come undone and hence a portion of the chains was crumpled. Typical of me, I couldn't help feeling, not to have noticed it. Then 'E lodged another complaint. I had been seen yesterday – one is always detected – getting water from a certain big house near this field. 'Waste of juice,' he said, 'going right over there when there is a trough in the field. Use your brains!' I could not see the force of this, since you can take a tractor to a trough but you can't make it drink unless you have a filler with you.

While going on with my harrowing I thought over that admonition – 'Use your brains.' I am not a brainy man in any marked degree and have never passed for one, though my capacity to use what brains I possess and to pick the brains of others is second to none. Still, brains was not the right word as used by 'E. I suggest that the word Ingenuity would better fit the case. I possess some Imagination; that is I can occasionally see what is there: but I have little Invention, which is the power to see what is not there. And I fancy that the faculty of invention goes with the faculty of ingenuity and improvisation. But these things are also a matter of habit and experience. An extremely brainy farmer is not likely to be much better and could quite easily be much worse than a stupid man who is born to the tradition, does what he has seen his father do, and which he has been made to do from an early age. The overcoming of mechanical and other difficulties will come to him quite naturally, ingenuity will be second- if not first-nature. What would puzzle me will be simply obvious to him. For what is obvious is not a question of brains but of training.

At a certain gold-mining district in Africa the natives were accustomed to fill buckets with earth and carry them to the inspection yard. One day the British overseer introduced wheelbarrows for use instead of buckets. The natives looked glum at the prospect, and on returning later the overseer found them *carrying* the wheelbarrows on their heads. It was not obvious to them what function the wheels would perform. It is obvious to me when I write a letter or a book where I should put a full-stop. It is not in the least obvious to agricultural labourers. When using the first person singular it is my *habit* to write it with a capital I. It is not their habit. They very often use a small i, as in French or German, since it seems less egotistic.

The boss of the farm which I have written about in Part One was a member of the Home Guard. One day he turned up at a meeting at which several proper military men, including an ex-colonel and major, were present. He found them in a quandary. They had wished to move the large desk which was at one end of the room, to the other. But how accomplish this? There seemed no solution. It was not obvious to the Army. Then Agriculture came in. 'The very man we want!' they cried, much relieved at sight of the boss. 'We were wondering how we could move this desk to over there.' Too astounded to speak, he said nothing. In complete silence he walked over to the desk, removed the top portion to the floor, carried the two other portions to the required place in two movements, and then placed the first piece again where it fitted. The job was done, the problem solved – amidst the applause of an enlightened Army.

Thus I saw that I must form the habit of ingenuity and improvisation. I was shocked into doing so. Let me no longer, I said to myself, be one of those people who can't do things for themselves, but have to get others to 'do for them' as the phrase goes. I date that resolution from the moment when I had found myself flummoxed by that simple coupling job with the roller. So the next time I found my tractor in need of water I did take it to the trough – and used my *hat* as a filler.

11. Operations in Progress

We were into May now, a most beautiful May, but I cannot say that I noticed it much, beyond an occasional glance at the turn-out. Nor did anyone else. It is your townsman who is conscious of the seasons and who talks about spring. The agricultural labourer does not notice it. He does not think in terms of months or seasons. He sees it in terms of work. This will have to be done now, then that; it is drilling time, or harrowing and cultivating time, ploughing time, hoeing time, hay-making time, harvest time, and so on – the New Year being in October. He does not know the names of the flowers so well as the country-loving townsman. He does not rejoice in the spring nor become melancholy in the autumn. The scent of hay is not grateful to him. And never, never does he think about 'the summer holidays'!

I could see four operations going forward from a certain high field which I was rolling on 7 May (to take the exact date from my notebook). Away to the left there was a curious activity in progress. A fire was alight under a cauldron. One man, it was 'E, kept poking a stick in the pot. Beside him the shepherd sat upright with a lamb in his lap. Dick was in general attendance. It was rather a lowering day, and the scene appeared as a mixture between an illustration in *Alice in Wonderland* and the Three Witches on the Blasted Heath stirring that remarkable pot boiling twenty-three separate ingredients. Having to ask for certain instructions, I approached and found that they were cutting off the lambs' tails – a bonus of threepence each going to Robert.

On another field Harold was planting potatoes with 'E's daughter and one boy. No more assistance was necessary, for a potato-planter was being used. It is a contraption fitted to the plough – in this case a three-furrow. One person sits on the plough and drops potatoes on to a sort of conveyor-belt which passes round with pockets to hold potatoes and then channels each into one of the three furrows which are opened and covered at the same time – a remarkably neat affair. A tractor-driver, with two assistants or one, can sow a three- or four-acre field in a day. Remembering what it was like planting by hand, I certainly applauded it, and I am wondering when we shall see a picker-up of potatoes.

Further off I could see the land girls couching. Couch grass is an irrepressible and desperate weed. With hugely spreading roots it clings to the fields. You cultivate the field, drag it, chain-harrow it, pulling up enough couch to build a rick – which you then burn in bundles and lines. But you can get more up – and then more. I refuse to use space in writing about it, but I had plenty to do with the stuff, both in getting it up and burning it when I wasn't using the tractor. It was a job which went on all the time – a ceaseless couch-battle. It is the farmer's curse. But I gather from a neighbour of mine that it has non-agricultural merits of a pleasing character. A great fellow in the use of herbs, he told me that if you cook some couch-roots you can cure lumbago. But this may not be universal, I fear. He seemed particularly sensitive to roots. Once when he got boils he dug up some dock-roots, ate them, and never had boils again.

How much has to be done to a field before its bed is fit for sowing! Ploughed twice perhaps; cultivated first one way then criss-cross; dragged twice; chain-harrowed and rolled; the couch burnt. Does the general public realize that all this is done to that field seen from the road, looking so silent, so deserted, as if no one ever went near it? Does the man on the road know that it has to be scratched and beaten and turned over like a rug, and scorched and burnt and knocked about? Does he know that before we can live even by bread alone, before bread can begin at all, all this must be done? I did not, when I was a man on the road and in the train.

The carter was busy drilling clover-seed in a field of young corn. The clover would not come up with the corn, of course. It would follow after the field had been harvested – a new fresh green push between the ruined stalks.

Thus I could see work progressing all around me, while I also was doing my share. I was well in the centre of my world now, and my main feeling was that of being privileged to be there.

I commanded a view also of another field – the hundred-acre which we had drilled in April. It was no longer brown. It had turned green. The field was carrying on by itself. No clumps of men on it as during the drilling time, no carts and sacks and tractors, no operations. But it was the silence of vast schemes not discerned by the eye, not heard; invisible, inaudible, and, it would seem, motionless; yet all in motion, a lofty design being built up, and exchanges made between water and air – that which is fluid being made solid, and that which is solid being made soft.

12. While 'Making a Show'

I was surprised at the amount of rolling that had to be done, especially on grass and young corn. When taking the heavy roller, not to mention the wheels of the tractor, across the tender shoots of corn, it made me smile to think how the con-scientious citizen out for a day in the country will edge his way beside such a field lest he tread on 'the young corn'. It is a bit of a paradox, certainly, that by crushing down the supposedly feeble green ribbons with a heavy roller you thereby make them fit to stand up all the better. But of course the ground is thus made firm, which gives the corn a steady grip, and as for the effect of the roller on the shoots, they are too soft to be injured by something hard, and we all know that elasticity of body, even of the body politic, overcomes all things.

With regard to chain-harrowing the green fields, I had pre-viously thought that pastures were just pastures off which the cattle fed, and that was all there was to it. But no, you cannot leave them alone, they also must be cultivated. The cow-droppings must be spread, otherwise you get a 'sour' patch; too rich. The innumerable mole-hills must be knocked over and dispersed, otherwise your pasture will quite soon disappear al-together, owing to this mole ploughing. The grass itself must be scraped so as to let the air in. Hence this work which looks so uneconomic, pays in the end. For after all, what is this green field but milk, cream, butter, and cheese?

Thus these days passed quickly. Some severe-minded persons say that tractor-driving is boring. I did not find it so. I have, of course, had to do some long fool-proof jobs on big fields, but if it was boring it was not as boring as some other jobs on a farm that have to be done. Moreover, on such occasions one can remain more or less physically fresh and therefore mentally fresh, which makes all the difference. In any case, during these early days of mine there was no question of the time dragging while I grappled with my preliminary and consecutive difficulties and mishaps. It was the other way round, my object was always to get something done, to make a show before anything went wrong – before the Van appeared. One day I had been told to roll a certain field. There was a breakage in the morning and I did not get on to the job before early afternoon. Could I do it now in four hours? I wondered. I just managed it. All the time I was fighting against Space – so Time fled.

Above I have used the phrase 'make a show'. It is an amusing one, so I repeat it. Whenever I started to do any job in company with Dick, he always said – 'Don't you think it would be better to do it this way – *it will make a better show.*' That was my idea also, whether with him or by myself, to make the best impression. And I often used to think how differently I would do certain jobs if I were my own master, with no consideration save the nature of the job itself. Sometimes I would go slow, doing a given piece very thoroughly, since no one would come and say – 'Haven't you finished yet?' I would skimp another field which really didn't need much attention, since no one would say – 'Look, you have left out that piece!' Vast indeed would be the difference. But for the moment I want 'to make a show'. Having got stuck in a gate one day and thus wasted time, I was late in getting started on a field which I had to roll. So in order to make the best show in the remaining hour at my disposal, I went up and down the field instead of round it. In due course 'E appeared and told me I was doing it the wrong way, and that I should have gone round since I would not then punish the corn by unnecessary turnings. I did not explain that I had gone up and down merely to make a *better show*.

Apart from any reasons just suggested as to why there was nothing boring about tractor-driving for me, it was often extremely pleasant on many occasions. It was sometimes necessary to take the tractor with some instrument from one end of the farm to the other. This meant quite a long round-about journey across fields, through gates, along leafy lanes and byways – delightful. Anyone who has experienced stooping or standing for hours at one stationary job understands the difference only too well, and if thus engaged will cast envious eyes at the tractor-driver passing by on his unmonotonous way. And there were some fields that it was a joy to roll. There was a lovely forty-acre field called the Park, where the soil was very soft, and when I rolled the corn I experienced no noise, no clatter, no bumping, no dust. Perched on my comfortable seat, with no animal to bully and shout at, I could glance now and then at the beautiful parky view around, at the gleam and sheen upon the meadows and the groves, at the chestnut trees with their Maytime torches, at the sequestered House beyond with its Old Garden enwalled from the world's woe.

I must add that at other times it was quite the opposite, and I became thoroughly fed-up with the roller. There were some very stony and uneven fields which I rolled after dragging, when there would be an unholy clatter all the time, and dust would cover me and blind me. On days like that the coming of dinner hour was a great moment, when I stopped and the clatter and rattling ceased, then switched off the engine so that its noise and belch also ceased, and a great calm fell suddenly upon the scene. Turning my back on the tractor I would walk away in the delicious silence towards some good spot for my meal. On a day in May I had it beside a chestnut tree. It displayed a magnificent show of flowers, and when the breeze blew, the petals floated down quite startlingly like a shower of snow. The tree was very large and old. I went and stood under it. A massive trunk. The few holes in the thick canopy of leaves looked like blue stars. I do not think anything in Nature is more mysterious or more effective than a big tree. It is not only that so much proceeds from so little, though this aspect of it is a supreme exemplar of Nature's method of turning thin air into hard and lofty substance: there is something more about a great tree. Standing under this one and looking up, with knitted concentration, quite baffled, I got the impression that it emanated – Goodness. It stood there firmly like a noble Thought, which, if understood, would save the world.

During these dinner hours that so briefly dashed past, when I sat beside a tree like that, I often remembered the Forest of Arden where it was so inviting 'under the shade of melancholy boughs to lose and neglect the creeping hours of time'. That phrase has often haunted me. Not very pleasantly perhaps; for being lazy by nature, I am afraid of idleness, and have never been happy when neglecting time. But now that time was no longer my own I could think with guiltless longing how wonderful it would be to lie down under such a tree, and, neglecting all things, dream my life away.

13. A Free Day

On the following Monday I turned up at the yard as usual just after 7 a.m. No one had yet arrived. Some ten minutes passed and still no one appeared. Going to the dairy where work was in full swing, I found 'E there. He was surprised to see me – for it was Whit-Monday, a holiday! I hadn't realized it. We had worked through Good Friday and I had heard no mention about a holiday on Whit-Monday – nor did I realize that it was Whit-Monday. What a break! Yet, how frantic the thought that I had *got up* out of bed when I could have remained there – a most bitter thought. For this early rising was the very devil. I have never been a late riser and have always held before myself the ideal of early rising, if not the practice. But it is one thing to rise at seven and another at a quarter to six, work all day and get back by six in the evening, and then do the same thing again next week. That was now my routine. I lived in a bungalow 'in

the wilds' again, though with some near and very kind neighbours. It was twenty minutes' ride down to work, and at least
three-quarters of an hour uphill back. I could not therefore rise
later than five forty-five, for I had to have breakfast, shave,
prepare two lots of sandwiched meals (three if there was overtime), and get down to the farm. As I never succeeded in going
to bed before eleven, every single morning's getting up was a
little battle. My alarm-clock would go off and I would have to
tear my eyes open. Then I would *not* get up, not at once. I
always held back till it meant a rush afterwards. I would lie
there, facing Time, as it were, feeling that if I lay quite still
perhaps I could hold Time, get it to stop, as a man might hold
the end of a hose and keep the water back.

Thus I fumed at the thought on Whit-Monday that I had
missed the chance of not having to do this. How different was
my life now from what it had been! Most of my work had been
of a free-lance kind. In those days I never knew when Whit-
Monday was coming or when it had come. Once, in my very
early days, I remember being asked would I like to dine with
certain friends 'tomorrow'. I couldn't think what was on and it
was only after I had excused myself that I found that
'tomorrow' was Christmas Day. Week-ends meant nothing to
me. Now I was privileged to know what these things mean to
others who are owned by masters for nearly every day all the
year round.

So now I had the gift of a whole free day. I could enter
another world for a change, the world of books. You will never
hear me, having done 'an honest day's work', denigrating intel-
lectuals as such. To work day in and day out with the mind
only, and never with the body, is as unsatisfactory as to work
only with the body – granted. But to sneer at intellectuality is
madness. If a person does not develop his mind he is denying his
humanity. For there are only two really human traits – the
heart and the intellect. To the extent to which a man does not
develop his mind (hence also his heart), he is unhuman, not a
man, unmanly – however much he may be a 'he-man'. Since
being in the agricultural world, no subject has so continuously

and so spontaneously presented itself to me as the problem of education. Up till now the powerful Few have not wished to encourage the Many to become aware of Mind, and most obligingly, the Many have therefore despised it and sneered at 'book-learning'. But we have to pay so dearly for the faculty of mind that if we do not make the best of it, we might just as well be animals. This gift is our specific means of becoming more – *alive*. Two things are essential to the real life of man, and neither can be supplied by Act of Parliament: love and intelligence – all else is the machinery of life.

14. A Harrowing Day

If getting up early was a curse, the ride down to work was a blessing. It was often an inspiration. I have always loved movement, whether on bicycle, skate, ski, car, or train. Yet perhaps the bicycle is best of all – on a long slope downhill. Add to this an early summer morning, and you have entered heaven. The houses are asleep, and the people have not entered the kingdom, they will not enter it; but the Gate is open, and the fair place lies before you, unstained, unshamed.

My journey took me straight through the village, past the post office, the grocery shop, the forge, the rectory, the inn. A great copper-beech rose behind the rectory wall, and on the left stood a row of chestnut trees whose mid-May blossoms held up their brief lights until they went out, and over the way a laburnum, till then absolutely insignificant and unnoticed, now aristocratically rose up to pay its dues and taxes, a flaming fountain of yellow flower, further enlightened by the morning rays.

Arriving in the farmyard, did I find 'E in a pleasing frame of mind? Hardly. On the Tuesday morning I made straight for the oil-can, meaning to fill it – for seeing to the oiling of an engine is one of my strong points. But he yelled across the yard to me to put it down, that it was no good, that it leaked, that he wouldn't have it used, not by me 'nor the King of Honolulu, nor anyone'.

This unexpected display of wit and learning rather eased the atmosphere in the yard and the others tended to relax their features somewhat. After I had got my oil I wanted some petrol, for which purpose I had a special bottle. All the tins were empty, so it was necessary to get some out of the tank in the lorry. This could be accomplished by sticking a rubber pipe into the tank. You could achieve a flow if you sucked your end for a minute or so. True, this meant petrol in the mouth, but you could spit it out. The operation looks a trifle absurd, and 'E, watching me kneeling down and sucking away at the rubber tube, loosened up and laughed, saying – 'Collis is drinking beer,' and laughed some more. As a wisecrack, no great claims could be made for it perhaps, but the sight of 'E laughing caused a further relaxation amongst those present, and something in the nature of mirth swept perceptibly across the yard.

How about mishaps these days? Well I made a point of examining the plugs now before starting up. They very often needed cleaning, and it saved a lot of time in the end. Indeed I became a champion taker-out and dismantler of plugs in quick time (never even dropping the little screw on top!). This meant, by the way, that a clean hand became a thing of the past for me. I have always had a partiality for clean hands and clean feet. Though often going without a bath for a month now, I still never went to bed without washing my feet. But my ideal of clean hands suffered modification. I actually started my agricultural career wearing gloves, and kept it up for some time. I quite abandoned this now, for you cannot deal with nuts and screws with gloves on. And now – such are the tricks of human psychology – I became proud of my grimy hands. They were real workman's hands. Once, later, when I was pulling beans with Harold on a wet day, our hands became very clean. He looked at his in disgust and said – 'No one wouldn't think I done no work!' And I began to appreciate the real meaning of Edward Carpenter's remark – 'I confess,' he wrote in his Autobiography, 'I love to see a *dirty hand*.'

Though plugs no longer troubled me, other things cropped up of course. Water sometimes got into the forty-gallon paraffin tank in the yard, and subsequently into my tank. This meant a stoppage after a few hundred yards. But I soon learnt to deal with that, though it meant stopping every ten minutes to clean out the glass basin under the tank. Unfortunately, when anything went wrong with the magneto I was done. I could only gape at it, fumbling without the slightest confidence that I could detect what was wrong.

One day, though the plugs seemed all right, I couldn't start up at all, couldn't get a spark out of her (machines are feminine). Harold came over, and we tried everything for over an hour. There was no chance of making a show before the Van arrived. I hoped it would arrive while Harold was with me also unsuccessful in diagnosis, and I knew that 'E himself would not know what was wrong, for his knowledge of machinery was very superficial. But the Van did not appear by the time Harold had given in, and I went off to get hold of Jimmy, hoping it would not appear before I had returned with him. But it did. Just as we approached the tractor 'E drove up, and got out in a fury, waving his hands about, refusing to listen to any explanation or excuse on my part, and saying 'You might as well go home!' We then proceeded to the tractor and Jimmy dismantled the magneto and found the trouble. Impressed by the complication of the work, which took us some time, 'E calmed down considerably. When the Van had gone away again, Jimmy said – 'He do fly up in the air, don't he!' And then added, greatly to my comfort, 'We've all been through it.'

Later in the day Harold asked me what that trouble had been which we had failed to detect, and I explained. But I was surprised that he had not asked Jimmy who must have passed by him on his way back. The fact is they would not have spoken about this, for they seldom spoke to each other, Jimmy being far more resourceful when confronted by any real mechanical difficulty.

Jimmy, under thirty I should say, was a very cheerful fellow, and equally good-looking. Everyone was glad when he appeared on the scene, his smiling face and pleasant turn of greeting warmed up the temperature a lot. He did not very often appear, for when he was not lorry-driving he nearly always, except during the heavy seasons, managed to work in the barn, doing this or that, no one knew what, and they resented it of course. For he was able to get away with it. He was in a powerful position, for he was the man whom 'E was always falling back upon. All the others were amateur mechanics, which is all right up to a point, but modern farm machinery calls for a genuine engineer on the premises. He regarded himself as a cut above the others, despising them for their obsequiousness. He didn't belong to the agricultural milieu. He felt superior. And as a human being he was superior. They didn't approve of him, but liked to see his cheerful face all the same.

Before going off, 'E had told me to go next to a certain field and drag it for couch. On arriving I found him and the carter there engaged in manuring. The harrow was in the middle of the field, and I went over to it and began to couple-up. I was in doubt as to which pin would fit this instrument, and was bending over the thing when suddenly a small tempest of a man's body struck against me, an arm shot past me into the tractor floor, grasped a chain, pulled it violently back, hurling several things with it on to the ground, and the voice of the carter using the customary expletives, said something unprintable. He fixed the chain to the harrow and then went away. But his violence, his apparent rage! Why? I asked myself, why this unpleasantness over what was by no means a momentous matter? I was far from amused at this incident.

It was a small field so I soon finished this job and went away with relief to the other field which I had not begun in the morning. I hadn't been there very long when Robert came up beckoning to me, and started yelling. My dog, it appeared, had just been seen going after his sheep on the Down. Now, my dog didn't run after sheep as a rule and in any case I had seen him a minute ago. But Robert insisted, shouting at the top of his voice, that he had been seen by Harold who had reported it. So I went and looked but could see no sign of him near the sheep. On returning I saw him coming out of the hedge in the field I was working on. He may of course have been on the Down, but was unlikely to have run after the sheep much if at all, and I reflected upon how colossal and critical a thing can be made to assume if you shout loud enough.

However, before the day was out Robert had cause to thank me. A number of the sheep escaped through a gap in the hedge and began to spread out all over the place. I noticed this, but I couldn't find Robert anywhere. So I drove them back myself, and filled up the gap. I did not experience any difficulty in getting them *all* to go in the necessary one direction and through the hole. For there is one pleasing peculiarity about sheep. If you can get a small bunch of them moving towards a given corner, the rest will follow as if the whole lot were tied together with invisible strings – and they will all rush blindly through the gap like water out of the drain in a bath. I wonder was it sheep, rather than swine, that rushed down that steep place into the sea?

While rolling this field, a very bumpy and stony one, I could see some distance off a lovely rich green field gleaming in the sunshine, all quiet on the agricultural front, and I suddenly wished I could be back in the old days when I could look at such a field seeing only its beauty and peace, and perhaps sit in it knowing nothing of irate farmers and men – a sudden nostalgia owing to my as yet unconsolidated position here, and my immersion in mechanics, my pushing and pulling with bolts and screws, spanners and hammers, plugs and carburettors, and the clatter and rattle of the roller.

15. Beauty through the Dust

Though it was June now there still remained some work to be done on fields which were to carry roots. It was worth glancing at the transformation of the fields around. The clover, from ankle-deep, was now knee-deep in rich, dark lusciousness – haymaking being round the corner. A field that recently had only showed lines of burning couch was now covered with a bright green sheet. The field in which sheep were earlier folded was now being ploughed by Harold and dragged and rolled by me. And I was amazed by the good crop of corn now coming up on another field which had seemed to me incredibly stony. 'Some seeds fell upon stony ground' – and did very well, it seems. Up to a point stones are an advantage, I learn, in terms of drainage. Yet looking at such a field earlier, so hard, so dry, so massively stony, the uninstructed spectator might well be pardoned for wondering how so tender a thing as a seed could derive nourishment there and cover it all with silky greens.

There in a corner stood the thresher covered up. How inactive it looked, how dead: yet capable of springing into intense liveliness as were the grass-covered drags and chain harrows lying about here and there like old ugly and forgotten thoughts. Over the hedge was a huge straw-rick: I had helped to put it there. And as I looked round and considered each field in turn, I was surprised to find that I had had dealings with every one of them – which gave me great satisfaction.

The sheep shearing was now in full swing, the large bales of wool being hung up in the barn. It was done by machine shears which completed the whole job in a week. 'E was one of the shearers. Hence it was a week held in the highest esteem by the staff. 'I wish it was three months,' said one of them to me, 'for then you know where 'E is all day.' A great advantage. No fear of the Van suddenly appearing. Especially at lunch hour. Officially we had half an hour off for lunch between nine-thirty and ten o'clock; and 'E had a way of appearing just when you had sat down for this delightful break, or were about to do so. The staff hated this. They liked to be found working, even though the break was legitimate. It seemed to give a bad impression to be found by the Van sitting down and eating – and of course no boss is ever seen eating. He often arrived just as we were taking that extra five minutes at the end. If he appeared in the middle it spoilt the break, for you couldn't enjoy your food while receiving instructions and holding conference, and you couldn't settle down again comfortably till he was out of sight. It was therefore delightful to have a whole week with the knowledge that the Van would *not* appear, knowing precisely where 'E was – shearing sheep in the barn.

I was on the last lap of the dragging and rolling now. It was very hot and the ground dry, so that the dust rose in clouds behind the harrow, and the roller was deafening. But at intervals I noticed that the weather was magnificent. The days were gleaming in a manner more often heard about than seen in June, and the surrounding fields and skies were shining with signs and answers and promises and prophecies and praise. The roller clattered, the dust rose, and the tractor gave choking trouble at intervals, but I could not help being aware of that glitter and that gleam. And I marvelled at the thought of night coming soon, the mighty opposite, when all that radiance would go and all those colours pass. A common experience, night following day? Yet we may doubt if between the pram and the bath-chair we will ever see anything more fantastic than this change. Every dawn is the re-enactment of the world's genesis, and the rising up of the light is the rising up of life. Hence in the radiance of the sunshine men shrink from murder. On days like these I could well understand Macbeth calling upon night to scarf up the tender eye of pitiful day, and with its bloody and invisible hand cancel and tear to pieces that great bond which kept him pale.

16. While Couching

Some of the meadows were now ready for cutting, so I took the tractor down to the yard to Jimmy, who would now take over. The cutter was power-driven straight from the power-take-off of the tractor. It is therefore a much larger and stronger affair than the ordinary cutter. It was certainly a formidable looking apparatus to fix up. It was necessary to remove half the floor of the tractor and join it to the cutter which has something like fifteen parts – shafts, pulleys, engine, blade, bed. A business of terrific screw-tightening and bolt-fixing. Had I been told to do the job (I was merely Jimmy's assistant) I would have been stumped by the jig-saw; but it didn't seem difficult as each part, taken separately, found its place. What struck me most about the mechanic's operations was that if a hole on the mudguard, say, wouldn't meet the hole in a given shaft by any amount of pressure, then he didn't give in but simply *made* another hole, piercing one by holding it in a vice in the barn. Again if, as so often happened, a screw was too big and would not fix into a given hold and no other screw would perform this office, he didn't give way to lamentation but put it in the vice and filed it off until it did fit. All very obvious to the initiated, no doubt; and once more I saw that the great principle for a mechanic is to have *resource*, and a sufficient number of tools and gadgets to make that resource practicable ... I have just said that Jimmy did not lament. I mean not practically. But verbally his lamentations were so frequent and despairing that I imagined he was hopelessly floored every time. But not a bit of it. He addressed recalcitrant screws and bolts as if they had hearts, cajoling and cursing them; but not, I soon discovered, with any feeling that they ever had the upper hand.

When I had sharpened the cutter-knives, I took a horse and cart and went to gather up some couch, for Jimmy was going to handle the cutter – at which I was sorry but relieved, for how would I handle any breakdown of that 'menagerie'? It was very pleasant with the horse and cart in the sunshine – always how pleasant going along quietly in the sun with a cart! And how different today working coatless in the warmth than weighed down with clothes in the cold – to me all the difference in the world! But not shared by the others. They preferred the winter, on the simple ground, they said, that the hours were shorter, half an hour later in the morning and off at five instead of half past in the evening. The heat of summer was regarded as a nuisance – whereas I'd rather have it than champagne. It was not surprising that the sun could give them little pleasure, since they wore underclothes, even pants, all the year round – so that one of the real joys of life, the specific one open to them, namely physical work in the sunshine, was turned into discomfort! As for working without a shirt – at this place it was quite daring to go without a hat. This sort of thing is not the wisdom of the ages: it is merely convention. In some particulars, of course, they are extremely wise with regard to clothing for certain activities, and I find that a case, even a strong case, can be made out for braces – though not on all occasions. But for the most part it is just a question of fashion. You do what the others do, and no one will break the fashion for the sake of comfort or pleasure. For nothing is so strong, so oppressive, so enchainingly tyrannical as the power of fashion. Almost anything can be done, anything could be done, and done daily and calmly, if it is the fashion. Then the mind turns the fashion into a *moral*. Robert was deeply shocked on one occasion when two land girls rolled up their dungarees above their knees on a hot day. 'E himself was far more broad-minded.

During this hay-cutting period I did a good deal of couching, in company with Alf and his boy who were newcomers. (I'm not bothering to put in surnames. For in practice I have a good working rule-of-thumb method in this matter. I call a gentleman, after knowing him a bit, simply 'Jones'; I call a lower-middle-class person 'Mr Jones', otherwise he is indignant, for he regards the Mr as his only title to fame; and with the working man I take a flying leap as soon as possible to the Christian name.) I don't know how Alf would have been described before Dickens, but now one can simply say that he had a Dickensian appearance and countenance, and leave it at that. Even his cap was Dickensian, even the back of his cap. He was a town worker really, from building and other trades, and was trying his hand at agriculture for the first time. He groused even more than land workers, but was more independent, and much less hard working. In the old days I had heard about the British working man always taking it easy and 'resting on his spade'. Perhaps this is true of the town worker. At the beginning of the war I did some A.R.P. work in Kent amongst a few labourers who were not agricultural. In the digging of a shelter I found that my pace was much too fast, especially for a wonderful man called Knight whose flow of tongue was unexampled in my experience. He required frequent intervals for a breather and some talk. 'The two bottom evils in the world, brother,' he would say, 'are the purse and the female,' and he welcomed as many stoppages as possible to develop this and other themes. But as soon as I found myself amongst agricultural labourers I saw that their pace was much faster and steadier, and that stoppages, if any, were furtive and seldom lasted longer than the lighting of a cigarette. Alf was finding the difference very marked, and gave me amazing examples of easy work and easy money from other trades. And it was clear that Alf's boy, about fifteen, had reached the conclusion that one shouldn't work at all on any account. All the same Alf was a nervous and inferior little man, and more apprehensive than anyone else at the approach of 'E. He worked in a feverish, jerky, busy manner. He pursed his lips, continually blowing outwards as if exhaling invisible smoke; it was evidently habitual, an unconscious technique to give the impression of earnest concentration and hard work going forward at full steam ahead.

When I joined him he had already decided to quit. ' 'Taint good enough,' he said. 'Don't do nothing 'ere but work, look-see. No one won't speak to you on this 'ere joint. Nothing but blank work for arf the money wot you get in the town. The missus can't stand it 'ere with them neighbours wot don't say a word, and I won't 'ave her locked up in no 'ome.' This tribute to agricultural and village life was followed by an expression of gratitude that I alone addressed him in a friendly manner. But I think this was only because I had taken the trouble to find out his Christian name. I said something about the others not being interested in things outside. He said that this was owing to 'the bloke wot nurses 'em, they get so as they loses 'art'. At this point the Van appeared at the other side of the hedge, and stopped for a minute while 'E regarded us with no enthusiasm, then shouted across, 'I don't want it raked up but picked up' – a distinction which, when analysed by us, yielded no clear idea as to what we were doing wrong.

I asked Alf whether in the days of unemployment he had been unemployed. He said no, he always found it easy to get work. But many couldn't, I said. He insisted that they didn't want it, that they were better off without it, especially with a large family when the 'Benefit' would amount to about three pounds. I mention this, not because 'better off' has any meaning there, but because this is the sort of remark workers make about themselves. And it is undoubtedly true that when the level of wages and the level of unemployment pay were nearly the same, as was sometimes the case, many preferred not to work. Only people who are ignorant of what work really is, and ignorant of human nature, can be surprised or shocked at this. Those who like their work are the only people who like working. We tend to forget how much work is unlikeable. We used to get it done at the point of the starvation bayonet. Terror of starvation is now a thing of the past. If the spur of necessity is entirely removed, much basic work will simply not be done – unless enforced. My knowledge of the working man is riskily unexhaustive, but what has struck me most forcibly is the fact that he now worries about money much less than the middle classes do. Money affairs really *haunt* the middle-class person. A sudden loss of job or income is a fearful blow, a family catastrophe, the break up of the whole machinery of life. But ever since unemployment achieved considerable dimensions the working man has felt increasingly secure. In the days when there wasn't a great deal of unemployment and the State left every man to look after himself, the fear of losing your job was often a nightmare (this, as short a time ago as, say, the publication of Galsworthy's *Silver Box*). When things got bad enough to be dangerous, Unemployment Benefit or the Dole was brought in and the *dread* of not being able to find a job and the next meal vanished. Then if a job fell through, the workman would say, to my astonishment I have heard him say it with the greatest cheerfulness (before the war-boom in work) – 'Well I'll go down to the "Labour" tomorrow and see if there is anything I fancy.' If there was nothing he fancied he would take the Benefit.

If the reader feels that the exceptions that disprove the above rule, if it is a rule, are just as important as the rule itself, I shall not disagree with him. I am content to make the one observation that the working people today, if not less greedy for money, are less anxious about it than the middle classes, and are less afraid of being broken – or 'broke'. Many of the latter receive a good deal of their income from investments. This brings with it nowadays a terrible feeling of insecurity – for, as Rebecca West has observed, there is a great difference between getting your money from some strange invisible source like investments, and getting it for definite work done or goods produced. In the latter case you do feel in unsettled times that your source of income may dry up. True, while things are all right, the middle-class person has more than the labourer. But this only makes him the more anxious. And even that little extra cash which he gets is spent to support visions and apparitions and ghosts of reality, and to wind round him scarves and veils of illusion, which he calls 'keeping up appearances'. When money fails or lessens he cannot cope with the situation, he is terrified of the Appearances disappearing. The machinery of his life breaks down, he is broken. But the labourer gets the Benefit and can cope. The onus really falls upon 'the wife' who 'makes do' a bit more. Middle-class people cannot make do, they are stuck in their fantastic swamp. Indeed fantastic: the labourer, accustomed to living within his means, is astonished and bewildered at hearing people with more means than himself speaking about '*my overdraft at the bank*'. He lives in a world mercifully oblivious of such nonsense and such failure in the art of life.

Up till this he had also been free from another word – *taxes*. Now that it is coming into his ken he is highly indignant. 'I'm not going to do no overtime,' he frequently declares, on the ground of paying Income Tax if he does. The tax is always spoken of as if it were equal to the amount earned! I'm told it hurt their pride to be taxed – though I don't follow this. Certainly they seem to prefer to make less money than pay a small tax. They prefer to marry in a hurry rather than pay a bachelor-tax, as is now virtually the case. The Beveridge business means a lot more paying out; and as insecurity is not their chief fear, one meets with no wild enthusiasm for the scheme. Actually, one never hears it discussed or even mentioned, indeed many seem not to have heard of it. It will be interesting to see how the working man takes to it when he comes in practice to realize its full implications. Accustomed to regard the State as something absolutely external, whose business it is to look after him and pay for his children's education and so on, he may not relish joining the privileged classes whose main privilege it is to pay taxes and to regard the State as part of themselves. But according to a section of the Press he is supposed to be clamouring for it. For all I know this may be true of the working man in the towns; and of course it is still not thought proper to consider the countryman as actually existing. 'A fortnight's holiday is now universal,' writes Sir Richard Livingstone, calmly turning his back on the whole agricultural world, just as a man called Commander Campbell never misses an opportunity to tell the twelve million listeners of the Brains Trust that their Christmas dinner, or any dinner, is entirely due – to the Merchant Navy.

17. Masters and Men; A View of Farmers

How hard it is to see the whole while merely grappling with the part! I had done a great many things to this field, but what interest had it for me after a few hours' work on the couch? I was just 'burning couch'. The labourer is too close to the earth to see the earth, to glimpse the whole or even the glittering of the part. As for Alf, it was just 'this bloody couch'. His knowledge of agriculture was as limited as his interest in it. He referred to Robert as 'the sheep man'. Once when we were spreading some caving-compost he had no notion that he was doing anything except throwing down some wet mushy straw to please 'the old man', and when I said it was manure he said – 'Oh, it's manure, is it?' While Jimmy was cutting grass on the neighbouring field, Alf thought he was cutting corn. And once he remarked to me – 'The old man don't do much farming, dun 'e? Just removing this 'ere couch.' He could see no relation between this couch-destruction and the preparation of a seed-bed, nor could he visualize any previous work on the other silent fields.

Sometimes Dick joined us, and his presence always enlivened the atmosphere by his humorously exaggerated grousing and take-offs of 'E. 'I hope you are making a good show!' we would hear as he approached. On such occasions I heard nothing good of agriculture. I enjoyed this, for I like unearnest people, and easily suit my mood to theirs. In fact, I like to grouse with a grouser. I don't like to spoil things by appearing too con-scientious to a grouser or too slack to a non-grouser, just as I don't like to be too sincere in the presence of an insincere person, and, I may add, just as often lie to liars.

Sometimes 'E also joined with the couching, for there was nothing he was above doing himself. The Van! – and if it was near the end of the day we wondered if his object would be to finish the field, which would mean going a bit past the hour for 'shutting out'. And we didn't like that, though it was the natural thing to do – to finish a job even though it meant an extra fifteen minutes. How often I have thought of this business of masters and men, arising both from my own experience and from what I have heard from others. The labourers don't think about the master. For he seldom thinks about them. They are to him simply 'labour'. 'I haven't got the labour,' he will say, not colleagues, not assistants, not even labourers. If a job is finished at five-fifteen instead of five-thirty, he doesn't say 'That's all right boys, we'll call it a day,' thus making it easy for himself next time he wants that extra quarter of an hour. Oh no, he says Go and do so and so. He can't bear the idea of losing that time; think of 'the money' I'm throwing away, he feels.

It is sometimes put forward that farmers on the whole are not amongst the choicest spirits of mankind. It is represented that they are mean, permanently disgruntled, hard, unsympathetic, greedy, and lacking in idealism and interest in the world. If there is truth in some of this, as seems likely owing to the frequency of the charge, it cannot be the fault of the farmers. That is obvious, since you and I, so vastly free from these faults, on becoming farmers tomorrow, would in due course have to be included in the charge, if it is true.

118

It is the effect of the Earth.

The Sea has a good effect upon men. On the sea we are *travellers*; we voyage in an element of alien mystery which belongs not to us but to fish, and where no man trespasses without fear of prosecution. He who ploughs the main does really plough in fear and praise, does really feel the mystery; so that even the humblest seaman becomes fascinated and cries 'Back to the Sea!' if he goes away from it.

The influence of the Air is often good. When an airman speaks we hear the language of the Ideal, either open or disguised; and some attain the perspective of pity and love.

The spirit of the ancient Earth is sterner. Hoary with cruel taxation from morning to night she exacts a singleness of purpose that shall not waver and shall not tire. Her demands are not only too great but too constant to allow those who battle with her any relaxation, any contemplation, any ideology, any interest in the spirit and the mind. She cannot permit her servant to get lost in reverie like a sea watchman, nor to hold the world in proportion like an airman. He must not pause beside Beauty. He must not open the book of Learning. He must not pay homage to Art. He shall be kept submerged in his great task by perpetual apprehension of failure and ruin.

18. Work on a Rainy Day

A series of breakages were holding up the hay-cutting, and I was glad not to be involved in it. Also some wet days came on. A good farmer is never at a loss to know what to do with his men on a wet day, and 'E had plenty of handy jobs waiting down in the barn and shed – oiling machines, doing repairs, sack-tidying, mixing artificial. I spent one morning removing sacks of beans. They had been left too long and were splitting at the bottom. I mention this job, for now in actual practice, I did really *spill the beans*. But the most usual job was mixing artificial – so much potash with so much sulphate of ammonia. We poured it out on the floor, crunched it up, and mixed it. Some of the mixture seemed to make a remarkable potion, burning boots badly (Alf had his soles destroyed), and I wondered whether it wasn't all a bit too scientific. Often 'E would give his instructions regarding the proportions to be mixed, and then go away. We all heard his words (perhaps four of us), but when we got down to it no one was sure whether he had said, say, half a hundredweight of potash to a hundredweight of ammonia, or more or less of each, or phosphate as well. In due course 'E would return and say we were doing it wrong, he had said less of one and more of the other. But curiously enough, he didn't seem to mind very much.

I did much of this with Alf alone. He seemed to like doing the sack-lifting or to dislike my doing it. I don't know which; anyway, he always refused assistance and even seemed to want to do most of the shovelling. It took us an hour and a half to mix and bag up a pile of manure. Once when there was an awkward three-quarters of an hour to go, we lessened the next pile by informal proportions, without, I felt sure, making the slightest difference to the yield of the ultimate crop.

But Alf didn't like working in the barn. It was too close to 'E. One afternoon it was half-raining. After dinner, as it looked like clearing, I went up to the field and carried on with the couch (not trying to burn it of course, but to cart it away). It began to rain a bit more but still not much. Now, as a general rule, if there is a drop of rain the English labourer (as opposed to other nationalities I am told) rushes for his raincoat and stops out-door work on the spot – so much so that some farmers dare not be seen putting on a coat themselves if a shower threatens, in case there is a general cessation of work on the job in hand. But out came Alf now. Seeing that the rain wasn't much, he had made a bee-line for the stable, got the cart and hastened away from the barn up to my field. He was considerably amused at his own haste and determination to get clear of the barn, and kept repeating, 'I weren't going to stay down there with 'e if I could 'elp it. 'E won't find me going down there, rain or no rain. It's better up 'ere. Peace and quiet 'ere, looksee. No one don't get me to go down there this afternoon, we're better off up 'ere.'

Observing my amusement at this, he repeated it over and over again with variations every five minutes for the first hour and a half. Sometimes I thought he was going to introduce a new element into the conversation, but no, it would just be – ' 'E don't get me to go down there if I can 'elp it. Don't want no work in that there barn with 'e around. Better up 'ere looksee.'

The Saturday mornings were long, for we knocked off, not at twelve-thirty but at one-thirty. This made our lunch hour an important meal and break. On one Saturday morning many of us were working at different jobs within visible proximity: Alf and myself spreading some caving compost; Dick over the way carting hurdles for Robert; the carter loading hay; Harold using the tractor. We were all about to break off for lunch at 9.30 when the Van was seen approaching. Better wait till 'E's gone, was the general feeling, so we went on working. He approached Alf and had something to say about his method of getting the straw loose, then over to me, finding that there was room for improvement in my scheme of distribution. He then passed over to Harold with whom he remained long in converse. But he'll be off soon, we thought, and carried on. He left Harold and went over to the carter. Then over to Robert where he remained some time in conference, all of us still working on, and then back again to say something more to Harold. Finally he moved off stage left, and when the Van was out of sight we all sat down – a most memorable break.

Dick was always in a tremendous hurry to be off, on every day, but especially on Saturdays, to see his girl. This morning he had been told to carry three wagon loads of straw to a given place. He loudly declared to us that he could fit in one load and a half, at most two, certainly not three if he were to make a getaway on time. So with a stream of suitable language he assured us that he would get two loads and no more – and he stuck to it, passing us eventually on his way down to the stable with time enough in hand to make his exit and then catch his bus. Meanwhile I carried on with Alf and Harold. 'Speed one-thirty,' they said. 'Speed one o'clock,' I said, since by one o'clock one could sight land, as it were.

It might fairly be asked how 'Patriotism' works in with all this, and 'putting all they have into the land', and 'willing work for the war effort', and 'splendid national service', and other B.B.C. phrases. Not very well really. I mean the phrases don't fit in too well, For the agricultural labourer, in war as in peace, is cut off from the world. He lives on a desert island. He is cast on a far shore. Upon him all the world rests: yet that world is to him a dream, and they are dream figures that he sees from his field passing on the road. They pay no heed to him, they think of him and thank him not at all. Who can blame him for not being able to think in national terms? Patriotism is not an unreal thing even when one's locality is not immediately threatened, it can be felt in masses such as you get in factories (or can it?). But not on the wide field, not amongst the cows, not under the pressure of the egoism of farmers. The labourer has nothing to prime him save his own ego and its persistent claims for a little freedom and pleasure.

19. What a Weed Is

It became hot again, though with occasional showers which held up the hour of haymaking. I was called now to a different job – that of hoeing some very small kale shoots in a very dirty field.

In towns men have become so far removed from the soil that when we hear that a man has *soiled* his hands we know that he is suspected of crime. But in the country soil is the acme of cleanliness and is only regarded as *dirty* if it has weeds on it. (And of course soil is so far from being dirty that if you cut your hand it is a good tip to plug the wound with a decent piece of earth, when it heals in no time.) What is a weed exactly? It is any plant which impedes or competes with any other particular plant we are interested in. It can be a 'flower'. Would you not call the scarlet pimpernel a flower? or the eyebright? or the poppy? But a field of kale, though it glitter with the scarlet, the red, the blue, the yellow and other shades of pretty flowers, is disgustingly dirty to the agricultural eye, and would still be considered as such though the rose, the lily, or the daffodil lifted their petals to the sun.

A weed may be considered as an exemplar of the paradox that the good that we would we do not, and the evil that we would not that we do. We do our best to care for the good plants, we spurn the evil weeds; but before we know where we are, the latter have sprung up unbidden and choked our plants. No one puts weeds amongst the kale, and yet they appear; while no kale would appear unless we put it there. Knock out the weeds, and after a shower they will rise up again. Knock out your plant, and even replant it, and it will die. In a word, weeds are tough plants, and that is doubtless why we cannot eat them, and why those we can eat are delicate and not fit for competition. Hence it is considered that only a lunatic will treat weeds as garlands. That is why King Lear, blasted in the storm, was found with docks, hemlock, nettles, darnel, and rank fumiter in his hair.

Thus hoeing is of great importance; otherwise many a field of kale, swedes, or mangolds will become submerged and all your work will be undone. Weeds should be treated, said William Cobbett, exactly as the Duke of Wellington treated the faction called the Whigs in 1828. But I fear I must acknowledge that there were times when I treated some of the smaller ones in the manner of Lord Nelson who deliberately turned a blind eye on another occasion.

The kale shoots were miserably small and weak looking, and it was impossible to believe that anything could come of them. 'Best thing 'e could do would be to plough them in, I allow,' was Robert's comment when he saw the field. But 'E knew better. So I carried on at what seemed a hopeless job. The ground was hard, the hoe light and blunt, and I made very little show. When 'E appeared and looked at my 'cut' he said that if I were doing it on a piece-work basis I would do a good deal more. You're telling me, I felt inclined to reply. For no one in his senses on the staff of any farm would go at the pace of professional piece-workers. These latter gentlemen provide an intimidating spectacle. Every yard covered is so much £.s.d. They know nothing of back-ache, having developed rubber spines. Time never drags for them, space being their only concern. They choose this method of work, preferring to go hard during certain months so as to be independent during others, and their own masters at all times. Some never take off, since work normally can be found all the year round: hedging and ditching by the chain in winter, sowing by the acre in April, dipping sheep by the score in May, hiling by the acre in harvest-time, thatching by the square, dressing mangolds by the acre or load, then hedging again. It would seem therefore that a farmer would be well advised to employ piece-workers for a job like hoeing, at any rate. But there is one snag, for their sole object is to cover so much space, and this can be done quickest by skimping the work and leaving in the smaller weeds. Thus the farmer, having paid a lot, finds the weeds still coming up in plenty – certainly here 'not worth the money'.

The day-labourer is careful not to compete with the pace of piece-workers. Given a certain job to do, for instance, he makes sure of not doing too much on the first day; for if he takes a big cut and does a particularly good day's work, he will be expected to do likewise tomorrow. He is not going to expose himself to the phrase 'you haven't done much today, have you?' if he can help it, when the boss appears. When 'E came out to me he said, 'Give me the hoe and I'll show you,' and then proceeded to give a demonstration which left nothing to be desired in either thoroughness or speed. He carried on for two minutes and then went off. The implication being that I should imitate this pace for the rest of the day. All bosses and foremen perform this exhibition, and while no one has the heart to spoil their comedy, it is held in derision by all the men.

20. The Real Inequality

Again the fresh beauty of the morning! The yellow flaming flag of the laburnum falls to the ground; the gorgeous candelabra of the chestnut trees have long since guttered and gone out. All effected at the rate of theatrical scene-shifting, it seems, as I cycle through the passing show. But the copper-beech in the rectory garden reminds me of the constancy of time. Its great trunk rooted in history; its leaves bathed in the memory of a thousand summers; the sunless branches in its tented shade; the slow dripping of the raindrops down into the glorious gloom of the soaking sod – are in themselves the Remembrance of Things Past.

... Thus in the early morning is the heart raised and the head cleared, as one steps on to the field of kale. And for an hour or so it is possible to remain in this frame of mind. But not for many hours. The morning goes well enough, but the afternoon sees a different man; the monotony of the task (give me that tractor again!), and the aching of the back, begin to numb the mind until it gradually stops working altogether, like a watch breaking down, and by the time evening approaches you feel little better than a rubbish heap of rotting thoughts, so that a hollow ghost stands where in the radiance of the morning had stood the living man. By that time one idea seemed the only true happiness on earth – the idea of just *sitting down*. Merely to get on to my bicycle and sit down on it – will I ever forget the pleasure! Yet I shall, that's the queer thing. There is nothing we forget so quickly as physical sensations – look how quickly people forgot what they felt when being bombed, and how women forget the labour of child-birth. In the years to come I shall often wish I were on the field, even the hoeing field. But for how *long* at a stretch? I will not remember what it was like, what the conditions for being on the field are. I shall never then be able to experience the excessive pleasure of sitting down, or of eating, for no man can force himself willingly – unless he owns a small farm – to work on beyond what he feels endurable.

This particular field was at its worst stage, the kale being small and the weeds large, so that they often both came up together. Alf joined me now and kept calling it ' 'ospital work'. He would plug along for a quarter of an hour perhaps, then say – 'Well, it'll soon be Christmas'; then have another go and soon stop again and say – 'Anyway it'll soon be Christmas'. Then he'd say 'I must go and see a man about a dog' and disappear for a short time. Farm work, he said, made you need plenty of sleep. I asked him what time he went to bed, and he said eight-thirty, sometimes nine, and often eight. He spoke of conditions in other professions, the sociality and also 'good grub in them canteens, not wot it is 'ere, where you get nothing to eat' (true word in war-time on the land!). Often enough, he said, the time is well spread out, there being an hour and a half for dinner, and a break for tea in the afternoon – ah, if there were a break for tea while hoeing! Would *money* thereby be lost? Personally, I think not.

Sometimes it was necessary to stoop down on one's knees in order to deal with some of the plants by finger. I mentioned to Alf that I felt rheumatism in my knees when I did this. Let me hand down his remedy to posterity. Whenever he got rheumatism, he said, in knees, elbow, or anywhere else, he simply rubbed in petrol and in a short time was cured.

This field was near to 'E's house, which had plenty of windows looking out over the farm. Alf didn't like them a bit, didn't approve of windows. 'You know why 'e's put them there,' he said, 'to see wot's going on. That's wot they're there for.' A little far-fetched, I thought, as an architectural critique, since one top window would do as a spy-hole. Still it is true that many farmers do like to have their houses built on the highest point, so that they can see without being seen. It is natural. And effective. They may never look from the windows, but the worker in the field feels uncomfortable if he is in sight of them – great eyes watching him if he sits down or makes an early get-away. For if the boss isn't there, the family is, and one or other member will notice and tell.

While riding home I reflected upon Alf's time of going to bed between eight and nine o'clock. And this tallies more or less with the bedtime of other agricultural labourers, though some make it a fairly regular nine-thirty. It is necessary if they are to rise early. That is to say they have no free time. This difference in length between the working hours of those on the land and those in the towns, is what has impressed me most; nothing, absolutely nothing, has impressed me more than this; and when I compare the hours of work put in by these agricultural labourers and those put in by professional men known to me, I say – Here is the *real* Inequality. It is not Wages; it is not Housing; it is not Education which is the bottom inequality, but the distribution of working hours. If the planners improve housing, pay, and education without tackling this matter, then the mental and spiritual life of the agricultural workers will not advance one step.

Recently in a public speech, Mr Ellis Smith, M.P., said that 'There is no reason why, at the end of hostilities, anyone should have to work more than six hours a day for a five-day week.' We need not suppose that he was thinking of agriculture or had ever heard of it; and to say that there is no reason why this should not be achieved immediately after the war is an amusingly empty phrase on the plane of practical politics; but as a general statement it is sound, and must be true. For every year we go on saving labour; and to save labour and yet keep the labourers working the same hours as before is an unendurable absurdity.

It is clear that the world would be saved if all men did work they loved doing. Such men have no time for quarrelling, for fighting, or for money-mania. There will always be few such men. We can never aim to build a society composed of such. But we could aim towards the ideal of work which engages nearly the whole man. In some factories today men use just – one finger. Not the body, not the mind – just one finger! But there is an occupation which can engage nearly the whole man and which if there were time given for the development of the mind, would satisfy the psychological needs of hundreds of thousands of people. This is agriculture. It could provide scope for bodily, mental and spiritual development. These are bald statements. I do not seek to embellish them, they are unquestionable.

When I got home I heard John Barbirolli conducting Beethoven's Seventh Symphony, over the air. What was agriculture for, it seemed to me, except that such a thing as that symphony and the playing of it should be made possible? To make bread so that it shall be possible for mankind to have more than bread and hear the scripture of the kings; to listen to a Beethoven, a Sibelius, a Tchaikovsky, uttering some far message of paradox and joy.

21. Haymaking and Combustion

The weather now made it possible for us to plunge into haymaking. I was soon to become thoroughly implicated in hay. Our first field was composed of sainfoin – for nowadays meadows are seldom composed of a miscellanea of grasses; they are crops. We went out and drew up in the field with full modern equipment, and went hard at it, the motor cars dashing full steam ahead. For hay is no longer *carried*; it is swept in. Two cars each with an attached sweep, feeding an elevator without cessation, can gather up fifteen to twenty acres in a day. All done in a great hurry. None of the scented peace and quiet which we used to associate with haymaking. The agricultural labourer seldom praises anything, or admits that he enjoyed anything in the way of work; and none, save the old, object to the introduction of any mechanical device. But haymaking provided an exception to this – here at any rate. One and all, they not only hated the present job, but glorified the past. 'We made *hay* in they days,' they said. It was regarded as a kind of holiday time then, their families in the field, great picnics, not to mention lots of beer flowing. Actually and truly a merry time. Now all swept away by the hay-sweep.

Thus we went ahead. The cars were driven by 'E's daughter and one of the boys. The carter kept the tiddler going across the field, the sails of its wheel sweeping up the swathes into long mounds convenient for taking up by the sweeps. Harold, Alf, Dick, and Jimmy received the hay at the foot of the elevator, while Robert built the rick assisted by myself and 'E or a land girl.

I speedily found that ricking under these conditions was no picnic. If four men on the ground are piling the grass on to the elevator, the man receiving it at the top has plenty to hand on. If I stood too near or there was a wind the stuff fell on my head – and at the end of the season I calculated that I had received about fifty acres of hay on my hat. I found that the material, from a hauling-about point of view, was more like wire than my former conception of hay. This was real exercise – but far from boring! Harold, who though officially the tractor-driver, was always one of the best workers at any other job he did, liked to have his game with me. He set the pace at heaving the hay on to the elevator, and catching my eye, would, with a broad grin, in unison with the others, send up a succession of small haycocks in an endeavour to submerge me. On one occasion later on, when we had to build a new wing on to our rick and I was the only person at all near the elevator, a special effort was made to drown me. It was nearly successful, for failing to remove the first lot, the subsequent waterfall came on top of me and I almost disappeared. But by sheer force I rose above the surface, and both on this occasion and on all others managed to keep my head above hay.

Making hay seems to me to be about the most tricky of all the agricultural operations. A weight of decision rests upon the farmer as upon a general in a campaign. If the hay gets a lot of rain it will be spoilt, as everyone knows, though I did not realize until I experienced it that it gets so black that you look like a chimney-sweep after dealing with it. It can be spoilt even easier by sunshine, a thing I had not realized at all; for if it gets too much of it, all the good will be scorched out. And if, in order to avoid this, you lift it too soon and it is slightly green, then the rick may move away, disappear from the field altogether: its means of locomotion being the same as that of an engine –

internal combustion. It will begin to heat, getting hotter and hotter until it explodes, catches fire and is seen no more. Such is the marvellous chemistry of the earth, that if we play with her we play with fire.

It happened that our first rick caused trouble in this manner. It had seemed dry enough, but next day we found that it was getting extremely hot. So much so that ultimate combustion was feared. In order to prevent this and let the air in, we dug a hole from the top right down through it. The odour was most remarkable – like very strong strawberries, I thought. But no comparison will describe its richness – at another time I thought it smelt like beer. We took turns with the hay knife, jumping down into the smoking crater. As we got lower we found it very hot down there, and none of us could stand it for more than a few minutes, and we came up pouring with perspiration. It was a fine morning but with a very cold wind, and the change of temperature after one's shift at this strange mining operation was quite alarming from a chill-catching point of view. We dug two of these shafts, and before building on top again, laid hurdles across the pit-heads. Just before this was done I got down into the shaft we had finished first, being rather fascinated by it. While I was down there Robert began to put a hurdle across the top. I pretended not to notice this until he had put it on. Then I shouted out as if fearfully alarmed at my caged condition, and 'E, much amused, said 'Collis has got left behind!' 'Let him bide!' shouted Robert, pretending to be angry. 'Let him bide! Some volks are better down under, I allow,' and threw a bit of hay on top of the hurdle, at which I shouted – 'Hey, Robert, I'm suffocating!' At which, with a great show of relenting, he opened the hurdle for me to climb out, saying – 'I reckon we can't afford to lose 'e quite yet', and so I emerged amidst general laughter. For, if work was going forward all right, 'E was by no means averse to a bit of fun, and actually liked an agreeable atmosphere far more than others realized, and was totally unaware of the nervous atmosphere he himself created. (He had two sons, as I have mentioned, and one of them, Reggie, inherited his father's suppressed sense of fun,

130

while the other, John, afraid of being left behind in life's struggle, was in such deadly bossing earnest that it was with consternation that one watched him.)

Our next rick was also slightly damp, but this time we were taking no chances and made two holes in the middle as we built. This was done by filling two sacks tight with hay and building on top of them, raising them as we rose. By this method two clean clear shafts were made right through the rick, up which the heat could pass. While building, one or other of the sacks continually kept getting submerged and difficult to find. It is sometimes customary to call such a sack 'the old man', and 'E himself, quite aware that he was often referred to by this appellation, added another light touch when a sack got sub-merged by saying 'the old man is deaf and dumb, 'e don't say nothing when you tread on him'. And subsequently I would ask – 'Where has the old man got to now? I must rescue him.'

This particular dampness we were guarding against was owing to rain that had come on since dealing with the first rick – combustion can also be caused this way. There were constant stoppages, one of the sweeps breaking down every quarter of an hour, the engine for driving the elevator breaking down, and the elevator itself having a stoppage. The wetness of the hay itself tripped up the sweeping, and Robert declared that had four horses been used instead of the power-cutter (which had broken down several times) we could have carried it by now, dry and all.

22. Colloquy on the Rick

The reading public is so accustomed these days to hear praise of the countryman – the swing in this direction taking place before the war broke out – that it is almost a shock to find that this is not yet realized by country labourers themsleves. There are still bitter feelings on the score that the townsman looks down on them. A number of us were couching on the following Saturday morning, before the dew had dried on the next hay field, and the subject came up. Some derogatory remarks were made concerning Jimmy, because they were annoyed that he always seemed to get out of doing jobs such as this 'ere couching. They began to refer to him as 'a town bloke' and to say that he had no right here at all! This led to the complaint, made by Harold, that before the war the town folk 'wouldn't look at you, now they love you', owing to present importance of food grown in England. It was clear that they thought that the present praise was mere lip-laudation caused by the war.

Would 'E want us to go on after dinner today? – that was now the great question. There was a tremendous distaste for working on Saturday afternoon. No one knew what he intended – no one ever knew anything in advance. All said – 'I'm not coming out after dinner, I'm not doing no work on Saturday afternoons' – Alf being even more emphatic in his declared determination that he would not return after dinner. Yet, in the event, he did – and brought his tea with him. So did all the others – for none trusted the other to stick to his word.

It surprised me that, hay being what it is, feelings about overtime should be strong. But they did not seem to think about the hay, nor to be even vaguely aware that three of the most fearful battles that the world has ever known were at the moment in progress. As for myself, I had brought out a certain amount to eat for dinner, but nothing for tea. That made a gloomy prospect – for whenever I was caught in this way, it never occurred to 'E to ask if I had enough food or bring me out any if I had not, unless I definitely asked him, and then he would bring out a very small piece of cheese and a very plain piece of bread. On this occasion I asked Dick to bring me back something, and he said he would but didn't – for his mother was not in. However, Alf brought me out some chocolate.

We carried a clover field that afternoon and evening. It was the biggest job I had done to date, whether with hay or with anything else, for we did not finish before nine, and there were no accidental stoppages. A seven-hour fall of hay from the elevator to be hauled round, and a steady rainfall of clover-

132

leaves with it. This latter was a part of the business I hadn't bargained for, the downfall of small, dry leaves which comes with clover – and I had not yet properly developed the one and only possible technique against this, namely the tight silk handkerchief round the neck, met by a tightly zipp-fastened shirt, and well topped with hat.

While I stood there on the rising rick the thought crossed my mind that if a painter were to come into the field and sit down and start making a picture of this 'rural scene', I would feel it to be a vast impertinence. And I thought of the picture eventually hanging at an Exhibition to which excessively men-about-town, and women-about-town, totally removed and uninterested in the immediate reality, would come and appraise the picture and see the labourers in terms of paint.

Presently Robert all of a sudden shouted across to me – 'Before the war you wouldn't be on this rick, and if you'd seen I and t'others working here, you'd have thought us a lot of mugs, I allow.' Then he added – 'I think after the war we should change jobs and I'll take my ease.'

'Well,' I said, 'I'd like to see you take on my job which seems so easy, but you don't know what it is.' (For I thought I had concealed the fact that I used a pen.)

'Oh yes I do,' he shouted, 'it's a p—'

'What's that?' I asked, not making out what he had said (it sounded like pig or pork or something).

'A poit, a writer!' he yelled. 'I could go out into that field,' he continued at the top of his voice, 'and write a hundred pages as good as any, but I wouldn't do it. It's too easy. I wouldn't do it. If I did on it, at the end of the day my fingers *would tingle with shame.*'

I turned and looked at 'E who was laughing. Whenever Robert had an outbreak of any kind, 'E always kept up a continuous over-emphatic nervous laugh, in order to keep the matter on a humorous footing.

'Robert wouldn't take no easy money,' he said.

I admit that this sudden attack – though it was really in the nature of an exhibition – rather nonplussed me. I would have liked to advance a more comprehensive philosophy of art than that put forward by Robert, but did not feel equal to doing so under the noise of the elevator, even if I could have found any words that would have been intelligible. Moreover, I was so subdued to what I worked in at the moment, that I could not help feeling a certain justice in his attitude, and I only said feebly, 'there is a good deal in that', to which he roared back – 'there is far too much in it!'

I felt, however, that I could not quite let the matter rest there, so reducing the terms of the Argument from literature to science, I said that the man who sat down (that deplorable position) and invented the elevator, for instance, had his uses.

But this mute, inglorious Milton was not prepared to lend his support to this view; having already disposed of Literature, he now swept Science aside with a single phrase – 'It took more brain to put it together than to invent it, I allow,' he said.

Since becoming submerged in the land I had frequently reflected upon how great is the difference between what the man on the road sees and the man in the field experiences. From the road, how delightful the sowing of that hundred-acre stretch of land appears; how calm, how leisurely. The tractors are quietly going round with their drills, the horse standing with the wagonload of sacks is half asleep, the group of men in the middle are conversing at ease, a man is bending over a sack in no haste. Enter the field, draw close. The boss is in a state of great anxiety owing to the threat of rain, the horse won't stand still without being yelled at, the man bending over the sack is in difficulties about getting the grain into a too small bucket and is late in having the stuff ready to feed the approaching tractors, the driver in front being in a great hurry because the one behind is catching him up – the operations proceed amidst flurry, speed, noise, haste, anxiety. From the road, how easy and pleasant it looks on the hayfield; the hay-sweep gently coming in with its nice little bundles, the pitchers throwing the hay on to the elevator with no trouble or effort, the men on the rick in an easy rhythm of leisurely movement, two men chatting together. Enter the field, draw close. The bundles are huge, the sweep has come in too soon and the hay won't come out for the pitchers without tugging, the receivers on the rick are more exhausted than the pitcher below since while hauling with all their might they stand on an unfirm floor; and the men who are chatting are simply saying – 'How's the time going?' 'Only three-thirty, I reckon.'

What the man on the road sees is not the immediate reality any more than when, with the wind blowing away from us, we see an aeroplane hovering like a hawk silently above some trees, or another glamorously glittering in the sky, innocent as heaven's cherubim horsed on the sightless couriers of the air.

Yet here we must pause. The man on the road does not see the immediate reality: he does see something which they in the field do not see, he knows something that they do not know. He sees the Whole. He may see only enough to call it picturesque. The artist is the man on the road with vision. He truly sees the whole, he perceives the Divine Harmony. His task is to reveal the whole to those who are submerged in the part, to unveil the harmony which is really on earth, and thus lessen the burden of life. He does not know that those two men are only asking each other the time, for he sees them in the light of Eternity; and though they may be in hell, he seeks to show that they are also in heaven.

I recently came upon a quotation and comment made by my brother Maurice Collis which deals with this theme. He quoted from the art connoisseur, Mr Max Friedlander, as saying – 'Art creates a second world in which I am not an actor but a spectator, and that world resembles Paradise.' And my brother goes on to add that 'this provides the most valid reason for the existence of art, which can unveil us Paradise while we are yet on earth'. I would prefer to phrase this with a slight difference and to go a step farther, in company with the great mystic Boehme who said – 'Paradise is still in the world, but man is not in Paradise until he is born again.' We should not say that art creates a *second world*, but rather that the artist uncovers the real world into which we could enter. We should not say that through him we may, *while yet on earth*, see Heaven, for we shall never find heaven save when we are on Earth. It is here. It can be seen when the eye is purged to see it. Sometimes in the stainless, shameless hours of early day, we realize this. As we cycle through the village, which is not awake and never awake to the Great Possibility that lies before it, we become aware that all sins have been forgiven and that Paradise is daily offered to mankind. The artist works for the time when men's vision shall be so purified, that seeing through the outer vesture, they shall have the strength to grasp the farther goal.

But while standing under the elevator, it was not with any feeling of surprise that I heard a man shout at me that his fingers would tingle with shame if he applied them to the task of Shakespeare or Plato. For if I, who by the chance of opportunity can see round the corner of a hay-rick, could nevertheless in the extremities of toil become so submerged in the Part as to think a painter's appearance an impertinence, how much more understandable is the attitude of men who are never in a position to see the Whole. Indeed, I am well content to have such remarks suddenly hurled at me; and, through me, at other artists, so that we may re-examine our place, accept our responsibility, and be true to our function in the scheme.

23. Typical Scenes

On the Monday, when we broke off for dinner, Robert produced a cake which he had brought out for me from his wife, possibly feeling that he had overdone it on the Saturday, or out of good nature, having witnessed the lack of tea I had had (no one having offered me as much as a slice). The business of actually passing the cake over to me was tricky, for it had to be achieved without anyone observing it. That would never have done: a proceeding so unusual and extraordinary would have led to gossip. To me it didn't seem so unnatural as all that, and, always a good receiver, I gave him pleasure by showing great pleasure at seeing it.

After dinner there was a hold-up owing to the breakdown of the battery in one of the hay-sweep cars. The current had to be transferred from the other car. Jimmy was late. 'Where is he to?' they asked, feeling helpless without him. Everyone seemed to have some idea how to do it, no one a clear idea, and experiments failed. Harold put forward one school of thought, Dick another, while Reggie and John fiddled with this and that, peering closely at the gadgets with unexampled concentration. Wires were strung between the two cars and there was a great deal of trial and error – chiefly, error. Harold wound away at the crank furiously. 'E said – 'I don't profess to know. I've too many other things to think about.' Robert advanced a decided suggestion of some sort, but no one took any notice of it, and he strolled to the hedge and carefully examined a hurdle blocking a hole. I stood beside him and made some remark sympathetically indicative of sage council rejected, and he gave me to understand that his patience was nearly exhaused. And so it went on until the mechanic eventually appeared, with that confident smile belonging to genuine engineers in a world given over to ignorance. And sure enough in a few minutes the job was done and the lifeless car was suddenly reborn.

As we went towards the rick, Robert pronounced on the folly of having machines, upon the waste of time they caused, while with horses the whole thing would be half-done by now; and ended by declaring that if he was a farmer he would let all machines 'go to hell'. 'All except your tractor,' I remarked to Harold. 'I don't want it,' he said quickly. He didn't mean that he didn't want it, but said so for the benefit of the company, because the tractor-driver is generally regarded as having a soft job 'sitting on his behind all day'; and since Harold did not see the matter in this light he wished to disclaim any desire to cling to his heavy burden.

We carried on. This particular afternoon was the hottest we had during the fourteen ricks we put up; in fact I have subsequently set any other gruelling job against this as a measuring rod of the just endurable. My longing for tea-hour cannot by any technical device be brought before the reader nor even felt by me now as I write.

The military were stationed in the neighbourhood, and after dinner an officer came into the field, took a prong, and joined the pitchers at the elevator and continued all the afternoon. At length it was tea-time, which was always heralded by the approach of 'E's other daughter or wife or both coming out with tea for the family. 'E did not make any remark of any kind to this voluntary helper, nor offer him tea. He was pleased that he had come, appreciated it, and felt grateful; but he was incapable of so simple a social gesture as that of offering refreshment.

It took us only another hour after tea to finish the rick. But today this did not mean that the final raking-up, the horse-raking, was finished, which was Dick's job. Now Dick's ruling idea was always to stop as soon as possible, but today it looked as if we would stop and go home while he alone remained to finish off the horse-raking. He was much perturbed by the enormity of this possibility. Would 'the old man' want him to finish? he wondered; and the job would take some time for he had only half-covered the field.

'Shall I shut out now?' he asked.

'E hesitated an instant and then said that he *didn't mind if he didn't finish,* meaning that he did mind but would not press him to continue.

Dick thereupon said that he would *just as soon stop,* meaning that he would infinitely prefer not to go on.

And he did stop.

There were compensations for working on the rick. A wise man will keep on firm ground if he can help it. Harold never had been on the rick and said he never would – I think he was chiefly afraid of giddiness. Still, I prefer the rick, for the simple reason that I like rising. When beside some trees it is pleasant to become level with the branches, and one gradually gets a good view of the surroundings, of that quiet field, that green hill far away, that village church growing from the grove. But we were

too far from the sea to catch sight of it. And that is what I
missed. If only we were by the sea! I constantly thought,
nothing would matter, no work would seem too long, no crisis
would be upsetting. Mountains that stride down to the sea!
cornfields cliffed by the shore: summer in the sky and winter on
the waves: the sun-path laid across the dawning deep: the ridged
and raving waste enstormed: the dark, cold winter dusk when
far, far away on the horizon a long huge black wall of cloud is
reared, and just below it soft red rays beam out as from the
gateway to another and a brighter land where all is happiness
and every tear is wiped away! – thus my mind's eye conjured
the sealess scene. For I was born by the sea, and lived by it, and
heard from my bedroom window its unfaltering fall upon Kil-
liney Beach. And though I care nothing about immortality, and
nothing about what happens to my bones, I do respond with all
my heart to the wild and sweeping poetry in Timon's frantic
apostrophe to himself – 'Presently prepare thy grave; Lie where
the light foam of the sea may beat Thy gravestone daily.'

24. Departure of Alf

A few rainy days held us up, and on approaching Alf one morning, his first words were 'I've 'atched out'. He had given notice
to quit. I was surprised at this, for though he had always said he
was going to give notice, he was wonderful at not sticking to his
word. Since he always said that he was not going to work overtime but invariably did, I thought his decision to give notice
would remain strictly in the realm of the imagination. But evidently he had had words of a sufficiently stimulating nature
with the carter to give him the necessary impetus to quit the
agricultural world.

This particular contretemps can hardly be blamed on the
carter. Alf had developed a habit of getting down to the
stable, when he had a horse and cart, on the tick of five-thirty.
Now the carter had to unharness and take the horses out to the
field, and needed about ten minutes in hand. He couldn't get

away on time when Alf only arrived in the stable at five-thirty. Alf's reason for not arriving earlier was clear and deliberate. He was afraid of being given an extra job by 'E to fill in the ten minutes, which might work out into fifteen or twenty minutes before he could get off. 'I'm not going down yet,' he would say, 'I don't want no new job. 'E'll be there, and 'e'll find me something. It don't do to go down too soon. Better up 'ere, looksee.' But this meant being finally turned on and cursed by the carter – which proved too much for Alf. So at last he gave notice.

He did not leave his cottage straightaway, and as he had often pressed me to look in, I did so one day. His wife, I found, had him well in hand. 'Don't speak with your mouth full,' she said to him, to my embarrassment. She was a regular town person and said how much she missed 'our street'. The neighbours had 'got her down proper' by spying on her and telling things against her to the tradesmen. But his tea was the curious thing. She only allowed him new potatoes and bread.

He said he would let me know where he went when they departed. But he went without a word, no one knew where, for he left no address – on account of bills it was said.

Thus passed Alf from the agricultural scene, a town worker who found that after all land workers do not live luxuriously on 'the fat of the land'. That idiotic phrase is still heard in war as in peace, and I was glad to see a man, accustomed to the canteen-fed factory life, find out how he liked instead the piece of bread and cheese in the rain by the straw-rick. His departure was pronounced on with a certain glee by the others. He had come to the wrong place, they felt, for a soft job. It is natural for the countryman to enjoy seeing a townsman find the work too much. 'A counter-jumper' is a term, often used, carrying considerable contempt. Not that it was used to describe Alf, who did not belong to that class, but they regarded him more or less with amusement.

25. My Own Rick

The rain passed and we continued to parcel up large fields of hay into neat solids. It is very satisfactory to look at a finished field, at the solid ricks in which all the hay is now encompassed, and the ground itself looking like a well-swept floor. (There were no stray bits left on the field at this farm, no waste; even straggling wisps were collected and elaborately added to the rick at the last minute.) When the sun begins to slant after tea, the stacks achieve a wonderfully clear-cut appearance, and seen from a distance cast shadows that seem themselves substantial.

It gave me much pleasure to look at a stack standing in a field, and be able to say to myself – 'I put that there, or helped to put it there.' Still more so, very much more so, if I had actually been the rick-builder. And, in truth, Robert did permit me to build one before we had done our fourteen. In a jocular way he had said that he would make me build one, and this had whetted my ambition, and seizing a favourable opportunity, I held him to it. I was extremely lucky. We had done several fields with short hay and a strong wind. I got a field with good long hay and no wind. Robert did not wish me to succeed. But he did not hinder me at all; on the contrary, he helped me in every way, adopting a fatherly manner as the best attitude. The others were anxious that I should succeed in order that Robert would be annoyed. And so, from the ground I received many signs and gestures indicative of the state of my corners and walls, with shouts of 'harder! harder!' when I was not making the perpendicular, and 'not so hard!' when I was going out too far. The thing in building is to get your walls up straight, which I found easier to understand than to do, since there is a strong psychological feeling against putting the hay *out* – one always feels it will fall over, not realizing how strongly it will be bound by the hay that goes behind it (for hay binds like brambles, as you find quick enough when you try to take it out). This tendency against the perpendicular is most strong at the corners when it is most necessary to oppose it and be bold. The great thing, I found, was to put two helpings at the corners, and not be faced with the psychologically distressing sight of a *sloping margin*. However, all went well, and I roofed it in the approved Gothic style. It needed no props – and, believe it who will, 'E was heard to say – 'One of the best ricks we've done.' It was on the highest level of the field, and so as we went away in the evening when it was getting dark, it looked wonderful, to me, against the sky – all those untidy bundles that I had been dealing with throughout the day now compressed into a pure solid, the pointed roof traced blackly and with geometrical straightness and sharpness against the light. Going away from it, down the sloping field with the others, I tried not to turn my head too often to have a look at it.

These were long days. By the time I had pushed my bicycle back up the hill, it was generally just in time to hear the Nine o'Clock News – news a thousand miles away. It would be eleven o'clock before I got into bed. Here was a real occasion of taking the weight off my feet – which had been on my feet for over fifteen hours – and doing so was a definite sensation, wonderful. Full days; happy days; days free from indulgence, free from choice, free from domesticity, free from dreams, free from lost hours, unrewarded labours, mistaken projects. How many men is each man composed of? How many men am I! It is a far cry from this to Bloomsbury where I lived seven years. A far cry from that field to the British Museum Reading Room in which I passed so many hours in search for truth. Hours ill-spent? – I searched for the truth and did not find it. But if I find it here it is because I sought it there. If now I look upon the common earth and read the Riddle, I had to forge my weapon first, and wait and wander till my hour should come.

One night I woke up at two a.m. (I looked at my watch) and moved away the books that I had put on a chair beside my bed; for in forking away the hay I was afraid that I would fork away the books as well, and either lose or damage them. So I piled them together under the chair out of reach both of the falling hay and of my prong. I did this with serious deliberation, being quite awake enough to note the time, but also feeling certain that hay was falling and that I was experiencing some difficulty in not damaging the books; in fact I dared not dig my prong in properly because of them. And sure enough in the morning, when I woke up fully, I found my books piled up under the chair safely out of reach of any hay that might fall.

26. *Meditation while Singling Mangolds*

The period between haymaking and harvest is rather an uncomfortable one. We are between two worlds, as it were, one dead, the other as yet powerless to be born. Slack off then? Pause in well-doing? Far from it. Now is the time to get down to the remainder of the hoeing before it is too late.

There was certainly still plenty to be done here on fields of kale, swedes, and mangolds. In fact it was only now that we began to single the mangolds. The shoots, sown by drill, come up close together in long lines. They cannot be left like that but must be given room to expand – that is they must be singled. About a foot must be left between each shoot. Thus while hoeing weeds away you also hoe out a vast number of plants – a wholesale destruction which gives one an uneasy feeling, for what good can come of these miserable little shoots you have left at such a great distance from each other? Frequently the shoots grow in pairs, and as it is impossible to use the hoe for separation it is necessary to stoop right down and separate them with your fingers. Thus singling is hoeing multiplied. I have not written enthusiastically about hoeing, though actually at times I have enjoyed it. I cannot remember any time having enjoyed singling mangolds, and as I frequently had to do many hours of this alone, I again began to feel time drag. And again I was shocked at the contrast of my attitude now towards the clock with what it had been in the old days. For I used to think then that all I needed was time to get on with my work, and money so as to be able to do that work. For me the money was time. For the business man time is money. For the hoer money is not time nor is time money; to him time is simply an enemy. And when we go a step further and enter prison, we are confronted with the most terrible phrase known to man – *doing time*.

Still, while performing jobs of this sort I have come closer to understanding the history of mankind. How easy it is, I said to myself one day, how easy while singling mangolds to understand the rise and fall of civilizations!

How did it all start? Who conceived the town, the city, the metropolis? Into whose mind first sprang the idea of the machine? Who first framed the fabric, turned the wheel of civilization? The countryman, of course. He was the first townsman, the first mechanic, the first industrialist. It was he who dreamt the dream of conquering Nature and of escaping from her. He built London and New York.

He stood on the field, spade in hand, trying to till the soil. A hard job with only that implement. So he invented a horse-movable spade – the plough. He stood amongst the ripened corn with a sickle. He could improve on that, so he made the scythe; and he went on improving all his devices in his conquest of nature – he was the first mechanic. And as he toiled in the fields, often covered with mud, or wet, or freezing cold, or his back splitting as he stooped over the mangolds, he began to think how wonderful it would be to get away from this struggle, to escape altogether from Nature. So he devised something more than a village, he built a large number of houses with intervening paths – a town. He went further – he conceived the idea of the Great City. How marvellous it would be, he thought, to make a place so vast in extent that you could not even see the soil, to make the paths therein so smooth and clean that you would not get a speck of dirt on clothes or boots, to see delicate women walking along who did not know the difference between a bangle and a mangold, to have lights turned on by a switch and hot water by a tap, to have shops making a blaze of light in the darkness, to enter glorious buildings in which you would find entertainment and instruction, and great churches like jewels so that the eyes of those who gazed on them grew dim.

Gradually the edifice of civilization was set up – in the image of the countryman's desire as he stood on the desolate field. But as the years passed and generation succeeded generation the townsman began to forget that he had come from the country, and the countryman that he had made the town. And because the people in the towns were more comfortable and better looking and with wider interests than those in the country, they began to feel more important and to despise the very people upon whom they relied for three meals every day. And because they felt important and began to look it, the countrymen themselves were impressed and thought them wonderful. As the process went on it was the man in the *street,* the man in the city, the *citizen,* who came to be regarded as the only person who counted, while queer derogatory names were found for the men in the fields. The citizens multiplied immensely, became far more powerful than the peasants, and decreed that town wages should be much higher than country wages. Seeing how matters stood, many agriculturists cried, 'Away from the land!' shook the mud off their boots, and joined the citizens.

But as time went on a strange unease began to afflict the people in the towns. As they walked through the everlasting streets they began to pine for the open fields, for the blessed sun, for the realities and simple joys they had left behind. They began to declare that civilization was rotten at the core and perished at the roots, and that nothing could save it except a great Unindustrial Revolution. Not only citizens, but 'City Men' began to say in their cups that their work was a farce and that they would rather 'keep a pig'. Intellectualists insisted that they were 'really peasants at heart'. A cry of 'Back to the Land' went up, not from those on the land but from those in the towns.

And when at last they returned to the soil from whence they had come, they often found that it was no longer there. Their neglect had brought about such appalling erosion that Gobi and Libyan deserts now confronted their astonished gaze, while in other places whole cities were washed away by rivers swollen with water pouring from despoiled and abandoned forests.

Thus my meditation as I stooped over the mangolds. The same conception had occurred to me forcibly earlier in the year when one evening I suddenly felt a great desire to visit a town and dine in an expensive hotel. Changing my clothes suitably I went in. I found a very nice hotel. So great is the difference between the agricultural world and the world outside – a strange, dream-like, picnic of a world it looks from the field – that I blinkingly looked round at the lounge as if seeing such a place for the first time. The good lighting, the polished floor, the groups of clean and well-dressed amiable-looking people held my attention. I poked round the place, and finding a bathroom, entered it. Overcome by the cleanliness of the room I thought it would be grand to have a bath – and I had one. True, there was no bath-towel; but the bath-mat seemed to me startlingly clean and it would do – and it did very well. It was now time for dinner and I entered the dining-room and sat down. I was greatly taken with the spotless table-cloth, the seven pieces of cutlery (I counted them), the vase with the roses in it, the perfect floor, the panelled walls, the electric candlesticks. The other tables were occupied by miscellaneous people, all looking well set up, pleased, and expectant. Waiters began to come round, dressed in white jackets and black trousers. Four courses were brought to me with great expedition. I examined each plate in turn – very nice, one with a picture of water-cress on it. I looked round at the smiling faces of the people, all wearing expressions not seen outside; and at a waiter bending over a group with the deeply knowing and confidential smile of a man who can produce wine. I looked at the foods that were brought to me – some meat, peas, greens, and potatoes. Doubtless they came from the land, but it hardly occurred to me to make the connection, certainly no one else in the room did so: the food simply came – no, not even from the kitchen – from behind the screen from which the waiters, like magicians, emerged again and again. For this, I saw, was a dream place, not subject to reality. If a ploughman, I reflected, were to come into this room suddenly, as such, he would be thrown out, or 'asked to leave'. And that would be right. I would be the first to cast the first stone at him. It would be an unforgiveable intrusion. For he would have broken the spell, destroyed the film and the fantasy of the agreed illusion, infringed upon the dream mankind has dreamt on the bitter field – this escape from Nature, this shelter from the storm, this palace, this paradise.

The whole thing was so fantastic and delightful, and knowing that a bus would soon be due outside, I kept a firm watch on myself (like a man over-drinking) lest I linger for ever here and become lost to the agricultural world. However, I pulled myself together and went out into the pouring darkness and caught the bus and then took my bicycle for a final part of the journey. I was soon passing our farmyard, which adjoined the road. There it was – deserted, silent, a pocket of gloom, a nonentity of a place, something to pass by. Was it really possible, I asked myself, that this slushy yard, so humble, so lacking in all the props and appointments of Power, was yet the foundation of society? Yet so it was. Upon this the fabric rested, upon this was erected all that glittered and all that shone; and I knew that the lighted palace from which I had come where the Figures paced on the polished floor, and the Magicians emerged with food from behind the screens, could not otherwise exist at all. I got off my bicycle and gazed into the farmyard – at the stable door, the pile of manure, the muddy pool, the old binder in the corner, the oil-cans and sacks, the three wagons and the two carts under the shelter. I peered at these things through the dreary dank of the dripping darkness, with some intensity, as if aware that here only, in this place, and in such guise, could I find the roots of grandeur and the keys of life.

27. A Critical Moment

Most of my hoeing was done in company with others. Working at this job in company is not only better for the labourers but better for the farmer – far more ground is covered by a worker in company with others than if alone. The spirit of competition always enters into it, for no one likes to be left behind if the work is being done in parallelled rows as is usual. Thus the pace is according to the fastest worker. And if just two people are taking a couple of rows there is the same tendency to compete – no one knows why. Once I did this absolutely deliberately. One of 'E's daughters often came out into the fields, and also imi-tated her father in every particular. Finding myself on a parallel row with her, I worked during the greater part of a morning at an absurd rate, continually passing her as I went up and down the rows.

Harold, Dick and I did a good deal of hoeing together. 'Anyway, it's a bit of a change and break for you,' I said to Harold. 'Yes, but the wrong kind of change,' he replied. All the same he always worked the quickest at this job as at many others. We were working now on a field along which the main track ran. Hence the approach of the Van was easily seen. When it was discerned approaching, our pace would quicken; not too fast, since that would look bad, too obvious; but appreciably, while we asked 'Is 'E going to stop?' If the van stopped then we might expect 'E to alight and come across, look on, make a criticism, and possibly join us. This was always a criti-cal moment when the Van was seen – 'Will 'E stop, join us, and spoil the morning?' became the great question. One occasion was rather amusing. Harold, Dick and myself were going along our rows side by side across the field. Our cut reached to about the middle of the field, when normally we would turn about. We were working towards the track when the Van appeared coming up, and then stopped. 'E got out and went over into the next field to speak to Robert, and there he remained for some time. We couldn't see him, but had to suppose that he could see us. At last he appeared again. Would he now come over to us? But no, he got into the van. But it didn't start off at once; evidently he was watching us. We were still working towards the track, towards him. We came to the end of our cut. We should now have stopped, picked our new rows and gone back. But Harold said 'Keep on, don't stop, keep on; if 'e sees us stop 'e'll come over, sure thing. Keep on and 'e'll be off.' And though we had come to the end of our cut we kept going now on ground which we had already hoed ('E wouldn't be able to notice this at the distance), and continued keeping on until the crisis passed and 'E got back into the van and did at last b off.

28. *Labourers and Marriage*

In the mornings and during the early part of the afternoon at this time there were more than the three of us, for we were generally joined by the land girls from the dairies. At this farm the land girls seldom stayed long, new ones always coming and going; and for that reason it is difficult for me to include them in my canvass, as it were, in spite of the friends I have made, especially one. If it were asked what the Land Army did during the war, the answer is quite simple – they got the milk for the nation. Of course they did a great deal else as well – and would the potatoes have been lifted without them? – but the main fact is this that the nation would hardly have got its milk without their help.

Thus in company hoeing went much better, for there is nothing like chat for passing the time. I sometimes wonder whether economists, sociologists, heavy-weight philosophers, and world meliorists pay enough attention to the ordinary remarks of ordinary people. In the course of conversation, a land girl (who was in love with Dick) said to Harold – 'Oh you've nothing to worry about. You're married. You have all you want.' A perfectly simple and straightforward statement which was received by Harold without the slightest demur. It is worth bearing in mind the simple desires and natural aims of people, especially women. For whatever unfeminine feminists may preach, women, the most sophisticated as well as the most simple, invariably say sooner or later – 'All I want is to make a home.' The modern publicist who feels it necessary to make it quite clear that of course he doesn't imagine that 'women's place is the home' might just as well say that of course women don't really produce children. (It is the phrase that is wrong, and the conditions, not the actuality.) The idea that women could

149

actually bear children without at the same time being particularly interested in and gifted for dealing with the machinery of keeping them going (often called home life), ought to be too silly ever to be discussed. There is also a lesser difference between men and women – namely that women are more human than men. For that reason they find it difficult to endure non-personal, wholly objective work when performed alone. Thus agriculture (except on the stock side) is nearly as unsuitable for women as is nautical work. In spite of the fact that they are so much stronger than men in many ways, and because of that extra muscle which physiologists say is situated at the base of their tongues, agriculture will remain alien to them until far more people work on the land – for *indifference to the object* gets a woman down much easier than a man.

But Harold, beyond saying that he would like a thousand pounds a year, did not demur in the least to the statement that, being married, he had everything he wanted (he had courted his wife for eight years). For this is true of many men as well as women. It is especially true amongst the working classes generally, and still more so among agricultural labourers, all of whom always marry – it is simply not done not to have a wife. And for them, as for the working class as a whole, there is no marriage problem, no sex problem, no domestic problem. For the most part the woman simply toes the line, she has no other course. Or there may be harmony. Or she may be the stronger and have the upper hand. But there is no great over-conscious problem made of the situation. They dare not think about it for there is no escape. When things are bad they are terrible – for there isn't the hard cash to separate. On this score I have sometimes come upon the greatest bitterness in connection with the actuality here of one law for the rich and another for the poor.

On the whole, however, there is no time for the refinements of domestic infelicity any more than for the leisured infelicities. I have often thought how far removed this world here is from what one might call the Virginia Woolf world of upper-middle-class frustration, time to think (without effect), time to dream (without pleasure), time to feel wasted and lost: what can a bit more money do to make up for this! And, we may add, in the agricultural world there is very little time for the young men to indulge in refined vices. Hence Buchmanism would be inconceivable amongst them. Mr Buchman (sometimes called Dr), was an American psychologist who in the name of religion gathered round him a huge following of university students to confess their private vices. Such introspection is unknown to the young man who gets up at six-thirty every morning and is hard at it till six-thirty in the evening. (Also the religious idealism that genuinely accompanied Buchmanistic confessions is foreign to him.)

Moreover, they do not read. Readers who read a great deal as a matter of course can hardly realize the state of mind of those who don't read at all. It is very different, doubtless. Reading – especially novels – makes us all far more conscious of ourselves and of other people and of our emotions and situations and reactions. We are not conscious about everything in the absurd degree presupposed in novels, we do not dream of emphasizing life in that way; but when we read about problems which approximate to our own we then brood upon our own. The non-readers are nothing like as aware of their feelings as they would be if they read about the emotions of others and the domestic problems of invented characters – though I sometimes wish that they were a little more conscious of their unconscious, for an obvious motive disguised by a trumpery reason is irritating. I am inclined to think that a non-reader takes life easier if less fully. A neighbour of mine enjoys a drink at the pub. But if I ask him to come out he often has to excuse himself at the last minute – his wife having stopped it, being afraid of him getting into mischief. I doubt if this annoys him much, however, or if he lets it get him down, or asks himself whether he has married the right woman and so on. Not being steeped in books which touch on problems of this kind, he probably doesn't think about it at all. Life doesn't present itself in the form that it does to those whose minds are broadened and often corrupted by reading. I never heard my companions make a psychological generalization about life or women or marriage, and if I ever did so few of them took the slightest interest. The most they will run to in this direction is, to quote Robert for instance – 'She'll always come home on Saturday night'; or, to quote Harold concerning a certain girl who had an extra affair – 'If she done it once she'll do it again,' indeed he kept repeating this much to the annoyance of the girl's friend – 'If she done it once she'll do it again.' I never heard him make any other generalization of any kind, and I doubt if he ran to more than this sovereign idea that if she done it once she'll do it again. Dick did like reading and was much more alive to the world and the possibilities of life than most of the others; and talking of girls he said – 'I don't like the kind of girl you go out with three times, and then – "How's your father?" '

It is right here that farmers themselves, alone in the British community, know how to choose their wives. They are the only people who show wisdom in this matter. Thus in the agricultural world there is no such thing as a nagging wife. The farmer's position is extremely favourable for keeping her down. He is up early; he is on the move incessantly; he is always grappling with difficulties and anxieties; he is invariably in a hurry; he is continually let down by man and nature; there is nothing abstract or invisible about his work, it can be so clearly seen, it is hugely writ; he is tired and hungry at the end of his hard day's work. This puts him into an impregnable position. You can hardly be petty with a man thus fortressed. You can't suggest that a little pleasure would be nice, since he forgoes pleasures, the hard-working, careful man. The only thing to do is to out-do him in virtue and also renounce relaxation. This is the line taken by farmers' wives, and one wonders whether the nation, while handing bouquets to the men for the work done, fully realizes the part played by the wives.

William Cobbett, wise in everything, provides here also the prototype of how to choose your wife as a farmer. He spotted her in New Brunswick. 'It was dead of winter, and, of course, the snow several feet deep on the ground, and the weather piercing cold. In about three mornings after I had first seen her I had got two young men to join me in my walk; and our road lay by the house of her father and mother. It was hardly light, but she was out in the snow, scrubbing out a washing-tub. "That's the girl for me," I said, when we had got out of her hearing.' In due course they married and lived happily ever after.

29. Hoeing with 'E

When we had finished this particular field of kale and swedes – how quickly the scene had changed since I had dragged it, chain-harrowed it, cultivated it, rolled it, couched it! – we were sent off to another stretch of kale at the far end of the farm. We assembled and looked round – there was about eleven acres of it. The kale was submerged in a mass of thistles, mutton-docks, and charlock. How could we make any impression on such a field? we wondered. Harold said that the only sensible thing to do would be to plough it in. I wondered; for that is exactly what Robert had said about the former one I had been on – ' 'E should plough it in, it won't come to no good letting it bide, I allow.' But in a few weeks it had risen up quite well.

The farmer who knows his job is careful not to take advice from his men. When in a quandary concerning the best place to build a rick in view of subsequent threshing, 'E occasionally asked Robert what he thought about it; but on the whole he was superbly independent. He would have pleased old William Cobbett who, in a little-known book on forestry, remarks upon how foolish it is for a boss ever to consult his men before making a decision. 'Let me exhort you,' he wrote, 'to give simple and positive *orders*, and never, no, never to encourage, by your hesitation, even your bailiff or gardener so much as to *offer* you *advice*.' And again, 'Above all things, avoid asking their *advice*, and even telling them your *intentions*. If you do this, even with the foreman, they will all soon become *councillors*. They will deliberate ten times a day; and those who deliberate know not any sense in the word *obedience*. As many hands as you like, but only one *head*.'

153

This field was well situated, miles off the track of general inspection, and we had a pleasant time that morning, Harold, Dick and myself. It was very hot, and during the dinner-hour I procured a bottle of beer which we could tap during the afternoon. Thus the three of us started off in a good frame of mind, and having chosen a sensible 'cut' which would make the best show, we did not intend to over-do it.

We had the field to ourselves except for the carter who had now come to broadcast artificial, but was out of sight over the rill. But in a very short time we saw the van draw up outside the gate. 'The Van!' said Harold, 'The Van!' said Dick. And all of us became very interested in our hoeing. 'I reckon 'E's going over to the carter,' said Harold. But at that moment the Van did a terrible thing, it *came into the field*, and the gate was closed behind. 'That means he's going to stay,' said Dick. 'I bet he's coming to hoe with us,' I said; and sure enough in a moment we saw him, hoe in hand, coming across to join us! And without any greeting or the slightest attempt at a *bonhomie* approach. he joined us in silence, and a great silence fell as we worked. I tried to humanize the situation slightly by saying that I wished that the mutton-docks were mutton chops. This decimal point of a joke was taken up by 'E who added another one per cent of humour to the idea. And Harold laughed, though Dick preserved a dead silence. Not being able to think of any further motif for conversation we relapsed into silence again, which was not broken till 'E suddenly reprimanded Dick for his slack way of hoeing – 'You might as well leave the field as do it that way,' he said, which brought the bitter rejoinder from Dick about 'no appreciation if he did well', and a further rejoinder from 'E saying – 'If I speak civil to you I expect you to speak civil to me,' for he was convinced that he himself always spoke civilly, and as a matter of fact Dick was generally more uncivil to him than he to Dick.

Meanwhile the beer was in the hedge. It was permissible at this farm, during a hot afternoon, not to stop working, but at intervals to take a swill of lemonade or cold tea.

So I said to Harold – 'It makes one thirsty, this heat,' and when we got to the bottom of our row he went and had a drink from the bottle, whispering to me on return 'that's saved my life'. Dick and I did likewise on coming down again, each saying loudly 'nothing like cold tea for a thirst', feeling that the word beer would sound too much in the nature of a planned debauchery. By this time the carter had come near us on his errand with the artificial, having made it snappy since the arrival of the Van. He observed this drinking of the beer, and though he knew that I always had a beer-bottle with me normally for cold tea, he was aware from fifty yards off that it was beer we were having, not tea. How he knew this I cannot say, but I was informed afterwards that he did know it. He was knowledgeable about beer. 'There's nothing 'e don't know about beer,' they said.

At last five-thirty arrived, and we had had very nearly four hours of this without a break. On the tick of that hour the three of us stopped dead, and 'E had to stop also and go off to the van. Had we not done so we knew that we would have gone over the time. So we simply 'shutout' abruptly, without comment.

30. The Labourer's Theory of Knowledge

If any farmers happen to read this book they may feel that I have only given one side of the picture. This may be true. But since most books on the land are written by farmers, landowners, or agricultural specialists, I shall be glad indeed if through me the labourer's view finds expression. At the same time I can hardly help being also alive to the other side. Nothing would induce me to take on the job of running a farm of my own with its attendant responsibility and appalling anxiety. I know well enough that time, for instance, is seen from exactly the opposite end by the boss – he is always *behind*, he must husband every minute. And I know perfectly well that all labourers will take the fullest possible advantage of a weak man. All men, and all women even more so, are bullies. Precisely to the degree in which a person is weak, advantage will be taken by the other side; whether between labourer and boss, or husband and wife, or parent and child, or master and pupil, or governor and governed. I always see this fact of human behaviour with the clarity of an image. I see it in the form of a spring of great elasticity. If much pressure is exerted against that spring it can be held right down. If no pressure is exerted against it, it will go out and out and out. It is not good to keep it right down. It is not good to let it expand right out. We are all afraid of that spring. In their fear some men try to keep it right down – with bad results. Others exert only a tiny nervous pressure – and are swept away. The thing is to hold a reasonable balance. This image may not be clear or useful to others, but I take a chance with it, since it is clear and useful to me.

There is an interesting remark which I have often heard here and elsewhere, not uncommon anywhere when some boss or foreman is mentioned. 'The trouble is,' they say, ' 'e's so *ignorant*.' By this they do not mean that he lacks knowledge. They mean that he lacks *manners*. It is a significant remark. For what is manners? Manners is psychology. It is the understanding of the simple psychological needs of other people. It is homage paid to the strikingly simple fact that people like you to address them amiably, to show appreciation, and to say thank you at intervals. If a man does not know this and act upon it he is called *ignorant* by labourers under him. That is their philosophy of education. I recommend it to the educational pundits who are shocked at the existence of those schools that really do understand the importance of teaching manners. If I were not afraid of holding up my narrative I would enjoy nothing better than to dig down to the further fundamentals involved here. I shall content myself with observing that when we go one step further we find that manners lead to *morals*.

Let a farmer then, I would say, exert a reasonable pressure upon the spring, with the applied psychology of a good manner, throwing in many a 'thank you', many a greeting, many a word of praise (it need not always be sincere), not to mention occasional sympathetic inquiry regarding a man's mishap or trouble. The grossest advantage would be taken of such behaviour. It would be taken once. It need not be twice. For the farmer could then afford to pounce upon any man, with real fury, and could do so with ten times more force and effect than if his normal behaviour was unamiable. I would myself make it a rule to pounce whenever the occasion justified it, even if I didn't feel angry. And to any man, 'the soul of good nature', who feels himself to be an exception to my generalizations about bullies, I would say that those who intend to accomplish anything in this world should try to control their good temper just as others should control their bad temper. And should anyone wish to be reminded of a delightful and classic example of just how to deal with the insolence of mankind, he can find it in Mr A. G. Street's *Farmer's Glory*, when a certain labourer thinks he can easily force the young boss's hand, but is given notice instead.

31. Lack of Cooperation

During the following days we had the field to ourselves, without any appearance of the Van. Conversation included discussion concerning the hour at which we received our money every Saturday fortnight. The word Wages, by the way, is never used unless it is preceded by the adjective 'higher'. It is always 'I've come for my money' or 'here's your money'. The words *my money* are felt to carry the idea of *my rights* better than Wages. Yet the latter word is a much nicer one. There is a touch of poetry in it. Preachers used to say that the wages of sin were death. That was good rhetoric, so no one questioned it. Had the preacher said that the salary of sin or the fees of sin were death, he would never have got away with it.

The time at which we received our pay was between six and seven on the Saturday. (This business varies enormously from farm to farm.) It was a very unpopular hour. They couldn't go out unless they got back early. And their wives were without shopping money: or so they said – probably untruly. For they surely cannot live up to the hilt like that. I mean except in some cases it cannot be necessary. Yet it may be true. True when the wages were twelve shillings a week; true now that they are three pounds and ten shillings; true if they were ten pounds; while we all know that the thousand-a-year man is very hard up – for here is another 'spring'. However, it is a trait very pleasing to employers.

They could easily have had the hour altered if all of them had become vocally indignant in unison and refused to be paid at that hour. They did not do so. For lack of cooperation was most emphatic. They never combined. They did not stand by one another nor trust one another. Each of them complained to me about the lack of cooperation of the others, making also some denigrating remarks concerning either the behaviour or ability of so and so. Their unsolidarity was quite remarkable. Neither in small matters nor large did they dream of acting together. And if on a Saturday morning 'E was away they were careful not to knock off a little early lest someone would tell the tale.

There is a tendency amongst some passionate middle-class meliorists to give the working-class man virtues he does not possess. For instance, they emphasize his capacity for 'warm friendship'. This would be strange if it were true. For friendship rises from developed emotions and developed understanding. But I have not found it to be true. Indeed the very idea of *affection* almost seemed foreign and uncalled for. And even when a man leaves and goes off somewhere else he seldom bothers to say good-bye to his mates – he just packs up and disappears. No letter communication follows, no answers to letters if written – I have sometimes thought that this attitude amounted to a sort of melancholy sense of the folly of attachments in a shifting world. I was rather amused one day later on, during harvest, when a schoolboy of about seventeen who had joined us was going off next day. He came out into the field in the evening and stood around, wanting to say good-bye to people. But no one knew what he was getting at.

If there was lack of friendship there was no lack of civility. No matter what anyone might say about anyone else, there was absolutely no open hostility. I was sometimes surprised at their double-facedness. But the same thing in higher circles is called tact and diplomacy. In this capacity I have often thought that my companions displayed the greatest mastery, acting on occasion with a discretion worthy of a Cabinet Minister.

32. Dick and Education; Harold and Village Life

Harold now went off on another job, while Dick and I carried on. When Dick was in the company of 'E he was silent; when in general company he humorously groused; and when alone with me he would give vent to his ambition to see the world and know things and study. He had a terror of becoming like older men on the land he saw around. Desire to see the world is luckily rare amongst agricultural labourers. We were near a beautiful village by the sea, but I met no one here who had ever adventured so far. As for wanting to study – well that is still rare anywhere. Dick did desire it. He used to learn a little German every evening. He was eager to acquire knowledge. Were it not for the existence of Mr H. G. Wells it would be extremely difficult to know what book to lend such a man; but there is the *Outline of History*, so I lent him that, which he read twice. Here was the perfect example of the young man for whom there are no educational facilities in the villages. No chance given, no encouragement. He was not talented, not exceptionally gifted at all, and with little will-power and no real passion for learning. He wished to develop himself, that is all – and might quite easily be prevented from doing so by circumstances. In fact he was exactly the kind of person with whom educationalists are concerned. No one need bother about the man of great talent, the man of genius, the man of will. Such men thrive on resistance, on difficulties, on enemies; whether thrown on the rocks or the cushions of life, they triumph in the end. If this is not wholly true, it is truest in the realm of knowledge and literature, when the reading of *one* good book will set him on fire, and nothing will stop his advance. There is little need to help or encourage him. But the man of small will-power and small talent and mild desire for development needs all the help that can be given, and years of it. Otherwise circumstances prove too much for him, and he gives up. His work stops him, his girl stops him. In Dick's case, however, his girl was his chief source of encouragement, and it is conceivable that she may keep it up.

The actual handing of the *Outline* to him was certainly a process demanding discretion. It would never do, we felt, to be seen with the book. And my edition was large enough to fill a big haversack. I brought it out to the field and at the end of the day we went by the side of a hedge to make the transference from my bag to his. Just at that moment Robert passed. He shyed slightly at the sight of the volume, rather like a horse alarmed at something. But he was not indignant. 'You've got summat to get on with there, I allow,' he said in rather a low and hurried manner, and passed on.

Then Dick went off to something else and Harold came back, and I worked with him for some days. He had lived in this village all his life and was content to remain there and bring up his family in the same place. He had no more desire to venture beyond it than into the realms of the mind, and he said, though not boastfully, that he never read anything whatever – and though I believe in the mind I do not forget that such men are the strong pillars of this world. But he was not uncritical of village life as it now is. He spoke of his boyhood, which was not so long ago, when there was a good deal of life in the village, with games and expeditions sponsored by the Squire. For some years that has been a thing of the past, and the lads hang about with nothing to do. It is the old story. In the old days Inequality and Aristocracy, the Lord of the Manor or the Squire considering it his duty to give life to the village: then the ousting of Aristocracy and the trumpeted entrance of Democracy, until the man whose motto had been *noblesse oblige* in relation to all the villagers, now has the greatest difficulty in getting a single attendant to come in *and oblige* with a little housework. He is no longer able to think about the life of the village, and the villagers are unable to give life to it themselves. The French revolutionists went in for Liberty, Equality, and Fraternity. Since then a good deal of Liberty and Equality have been established. Has that led to more Fraternity? Do we all now embrace as brothers under the wings of Equality? No. There is less Fraternity. Each man is now out for himself and for higher wages. No doubt it is only a transition stage. We can hope for better days. The moral is clear: the people must have *leaders*. Every village must have a leader. If the old ones have perished to make way for democracy, then the sooner democracy supplies new ones the sooner we shall get out of this wretched transition stage. But it is clear that leaders cannot be sent into the village from outside. This is something that cannot be *planned*. You cannot farm from Whitehall, it is reiterated, you cannot cultivate the soil. Neither can you cultivate the soul. It would be as absurd to try and plan a Village Revival as a Religious Rebirth or an Artistic Renaissance. It must be done by the village itself. A village will cohere under a leading personality who belongs to the place. Otherwise it will remain incoherent.

From where we worked we could look down upon the Manor House. One old lady lived in it. She had lived there fifty years. But now it was passing from her hands. It was up for sale. She possessed two outmoded things – goodness and culture. When she passed, would they pass away also? I wondered.

33. Farmers and Incomes; Pleasing Considerations

At length Harold went off again and I carried on alone on this eleven-acre field of kale. Although at first it had seemed a hopeless affair we had managed to make an impression upon it. 'E had told us to leave the charlock and concentrate upon the thistles and mutton-docks. But that was against human nature, it goes too much against the grain to leave part of the weeds like that. For making a good show, apart from any effect upon your employer, has a personal bearing as well, and in a case like this one could not leave in the yellow, thus blurring the work, instead of seeing the green portion which one had done over against the yellow-flagged portion one had not yet tackled. I managed to make quite a considerable impression even by myself, and when 'E appeared he was actually surprised at the progress, and though he had not much hopes in the whole field being finished on account of pressing work elsewhere, he let me carry on – in which I encouraged him, for I liked this job; pardon my inconsistencies about hoeing.

When alone with 'E I always got on with him excellently. And if launched into a chat he would often continue on and on for some time, and not necessarily only upon agricultural topics. But I preferred to get him on to agriculture and thus pick up what I could, including such a pleasing item as that cows sometimes do better on poor hay than on very good hay in so far as, instead of stuffing themselves, they are abstemious and thus keep in better condition. Harold and I had amused ourselves while hoeing by calculating 'E's profits (quite a favourite pastime on this farm). Taking it piece by piece it had worked out under our hands into a huge sum, for we did not err on the conservative side. And I could not resist the temptation of getting 'E himself on to the subject of financial takings, and learnt, of course, that he had so far made – *nothing*. Such and such a field had cost him £1,000 to prepare (we had calculated that it should yield £3,000) so how could he hope for a profit? I listened fascinated as I always am by farmers explaining how they have not made and cannot make anything. I do not necessarily doubt their word, I have no head for this sort of thing. No one knows what a farmer's income is if he chooses to keep it dark. Very often he is quite as poor as he says he is. He may be extremely rich; but on no account must he ever admit it, since if he does he feels he'll be done down: and his men must not be led to think that he has made a huge profit, for then they might expect a bonus. 'E used to have a small farm, and he said that it paid.

So I said, just by way of falling in with his line of talk – 'There's no profit in these big farms.' But he didn't like that. For while he didn't want to be thought rich, neither did he wish to be thought poor and unsuccessful. So he said – 'It does and it doesn't. It depends.'

I continued here for nearly a fortnight. And very pleasant it was. This was hoeing without tears. The kale was large enough not to be tender, while the thistles, docks, and charlock were easy to snip away, and not so numerous as to make progress discouraging. The situation was pleasant, the view good, and the weather perfect. I rode straight to the field in the morning, without first going to the farmyard to receive orders. This made a much shorter journey, ten minutes less, as well as a far more agreeable way of starting the day – no complicated orders from 'E, which might need a repeat, nor sight of the carter with furious lower lip cursing at a horse as he backed it into a wagon. And if I was a little late I didn't worry, for no one would see me – on one occasion I overslept a complete hour without anyone being the wiser. Thus my early morning ride was for once unhurried. Also the approach to this field was delightful. I had to pass up the avenue of a Big Thus (not the Manor House) and along by the garden wall, one of those high, weathered, red-brick walls that recall to mind the spacious days of ancient queens. When I stood beside the kale, hoe in hand, I had a morning view of the quiet fields, the nestling village, and the tree-closed church. And I would think to myself – What better than to be here? what more simple or more sane? Then it seemed strange to me that men are packed in ugly towns. So few here, so many there! What fly they, and what seek? and having sought, what found? What found compared with this! This *is* our first and foremost home beside God's footprint and his fountain. We stray from it, we stray indeed: roofed and walled, paved and collared, we shut it out!

I spent many smooth and peaceful days here. There was a battered old straw-rick in this field which served as my armchair for meal times. I am very critical of armchairs and consider them more important to felicity than electric light and indoor sanitation. I am frequently amazed at the ineptly called *easy*-chairs which I find in the houses of my friends, chairs tilted back at an angle that used to be reserved solely for a dentist's convenience, so uncomfortable that only an athlete could sit in one, and in which no human being could possibly read or reflect. These chairs always seem to me about the maddest things in the present mad world. I must not expand; but I am free to say that though I do not need a whole straw-stack, it serves admirably as a good working model of what I require. It provides the perfect back and leaves the knees and legs with nothing to do but enjoy themselves. But perhaps I lack back-bone; it seems that I do in comparison with my friends who appear quite pleased with their chairs – and also with my friends here, for these latter will often enough sit bolt upright after hours of hard work, with apparent ease, while I look round carefully for something to lean against. They even seem comfortable leaning on their elbows, a position which to me is the extremity of discomfort.

My meal-time breaks were absolute bliss here – perfection in comfort, temperature, and view. In short, true picnic after picnic. Normally picnics are hell – planned pleasure, a seeking after enjoyment. How attain happiness? Only as a by-product. Only by walking smartly in the opposite direction. Then it can come for half an hour. Here the conditions were given. I was tired and hungry and with only a scheduled time for the break. Hence my bliss.

From these favourable dispositions I looked out upon the agricultural world with anything but a jaundiced eye. I passed in review the lives lived by so many thousands of people who are supposed to be better off – the endless number of those who do what is called clerical work, those who sell things on commission, those who type their lives away, those who sit on summer days in electric light, and multitudes of other slaves of slaves of slaves. I thought also of the artistic world, the painters, the writers, the actors and actresses to whom the word Security is unknown, and to whom steady remuneration for work done would seem like heaven, people compared with whom the agricultural labourer knows nothing of insecurity, nothing of poverty, nothing of hardship, nothing of anxiety. If only the land labourers knew the world beyond the field, I reflected, they would be content with their lot. Whatever their wages, they are always at least two pounds to the good on the townsman; they are not plagued by extras (rather given extra), nor by rent (a Civil Servant in London paying for one room as much as the agricultural labourer's weekly wage), nor by Appearance fees (he spends three pounds a year on clothes for himself). His housing for the most part is extremely good. It seems to me that any further emphasis on wages is less important than on the modification of working hours and educational activity within the villages. Then what an opportunity, what conditions for a sane life!

Another thing about the geographical position of this field was that by taking my bicycle down hill I could reach the village inn. While there is little to be said for beer in the winter, it is really wonderful in the summer combined with dinner after a morning's work. So I sometimes went down there in the middle of the day, taking my sandwiches and cheese (if I had any) with me. It was a pleasant hour. The pub was more delightfully situated than any other I have ever known, it might have been in a book; on one side was an orchard, on the other a copper-beech, while in front was a row of chestnut trees. As I write these lines I think of the pleasant and obliging couple who ran this place, owned by the old father in the background, upright, fine-faced, puritanical, and completely humourless. His daughter loved the place, loved the trees, and hadn't ever the slightest desire to go near a town. What's more – she loved the sun. Thus she stood out, let her stand out here, over against the average white-faced country housewife who has never seen the sun, never heard of it, never sat in it. On a lovely day she itched to close at two p.m. in order to get out into the garden and be in the sun. Her husband was the typical independent Englishman with the greatest contempt for B.B.C. blah, and newspaper talk, and official excuses for lost battles and inefficient organization; the kind of man who though a sergeant in the Home Guard was incapable of taking it either with that seriousness or self-import-ance which would have endangered his good humour and easy-going friendliness.

Very few people went to the pub at this time of day. All were having hot dinners at home. All except Giles Winterdrew. I'm not a novelisty sort of person who looks round for 'copy' and sees human beings as 'characters'. But I must mention Giles Winterdrew before leaving, for I suppose he would qualify as a 'character'. He was an old soldier, with a Napoleonic Wars look about him. He was tall and upright, but his joints were almost stuck, and his progress slow, as stick in hand, with set sallow face, he made for the pub every day. He arrived at about noon, stayed till closing time, bought several bottles of beer, and re-turned home with them. He then went to bed with these bottles and remained there till the next morning when he would again go to the pub, have his drinks, buy more bottles, and go home to bed with them. This was his whole life now. Beer got dearer and dearer and worse and worse, but he still bravely stuck to his disciplined routine. At last, for considerable periods, there was no beer at all. The framework of his life was shattered and he died.

But these days of mine were coming to an end, and on 'E's next appearance I was told to leave off now at this job. I had done about half the field, but there was too much to be done elsewhere, and 'E decided that for me to continue here 'would not be worth the money'.

34. Strange Job on the Beanfield

Returning to the centre of activity I found most of the staff engaged on a beanfield which was just below the scene of our former operations. It was a peculiar job. In striking and indeed appalling contrast to the beautiful beanfield I had delighted to look at on my neighbour's land at my first farm, this was a miserable spectacle, the beans being so hopelessly under the dominion of thistles and other weeds that they couldn't be cut.

We had to pull them up by hand. It was a job long remembered on this farm. Though each of us took three rows it was very slow work harvesting a whole field in this manner. But we went at it hard, pulling up the black bean-stalks, which were lower than the thistles, and making bundles of them. We were joined by 'E, and the pace quickened. He was next to me. 'Pull 'ee?' he cried, 'pull 'ee! it don't do they no harm.' And he dashed ahead, grabbing them up, both hands snatching out to left and right, as if he were picking up gold. I began to get left behind. 'Come on, Mr Collis!' shouted Robert (I was always Mr here with all the men) across from his row, trying to get a rise out of me. 'You're too cunning, biding up there on the kale, thee and thy dog. It be harder work on thease field, I allow.' While Dick, who was working on my left, whispered – 'Make a show, Mr Collis, make a good show?' and, imitating the actions of 'E who was just in front of him, grabbed at the beans with unexampled zeal. Thus we proceeded at the good work till tea-time and went on after tea. But on one occasion I was alone on the job for an afternoon and was about to go home when 'E came and said he wanted me to go on after tea. 'It's not a one-man job,' I said. I stayed; and later on the others appeared, and I gathered that my remark 'it's not a one-man job' had been repeated and gone round. I still think it was an absolutely sound remark, a critique of the purest reason.

During one hot but windy afternoon there was a snowstorm on this field. It was worth seeing. A blizzard just on this field alone. The wild, whirling flakes did not fall from above, they rose from the ground, for they were not made of snow but of thistledown. It was as good an attempt at an artificial blizzard as anything Hollywood could put over.

The final afternoon was memorable and long remembered by everyone. It poured with rain. Our business was now to tie up the beans into sheaves and stook them. We got drenched to the skin. 'E said that we needn't carry on if we didn't want to, but there was no definite and concerted movement to stop, so we went on. We were through by four o'clock. All of us drenched. Then, did 'E tell us to go home and get a change? No. He just stood round saying nothing and looking unhappy, while groups of us held little committee meetings. 'What are you going to do,' one asked another, and some said – 'I know what *I'm* going to do!' And without anything being said, we all dispersed. Some returned later and did up to an hour's work, while Harold who lived a good way off returned to put in a quarter of an hour. As for myself, rejoicing for once at my distant habitation, I hadn't the faintest intention of returning. And as I rode home I thought of the ridiculous scene when we had stood around in grave committee after the job was done, 'E saying nothing; and I thought if I wrote it down my word would be doubted.

35. While Hiling

It was not till 20 August that the weather permitted us to get down to the corn harvest. Now at last we were off. We all rather quailed before the formidable task ahead – perhaps thirty ricks. So we started in on the binding and hiling (not called stooking in this part of the country). Harold and Jimmy carried on with the two binders, and I found myself on the first day hiling with Dick over against Jimmy's binding.

The binder is an attractive instrument. Especially as seen from a little distance, its gently turning 'sails' noiselessly paddling back the lake of corn. At close quarters the ingenuity of the thing is fascinating. To cut at that rate is in itself an achievement; but also to take up convenient portions of what is being cut, and bind it, and then chuck out the bound sheaf – that is something remarkable. Yes, one feels, the cutting was a straightforward invention perhaps, and the elevating of it upward on a moving canvas: but to have it tied firmly into *separate* parts and then flicked out – how accomplish that with robot fingers? And as a matter of fact the two fingers which do every minute flick out a sheaf, have a rather disturbing effect – there is something too roboty about them.

Having cut the corn down it is necessary to stand it up again. There is hardly a layman who doesn't know about the job of hiling. It may be all he knows about agriculture, but that much he is aware of, and if he has helped in the fields at any time it is generally at hiling. Yet like all these things it can be done wrong. As the corn will now stand up only if it is propped up by leaning against itself, it will certainly fall over if not treated scientifically. No use doing it in an haphazard manner, for the wind will then lay the sheaves as flat as the cutter did. And the way to avoid this is *not* by clustering a lot of sheaves together – for then the ears won't dry. Not more than six at the most, arranged as a tunnel.

This first field of ours was a small one of barley. Barley is the easiest of all types to handle. It makes a short, light sheaf so that you can take two up, one in each hand with great ease and clump them together. Soft and pleasant to the touch, the bunched ears are like flaxen curls on silky heads.

This was one of the very first fields I had had anything to do with on this farm. I had couched and harrowed it with horses and with tractor. It was brown earth when I had left it, and as its situation was right away in a corner, I had not seen it since. Now it had changed to this, now the drooping pennants, now the flaxen curls; the transmutation that never falters and that never palls; the seeming simple cycle; the turn again of the hundred-thousand-year-old Wheel.

Next day we hiled wheat. Wheat-sheaves build well, as they are very stiff, but it is less easy to take one up in each hand, owing to their weight – grappling with two at once is fairly hard work. The bound stalks make almost a bundle of canes. People complain that hiling wheat cuts and scratches the arms badly unless you wear a jacket. I did not find this was true. You can hold them away from you, there is no need to clutch them in your arms. But I did find it often very hard on the hands when thistles were bound up in the sheaves – one would get on quicker with gloves. We hiled in couples, each couple taking three rows, and going round the field. Going round it, not up and down. Once when I was hiling alone early one morning I started by going up and down. When the carter came out I was asked, Was I backhanded? – which conveyed nothing to me till

I realized that everyone went round and round and not up and down, since all the sheaves are thrown out in one direction, and it facilitates matters to approach from the stalk end.

I soon sampled what it was like hiling oats, for now we got on to a very fine field of oats, the field which had seemed so incredibly stony to me when I had cultivated and harrowed it. I found oat-sheaves to be much the most difficult to deal with. They were huge and top-heavy, and very much inclined to fall over if poorly put together. One technique is more necessary in this case than with any other corn: you must *bump* them down on the ground. Holding one in the left, one in the right hand, you don't just *lean* them together, you bump them down on the ground at the same time as leaning them together, as if you hoped the stalks would stick in the earth like spikes – which in a sense they do, for a much steadier stook is achieved that way.

We made fast progress over these fields; the fairly frequent presence of 'E serving, no doubt, *pour encourager les autres.* The person coupled with him was not envied; nor was it good to be going round anywhere near him, since if he was somewhere behind he would soon be bound to pass, and if the ring was getting small, perhaps get round twice to your once. 'Look where 'e's got to! 'e's down the line already!' someone would say, while everyone kept an apprehensive eye on his progress. On one occasion, after the break for tea, when I was walking towards my hiling companion, who was Dick, I found myself also walking towards 'E who then signed to me to join *him.* Away we went, 'E and I, grabbing at and dragging the sheaves together at great speed – for, seeing there was no help for it, I even quickened the pace for fun, making our progress even more appalling for the others to witness, so that I could imagine them saying – 'Look where the bs have got to!'

'E was certainly a real countryman, descending from a line of farmers; but he was not typical in this matter of pace. No calm, steady, leisurely gait such as we associate with the countryman. Yet pace may be the wrong word. For the curious thing was that Robert always gave an impression of great ease and leisureliness, and yet did his jobs much faster than it appeared. Once when we were all spreading the hiles – that is throwing the stooked sheaves on the ground to dry out after rain – the pace was very swift as we went along forking down the hiles, and I found it difficult to keep up. Robert didn't appear to be making any effort at all, and moved forward with a casual ease that should mean that he would soon be left behind. He wasn't left behind. He was going slower, but he didn't lose ground – strange. And I frequently saw him build a straw-rick without seeming to exert more effort with his prong than if he were stirring soup.

36. While Carrying

Now for the carrying. My first experience of this entailed pitching sheaves into the wagons in the field. Dick stood in the wagon loading the sheaves which were pitched up by me on one side and the carter on the other. I had to grasp the technique straightaway. It did not take me long. The sheaves must reach the wagon with stalks pointing outwards, otherwise the loader cannot easily do his job nor the unloaders at the rick do theirs. The thing is to take two sheaves up on your prong and elevate them. The carter took three or four, just to show off and get his side done before mine. Being a very small man he always wished to emphasize his strength. 'Small men,' said Dick, 'have big ideas.' It was quite unnecessary to take up so many at once and it made it more difficult for the receiver. I soon found that I could keep pace with him by simply taking *one* up at a time, since you can do that in a jiffy, while in endeavouring to pick up two or three at a time you often muff the affair and fail to get hold of them with your prong, thus wasting time.

This job of pitching up for the wagons on the field is undoubtedly the easiest of all the harvest operations. The loader's position is not so enviable. For not only does he lack a firm floor, but every minute the wagon is jerked forward by tractor or horse while the driver cries 'Hold tight!' like a bus-conductor in Oxford Street. And the loading is a little art in itself, as a lot of people find to their amazement who have come along in the summer to Help the Farmer in answer to the typically urban ineptitude which exhorted them to Take Your Holidays On The Farm – a slogan met with hoots of derision by every agricultural labourer.

But most of my time was spent either on the rick or pitching to the rick; and thither we will now proceed. After the bed of straw had been laid down, as for any kind of rick except straw itself, the first arrangement of the sheaves surprised me. Robert stood in the middle, putting up what looked like a huge hile. What was the idea of this stooking? I wondered – till I saw the point, which was the obvious one that these bottom ears must be kept up somehow, and the middle filled as compactly as possible.

Until later when we began to use the elevator my job was unloading the wagons and feeding the rick. Quite a reasonable job even at the worst of times. And when the rick is low and you are well above it, not a great deal of effort is required provided the wagon has been built properly – otherwise there is the old intensely irritating difficulty of getting the sheaves loose, no matter what plan you improvise. The pitching on to the rick required another new technique. You cannot chuck them down anyhow, for they must lie with stalks facing outwards and crop inwards, and if they alight the wrong way then the men on the rick will have to turn them over and time be lost. Especially is this necessary, of course, when you are dealing out sheaves to the rick-builder himself. Thus in whatever position you may find them on the wagon, your pitched sheaf should fall the right way round if you wish to promote the greatest convenience for the greatest number of people engaged. This is not difficult. A flick of the wrist, as you pitch, easily makes the sheaf turn somersaults in the air if that is what is required. It did not take me long to get into this; for it is not true that all agricultural jobs require a lifetime's practice to make perfect.

An instructed spectator can generally single out an amateur by observing one particular – namely the way the prong is held by the left hand. Nearly everyone at first has an inclination to put the left hand round it so that the wrist is pointing out instead of the thumb. But I did not do that now. I did, however, at this time do something else which would have enlightened that spectator as to my unprofessional status, something that seems incredible to me now – *I wore shoes*. The discomfort I went through owing to this unnecessary nonsense, still riles me. Rubber boots, of course, were out of the question. But why shoes? I had the fixed idea that shoes in summer were light and cool and restful. But not only was the endless walking about hiling on uneven ground anything but comfortable in shoes, but now when I stood on top of the ripe ears of corn, the grain continually got into my shoes, and I had to keep taking them off to empty them, or stand feeling as if I had pebbles under my socks. Nor could I purchase a decent footing in them. And the remedy? Boots of course. I thought boots were stiff, heavy, hot, uncomfortable foot-pinchers. The opposite is true. They are comfort itself. Their weight doesn't matter in the least, the firm footing you get is a delight, and no grain ever gets in. When later I took to boots I never even wore rubber ones again, not even in the winter, for if you get leather ones large enough you can still wear two pairs of socks and thus be as warm as you are firm. One must have a firm footing in this world. A steady base is the first essential in agriculture – as it is also in architecture and in literature.

At no time did one need the broad nailed gripping boot more than when unloading the wagons, for one's footing was often precarious, and it was always a pleasant moment when one reached the floor of the wagon, and could stand once again with ease. We generally had two wagons and one lorry carrying the loads from the field. Thus no sooner was I finished with one lot than another was seen approaching. The unwritten law in this affair is that the rick-builders must 'hold' the carriers. That is to say they must always be ready for the new material sent in from the field. It would be a confession of failure if a wagon is kept waiting while the one in front is still being unloaded. Such a situation would get on the nerves of the rick-makers and also lead to the workers in the field being 'stood up'. On no account must such a calamity occur. Thus if three wagons are going strong the unloaders have to work fast. Sometimes one of us (there being two, myself and the man with the wagon last come in) eased up, and then 'E would become apprehensive of the impending calamity, and say – 'Let's have 'em!' At which Dick's brow, if this was addressed to him, would darken into night. Sometimes 'E would jump on to the wagon from the rick and unload a bit himself, throwing out the sheaves at the rate at which lesser men in lesser spheres deal out cards.

When the load came in on the lorry it meant that I had Jimmy as my mate in pitching. As I have said, he was a distinctly cheering kind of person to have around, his smiling face and good-humoured manner always creating a good atmosphere. He used to call me 'Sunshine'. 'Ah, there is Sunshine,' he would say, as if it were my actual name. I mention this, for I am not the man to miss an opportunity of showing myself in a good light. But I cannot subscribe to the description, I'm afraid. Never before have I been referred to in that way, and I suppose never again – so I'm anxious to record it here. I think I can understand it, though. I'm careful not to lose my temper unless a given situation psychologically demands it (so calculating have I become), any more than I ever allow pride to get in the way of an ultimate aim; and during these rather testing days I believe I almost deliberately kept to a cheerful and even smiling countenance. This may have been so, because subsequently, when actually questioning Jimmy about his appellation (which was far truer as a description of himself, indeed perfect as such), he said that 'it required guts to get up on a rick and smile in that way' – a remark which greatly pleased my vanity. And in all seriousness I took note of the fact that a modicum of even deliberate cheerfulness of expression has considerable effect.

Jimmy's lorry-load was much larger than that which could be put on an ordinary wagon, and it was always with great relief that we at length dug down to the floor. 'The parade' I used to call it, 'my old pal's parade'. He had a way of digging down as soon as possible till he stood firmly on a piece of the floor, however high around him the rest of the sheaves might be – 'I've already reached your old pal's parade!' he would say, while I was still several feet above it on my side. He liked my names for things. I used to call his lorry 'the green thing', and the wagon that was tractor-driven by Harold as 'Harold's caboodle', and he took a great fancy to this nomenclature for such serious agricultural objects.

37. Early Morning Jobs

Sometimes we started the day by making some thatch. We used a machine for this also. It is a kind of large sewing-machine which sews together the straw with which one feeds it into mats which are rolled up and put away until subsequently the thatch-maker unrolls them across his ricks. At a later period I thatched them myself. As I have never thatched with hand-made ones I cannot make a comparison, but so far the traditional sort seem much better. These machine-made ones are much thinner, and also strong wind easily turns the mats into *sails,* so that after a storm whole sides of thatched ricks are found half ripped off. We certainly made our thatch with a maximum of inefficiency. If you do not feed the machine with an even pressure the result is a mat with gaps in it, thus hopeless in rain. However, like all these things, I suppose that soon machine-made thatch will be well knit, and a sure device found for pinning it down on the rick.

At other times my mornings began very quietly, and there was not much for me to do except pull up some of the charlock that still remained covering the greater part of a field of swedes – for when I came back from that far field of kale I was astonished at the change that had taken place here and there, especially this stretch of charlock like a great yellow rug which had suddenly been spread out. Sometimes I had little more to do than go through various hiled fields and re-erect stooks that had fallen down, or turn them to dry out after rain. Indeed, after there had been a good deal of wind, quite a number of the stooks were down. On a certain oatfield I was pleased to observe that my own lines (I had particularly noted their position) all remained intact, which proved to me that even in this small matter deliberate, careful building pays.

While engaged in this I often came upon a rabbit who rushed out from the centre of a stook. For, instead of a burrow, the creature had found this a lovely ready-made house, warm, peaceful, and dark. Here might it dwell for ever. As one who often feels a longing to curl up in some little nook like that and shut out the world, forget it and be invisible from it, I was sorry for these deluded rabbits, and used to examine the little nest thus created, laying my hand on the warm patch just vacated, and for a moment almost become, in imagination, the creature.

Later on there were rainy spells before we had carried the oats, and consequently it stayed out a long time. Oats has to be left in stook for a few weeks before carrying, and it cannot be carried wet – whereas you can cut and carry wheat or barley on the same day, while if it rains you can rick wheat even while the water is dripping from it, I was surprised to find. But as none of this applies to oats, constant weather is most important; a lot of sun during harvest being more important than during hay-making – for though you need not make hay while the sun shines and do not want too much of it, the more you have with corn the better. We had no such luck this year. And on one oatfield, at a later date, which I was turning, I found that the ears of different sheaves were stuck together in fraternal embrace. I could not get them apart. It was a remarkable sight. The seeds had already germinated within the damp ears, and had sent out long shoots which, like green pieces of broad twine, were intermingling and clasping each other. A curious and unruly spectacle: as if Nature, unwilling to conform to man's requirements, was eager to cut out the harvesting, the autumn, and the winter, and start the work of spring straight away.

38. Scenes at the Pub

Though we did not get through without rain, we had some long, hot spells. Once more I was putting in a very full day, once more enjoying it even when I wasn't enjoying it, so to speak – for I like doing things in extremes. Again the very early rise in order to make enough sandwiches for three meals – and what lack of material there was! being reduced for the most part to fish paste and bread. Again the break for lunch at ten, and the coveted hour for dinner, at which time I counted myself the gainer, for I could sit down at once, wasting no time going home and getting back like the others. Then the long spell before tea at five-thirty. At many farms, when overtime is on, it is customary to stop for tea at five – but not here. The break for tea was the day's great event: it was an an event which at certain times on certain days did not seem actually *possible* (a feeling hard to express, but which I frequently had during hoeing, when I caught myself saying to myself, It is hard to believe, but five-thirty will in fact arrive and you will stop). My thermos kept my tea really hot, and drinking it was like taking whisky then: I mean this in the exact sense that as the first mouthful runs along inside, you *feel* it passing through, warming and bracing you in a manner it never does save after a long interval of exercise. Thus I harp upon these simple themes, not for the first time. For this is one of the main realities of the agricultural life, too dull to refer to often, but more central to one's experience than the peculiar incident and the lofty thought. After tea we all felt surprisingly revived, it was quite remarkable. The next two hours were no effort, and three would not have seemed too long – that is why farmers, who think of their men, stop at five and do two and a half hours afterwards instead of the two after the five-thirty break. Then again up the hill home, and yet another meal. And so to bed, the sheer pleasure of lying down being itself a physical luxury.

But I did not always go straight home. Very often I went with Jimmy and had beer at the pub. There was a certain inner room

– it was called 'upstairs' though it was exactly one step higher than the other rooms – in which darts were not played and where we had song and dance. For women could come into this room, but never went into the darts room, as that is a game reserved for the men. There was a table taking up the greater part of the room, but in the space left at one side we danced, for one man played the accordion. And the enjoyment was quite as great as if we had had the Hall of Mirrors at Versailles at our disposal (if there is such a hall). The atmosphere was distinctly cheerful and there was singing during the dancing and in between whiles. Pressed to sing I had to explain that I couldn't command a single note, but I performed my one and only parlour trick, which was a take-off of a Churchill speech, with Churchillian intonations and rhythms. I made an elaborate job of the thing, putting the man who acted rather as the comedian of the company into the role of a Lord Mayor, whom I could then address as if at a banquet at the Guildhall. To my astonishment this went down remarkably well, and I had to repeat my *pièce de résistance* again and again throughout the harvest and well beyond it, until 'Churchill' became my nickname. These were great evenings after our day on the field, providing an excellent contrast.

We did not always get this room to ourselves, for the military sometimes came in. One evening there was enacted here a peculiarly national scene. A corporal began to sing certain songs which eventually were felt to be too raw in the presence of womenfolk; and our company ostentatiously moved into another room, after first making some deprecatory remarks. But in a moment the corporal followed in a great state of indignation. He wasn't standing for the remarks that had just been made! He wasn't going to pass over such accusations! He had witnesses and he would have the Law on us, he would have us up for Libel! Very angry indeed, he supported his threats with two statements. The first was financial. 'I could buy this pub,' he kept repeating. 'I could buy this pub, and two like it!' The second drew its strength from domestic values. 'I'm a married man,' he reiterated, 'with a wife and two children.' Having thus established his impregnable position in society, he returned to his threats of Law and Libel.

This was received by my friends very quietly. They had not wished to hurt his feelings, and their one aim was to appease him. With the greatest civility they unsaid everything they had just said, and eventually shook hands with him – not so much in friendliness as in the manner that one tries to pat or soothe an obstreperous dog. The corporal took this with a poor grace, and the incident did not end at this point. The man who had been mainly responsible for the earlier remarks began to feel dissatisfied with himself for climbing down, and subsequently took the corporal outside and threatened to fight him, or did fight him, I'm not sure which. He had been ashamed of his earlier attitude of giving way to the man, and confessed privately to me that he 'liked a bit of a set-to'. Thus here in this corner of England, as anywhere else, was exhibited the national characteristic of appeasement and pugnacity. First appeasement, then pugnacity. If the first is not appreciated, so much the worse for the offender.

What with one thing and another these were great evenings after eleven hours harvesting, and when beer and lots of it was what we needed. In the nineteenth century people got drunk: today no one gets drunk. At least not in the traditional and proper sense as summed up by Plato. It would never do, he said, for a guardian to get drunk and thereby need a guard, and '*not know where he is*'. We were glad to know that we were where we were and not in the field under the eye of 'E. And there was one other great thing in favour of beer at this hour. To take more tea just before bed was not good, but after plenty of beer one could be certain of almost immediate oblivion in the best sense of not knowing where one is.

39. Scenes on the Rick

Pitching from the wagons was easy enough while the rick in question was still young. But the time came soon enough when we no longer chucked the sheaves down but began to throw them up. At this stage we often got on to the new wagon-load from the rick, jumping down. Once when I had reached the top of the ladder – which reached to the top of the half-built rick – and was getting off it I lost my balance, seized hold of a sheaf which did not support me, and fell to the ground. Everyone peered over, expecting to see me disabled; but finding that I had achieved little more than a slight cut and bruise, I immediately rose, replaced my hat, and without making any observation whatever, went up the ladder again and started unloading at once, as if I had merely chosen a quick way down to pick up something I had forgotten. This procedure was witnessed with some surprise (as I secretly meant it to be), but all the same I was careful never to slip up again in this manner, and I do not recommend anyone to try and use a top sheaf as a means of support.

When the rick grew really high our work from below became proportionally harder, since we had to throw the sheaves up higher and higher. Sometimes, either owing to bad timing on one's own part or carelessness above, one's sheaf came tumbling down again. But this seldom happened, for if the sheaves go up in proper rotation they need never be muffed at the top if the receivers know their job – that is, simply realize the necessity to give a *bold stab* of the prong into the up-coming sheaf (an almost infallible method, as I found when on occasion I was in that position myself). But sometimes, if there were too few people on the rick and no one was 'built in' on the rising wall, a point was reached when it became necessary to throw the sheaf right up if it was to be caught – an exhausting procedure. 'Come on now, Mr Collis!' shouted Robert at one such time, 'throw they sheaves up thease side. It'll give thee summat to remember when on thy tractor again!' At which I threw one so high that it would have gone right over the rick had he not just spiked it in time – an exhibition received with acclamation by Robert and 'E. But Harold, who was pitching with me, said – 'You haven't done nothing yet.' Having done the same amount as he, I replied – 'Then you can't have done nothing neither' – at which there was some hilarity, and we all continued not doing nothing until the rick was finished.

As there was still a lot to be carried, and as large ricks would save time, 'E decided to use the elevator when the ricks reached a certain height. I don't know whether this is a widespread practice. There is supposed to be a certain wastage of seed that way; but actually when a sheet is spread out under the elevator, most of the grain which falls out is caught and can be bagged. I was very pleased at this innovation, since when things began to get rather difficult they became exceptionally easy on pushing the moving stairs beside the wagon, and I called the elevator my friend, and it began to be known as 'Collis's friend'.

But this was short-lived. For just at this time some extra helpers came along, and I was called for on the rick, where I remained for most of the rest of the harvest. My job here was fairly equally divided between dealing with this new type of waterfall from the elevator, and binding after Robert. Binding is straightforward enough, and consists chiefly in laying a second layer of sheaves half-over the first layer put down by the rick-maker, other sheaves going behind yours, and so on. Of course if the sheaves are coming down very quickly from the elevator and falling all over the place, it is easy to get flummoxed and to bind loosely and badly. Thus I was always much relieved when a load was finished, thus giving us a few minutes anyway to sort things out if they had got in a mess. Harold, continuing his fun and games with me, always sent as many sheaves as possible up to me as quickly as possible. Having failed to bury me under hay he tried to bury me under sheaves, and certainly they some-times tumbled down in great quantities. 'I don't think much of this elevator idea!' I said to 'E. He laughed and shouted down to Harold, 'Collis says he's going to withdraw the elevator. He hasn't no use for his friend no more!'

Yet I still liked rising in the world and getting my view. At this time of year one of the most satisfactory of all agricultural sights meets the eye – that of sheep folding a field of clover. I could see them on a thick luxurious field which could have taken a second hay-cut. On one side of the hurdles was the dark green clover, and on the other all of it eaten away by the sheep who had at the same time thoroughly manured the ground. It is a sight which gives one such a feeling of benefits bestowed upon all by this most proper homage to the rule of return.

And I got a good view of the workers out in the field, pitching and loading. It was especially fascinating to observe 'E's boy, John, at work. It was phenomenal. Here anything at all in the nature of leisurely work was absent. His forking up of the sheaves was accomplished at the double. He dashed at them with his prong as if to bayonet them, hurled them up to the loader on the wagon, ran to the next and hurled it up, then jumped on to the tractor, and, before the others were ready on the far side, cried 'Hold tight!', brought the wagon forward a few yards, stopped it, seized his prong, leapt off, and rushed at more sheaves – as if something were biting him. How far this really pleased the parental eye, I don't know, but I suppose it did. But he had one relaxation. If a rabbit suddenly ran out from its hiding place in a stook, he would rush madly after it with his prong, no matter for how far or for how long, forgetting all else. This pursuit was entirely utilitarian of course, and emphatically pro-agricultural and calculated to promote exter- mination of vermin; but happily it dovetailed remarkably well, I thought, with his psychological requirements.

I was generally sorry when a rick was practically finished and I had to get down. As the roofing grew our plateau naturally became continually narrower so that there was less and less room to work in and the pitchers below had to send up the sheaves slowly. Soon there was only room for two of us, then only for one and Robert would say, rather apologetically, 'Better get down if you will', knowing that I didn't like some- how having to retire as a now useless tool. Once, long before roofing, our rick began to come up against the branches of a tree, which had seemed far enough away (over a wall) when we had planned our base. While the elevator was going full tilt ahead, Robert asked for a billhook and began hacking away at a branch, and in fact engaged himself for some time at this. My pile of material began to assume proportions. 'Hey, Robert!' I cried. 'You can't start taking up forestry while building a rick! What am I to do with these sheaves?' 'Let they sheaves bide!' he yelled, 'I baint gwine to have thease wold tree interfere with I!' Meanwhile I failed to grapple with the waterfall of sheaves – increased in volume from below for the occasion.

One rick finished, on to the next – with 'E measuring out the space for the bedding of straw (I saw now where that bent head and long cricket-pitch strides came from: the result of perpetually measuring out rick-floors). We generally built almost exactly one and a half a day. I liked it to work out so that we were finishing a rick after tea. For one thing, the intensity of the agricultural earnestness was relaxed and good humour often prevailed; more people came out then, and we had our land girl from the dairy and the atmosphere was even uproarious at times when Robert yelled about gaps and holes, pretending that I was responsible for them. And this was by far the best time of the day to be high on the rick. That is the hour at which one really does glance round at the view, when the soft lights come on and the hard ways of the world are diminished.

We were now on a field beside that piece of kale I had first hoed, those plants that had seemed so poor in promise. The miserable stalks that I remembered were now as thick as a man's leg and as high as the waist or shoulders – and again I marvelled at the march. We worked very late that evening, and it was an especially lovely one. The wind had gone down completely and all the shapes of earth captured in the yellow rays were sculptured by their shades. The sun set and the dusk gathered, and with it came a deeper silence, as when a clock stops ticking in a silent room; the clouds had got stuck and would never move again; the new moon stooped down so low above a tree that I could have hung my hat upon its horn. The final tricky part of the rick-making began when, the platform growing very narrow, I had to handle the sheaves with much circumspection. Down below I could see the roads becoming whiter and the fields darker and the woods more sombre, and as I glanced at them it occurred to me that perhaps after all this is how I would prefer to catch sight of Beauty – through the corner of my eye, while immersed in something else, while not seeking her at all.

40. My First Attempt at Rick Building

By this time I began to know what a rick is. It is a *solid* cottage. Its bricks are sheaves, its slates are sheaves, and it is filled with the same – on similar lines as Ghenghis Khan built his pyramids of skulls. They stand at this time of the year all over the countryside, and it looks very easy to put them there. But how would I get on, I wondered, if I tried the job of architect? Would my exhibit resemble the leaves of yesteryear? Yet such is my pertinacity and venturesomeness, that I determined to try.

As I had succeeded rather too well with a hay-rick, Robert was none too keen on a further success. Nor were the others, really. It would hardly do to let me get away with it. 'Build it on the sand, you mean,' said Harold, whatever that meant, when the subject came up. 'You'll be losing your job, Robert,' said Jimmy, and Robert not quite liking this even in jest said that 'come threshing' he would be only too glad to hand it over to me. Nor was 'E particularly keen, as my attempt might well hold things up. But he was always very sporting to me in such things. When we had started on a certain barley-rick, a favourable opportunity seemed to offer, and I weighed in on it. Actually it was idiotic to choose barley of all things, since the sheaves are so stumpy and as slippery as glass. However, I started and began going round. Here I made another capital error. I remained standing up, doing the work with my prong, instead of dealing with the sheaves by hand and going round on my knees as Robert frequently did. The corners were my chief difficulty. I had carefully watched Robert dealing with the corners, and I could *teach* how it was done, but to do it in full action without fumbling was another matter. However, I carried on round.

'Go forward with thy left foot!' bellowed Robert loud enough to be heard two fields away.

'Tread 'ee down!' said 'E, my second tutor.

'Keep 'ee closer!' shouted my first instructor.

Baffled by having placed a sheaf too far in I tried to push it out, but another fell on top of it before I could do so, and another bellow came from my foremost guide.

'I thought you said – ' I began.

'You're not giving me instructions!' he roared, 'I'm giving them to you.'

'Not so hard this side!' shouted further agricultural advisers from the wagon, who were careful to deliver sheaves in plenty.

Under these ideal conditions I proceeded. The Israelites, we are told in the Bible, were in the deplorable position of having 'to make bricks without straw'. I never understood what straw had to do with it, nor do I now; but here I was attempting to build with bricks *of straw* and with no cement. My tendency to keep the sheaves too far in became too strong for me, especially on one side, and my rick began to slope inward Gothically as if I were already roofing. Then in a too great effort to check this, my architecture began to take after Giovanni Gambuti who inspired the Leaning Tower of Pisa. Meanwhile the sheaves were handed to me far quicker than I would have ever dared hand them to Robert. And at last, under protest, I was prevailed upon to give in, and must chalk up the truth that I did not succeed in this venture. The pressure was too much. It is a good thing to learn under pressure, no doubt. Bertrand Russell said that his parents taught him to swim by holding him upside-down in deep water; but he added that he could not recommend this as the best method for everyone. In the same way I daresay I could have found easier conditions under which to build my first rick.

41. Meditation in the Old Garden

We reached our last wheat field now, and only two fields of oats and the hundred-acre barley lay ahead. Owing to a faulty packing of food one morning I had gone short at lunch, not daring to be short at dinner with the afternoon in front. As the morning advanced I began to feel exceedingly hungry, and was afraid even to look at my watch lest its progress would be too discouraging, and refused to give my well-known signal (using arms as clock-hands) to Dick whose sovereign thought was always the progression of time – it ruled his mind like a king. Unfortunately it worked out that it would be possible to finish the rick in the morning if we went on a bit longer than usual – which we did.

Actually I was glad of this because the next field to be tackled was right away at the other side of the farm – beyond the Big House. I saw that I would be able to have my rest and food in the garden. So when the others had gone I took a short cut and made for the Big House and entered the Old Garden. It was not open to the public, but it was open to the private, so to speak. No one seemed to be in residence at the moment. The door through the wall in the garden was not locked and I went in. I sat down on a seat backed by the high wall and fronted by a pool of lawn cliffed by ancient trees. Here I now ate my much postponed meal. I enjoyed it so much that when finished, and with cigarette in hand, I felt a great sense of physical well-being. It is not very often that one gets this feeling after agricultural work, but if the weather has been hot and the work hard-going as opposed to a slow drag, it is possible to feel really well afterwards. When this happens the mind sometimes attains considerable liberty and can move without hindrance. And, in my own case, as I had been doing what is called 'an honest day's work', my mind enjoyed still greater freedom. I could regard phenomena, natural or social, without guilt, without anxiety, without ideas conceived by others, without for a moment having to attain to the condition of that strangest of all birds, the bird with only one wing, Left or Right, the bird that cannot soar upwards and take a bird's-eye view.

In this mood I fell into contemplation of the Old Garden. Aloof in the melancholy shade of history, it gave out peace and cast the ancient spell. How did it come into existence? By some men being rich and others poor, by inequality, by privilege. Entering into the era of equality, shall we then throw them open to the public? The moment we do so they will become – something else. They will no longer be gardens: they will be *parks*. Instantly their essence will evaporate and they will no longer be what they were. We must face the logic; the moment privilege becomes public it ceases to be privilege, for you cannot have a privileged many – they would not then be privileged. So our question is – Shall we have a privileged few? Well, the many do not like this kind of place anyway; secluded reverie is alien to them, quiet reflection wholly unsought – they prefer the definite peopled park. But they also enjoy on occasion the parade of circumstance and the pomp of power. And I said – Let us not throw everything away in the name of Equality. Let there be privilege! Let there be pride! Let there be palaces though they be built out of the pennies of the poor! The time is coming when the flood-tide of the multitudinous Many shall flow through all the gates and into all the courts of pleasure; but even then, let there be here and there a too favoured Few, so that scattered throughout the land there may yet remain, enwalled from the world's babel, the sequestered place, the pool of silence, the repository of peace, into which the wanderer may come and bathe in the spirit of the past and hold converse with the mighty dead!

While lifted up into this pleasant mood as I sat in the old garden, I heard the distant rumble of wheels. I knew exactly what that sound meant. It was the approach of our wagons making towards that other field which we were to carry in the afternoon, and I must now get up and move out into the *medias res* of agriculture. And as I was happy in my thoughts at this hour, and in this place, so was I happy in *that* thought; for whereas the time had been when the rumble of wagon-wheels would have meant nothing to me save the faint murmur from a world of labour in which I had no share and yet upon which all my ways depended, now, though I might dwell for a brief period in the Old Garden and the Ivory Tower of my soul, I must presently depart from thence, and enter into and take my place at the centre of the world's work. And in this also there was happiness. In this there was freedom.

42. Imperfect Scenes

The weather broke. Not badly, but just enough to hold us up and make it necessary to turn the stooks of oats. 'E took hold-ups caused by the weather very well, I thought. He didn't let it make him lose his temper. And though we had more to do and fewer of us to do it than at many of the farms round about, we were ahead of most with our harvesting. 'E was respected in the neighbourhood as a man who at any rate got things done. Looking at him, I wondered what such a man would do under complete State Ownership. Would not this strong natural force be lost? Men who are out for themselves in agriculture, and not for the State, do more work and hence serve the State better than those who work for the State. A post as mere Manager would never engage the full force of these men; it would be largely wasted. This would be a bad thing if we go on the assumption that efficiency is the aim of life.

The sun returned and we carried on again after first spreading the hiles. One morning while I was engaged at this I found a dead hare which I picked up and put in my bag to take home for consumption. Next day while we were starting another rick, 'E began to talk about someone having been seen with a hare, the implication being that 'someone with a dog' had caught a hare. 'E was a tenant of the Squire who was much against there being any dogs about that might interfere with his shooting. 'Don't let the Squire see thy dog loose,' Robert had said to me, 'or he'll have him shot, I allow' – for Robert didn't approve of my having a dog as well as he. And now 'E brought up this subject of the hare and said that the Squire would be 'creating'. I said I had picked up a dead hare. He said he 'didn't know nothing about it', but that he had heard but 'wasn't saying nothing' as to who had informed him, but anyway if I wasn't careful the Squire would be *creating*.

I failed to take all this with the proper seriousness, and was inadequately impressed either by the Squire's alleged creative powers or about the hush-hush concerning who told the tale. I knew who must have told (not Robert), but said, with the maximum of indiscretion, 'the only person within sight was Robert'.

It was as if I had put a match to a piece of petrol-soaked paper. Up went Robert in flames. I could hardly blame him, for it was a poor joke on my part; but he certainly got excited, yelling and stamping with rage at this scandalous imputation, finally bringing up the occasion when my dog had been seen worrying his sheep, to which he had a Witness (the same being Harold who now looked appropriately sheepish). I'm no hand at shouting-matches and could say little under the circumstances except 'the trouble with you Robert is that you can't take a joke' which didn't do much good. 'Joke be b'd,' he said. But the thing then petered out, and I said no more, leaving bad alone, and not trying to add to or quench the flames.

By seven-thirty we had finished the rick, and with half an hour in hand we trekked off to another field and started a rick at once, for some of the others had gone ahead and loaded the wagons. At one time a loaded horse-drawn wagon stood waiting by the rick till we were ready to move it in. When we were ready we found that the horse wasn't. He had decided not to move, just refusing definitely to bring the wagon alongside. 'E got off the rick, went up to the horse, and saying – 'Up you sod!' jabbed the wooden end of his prong into the horse's ribs. It gave a leap forward, snapping the harness in four or five places and breaking clean out of the wagon. 'E gave it several more jabs, though this did nothing to improve the situation, since the wagon now remained exactly where it was before. Someone had to go and get fresh harness, and a considerable interval elapsed

189

before the wagon at length moved forward under the now docile horse – Harold leading him forward and giving him a friendly pat on the nose and neck.

This brought us to the end of an imperfect day. The following day also closed imperfectly. We were working at a rick near the end of the afternoon when the sky blackened and rain approached. It would be necessary to throw a tarpaulin over the rick. Harold and Dick were feeding the elevator. Suddenly Robert exploded. With extreme fury he yelled down to Dick – *not* saying, Get the tarpaulin, but Why the etc. etc., hadn't he got it? as if Dick had refused to do something he had been told. Dick's gorge rose and he didn't budge – at least not until he was told to do so by 'E. After this had been done and we had put the tarpaulin over the rick, Robert, still in a rage, advanced towards Dick with his prong as if to lay him out, while pronouncing an oath of the utmost extremity. Dick stood his ground, hurling back a drastic imprecation; while Harold, who was watching the business carefully, placed himself close behind Robert, fully intending to strike him down if he really did raise his hand against Dick. But Robert suddenly put up his prong and walked away.

Thus nerves began to get rather on edge as we neared the end of the harvest. The truth is Robert was afraid of rheumatism if he got caught in that oncoming rain, for on the rick we were not within reach of our coats. It was therefore very irritating not to have the tarpaulin fetched at once instead of having more sheaves sent up on the elevator. Robert was a fairly good-hearted man and he did not bear ill-will towards Dick after this, nor towards me about the hare – in fact he brought out some more cake for me. Indeed there was very little in the nature of sulking at this farm. 'E himself detested sulking and reacted at once when it was exhibited. 'I like a clear atmosphere,' he said, quite convinced that no man ever did more to promote a good atmosphere than he himself. Though Robert was not notable for his sense of humour or fun, he could laugh and I always got a tremendous loud guffaw out of him if I made some grousy kind of joke against something. But 'E, who treated him with great respect, never found him a good listener. Feeling the necessity sometimes to make some kind of remark while waiting between-times on the rick, 'E would speak about the market or the weather or even the war, but Robert hardly ever said more than 'Aye' or 'That's where it is' without looking up. And on a certain occasion when loaders and rickers were all on a level, 'E actually told us a story, and a very good story, about a bull, but Robert neither listened nor laughed, and gazed firmly away into the distance.

Elderly workers have always been critical of the younger generation. It is even more so today. Men who have worked very hard all their lives for a very small wage, now see young men, with a lamentable tendency to enjoy life, working less arduously for a far higher wage and with promises of security and what not in the future. Robert was a very skilled man, invaluable on any farm, who could do a number of jobs a good deal better than younger men; but it was clear to him that a grateful nation was going to repay him by making Dick's life easier than his had been. Elderly working men and women are much less critical of the social system than of the younger generation.

There was twenty minutes in hand before it would be officially time to leave off. So 'E found jobs for us. He instructed me to go to a certain distant field and pull up charlock. By the time I got there I had ten minutes before me, so I stood sheltering from the rain under the hedge and read a weekly paper, coming upon a review by Mr Raymond Postgate about a book on Detective Fiction, in the course of which he remarked that the photographs of the detective-writing authors betrayed, with one exception, definite criminal types: the one exception being thus mentioned, I supposed, so that if any of them reproached him for saying this, he could say it was the other fellow. Thus lost in these incredibly non-agricultural considerations, I now saw that it was five-thirty and I could depart.

But as I went home I reflected upon the situation as it must now present itself to the employer. In the old days wages were so low that it cost three shillings less to keep a man than a horse. Those were the days, he feels. Now he is faced with a heavy wage bill, the difference within one generation being immense. Thus it is only human that he should now feel – as probably he seldom did in the past – that every minute wasted is money spent on nothing. As I write, wages are still going up. It might be a good thing if they stopped now. For the fact is that it will tell against workers if they go too far. Not only will it make the psychological atmosphere uncomfortable, but after five or six years of increased mechanization and increased knowledge on a farmer's part of how many men he can *do without,* it will not be so easy to get a job on the land if wages are very high. Men who really want to work there, who would love it, may find themselves going round and being told by farmer after farmer that he 'doesn't want no more labour'.

43. *The Combine Harvester; The Leisure State*

We were now faced with the hundred-acre barley. It had been left too long in any case, so it was quite unnecessary to hile it. If the weather held we could cut and carry at the same time. But it was now late September and 'E decided to hire a combine to do half of it. And this was done. While we cut and carried fifty acres, a combine harvester did the other half.

It is a remarkable machine. A truly triumphant invention. No open-minded person could fail to admire the scientific ingenuity of the men who contrived it. It is a binder and a thresher in one unit. The corn which has been cut and taken up by the binder is taken up but not bound; instead it passes through a threshing operation so that the grain pours straight into a tank which is emptied into sacks and deposited on a lorry once every round of the field. The straw, instead of being ricked, is spread over the field as it comes out by means of a revolving fan like the screw of a ship – so what with the usual binder-sails and this screw behind, the contraption looks like a sort of paddle-steamer whose element is corn. It is very neat: for when you examine it closely it seems astonishing that the job of the bulky thresher can be encompassed in so small a space.

Thus it proceeds round the field, doing two jobs at once: that of cutting and threshing; and knocking out the necessity of three middle ones – carting, ricking, and thatching. An absolute godsend to the small farmer, I reflected, to the man who runs a hundred acres by himself with a son, a daughter, and one or two assistants. But in relation to big farms, I could not help feeling gloomy about its appearance. It is rather as if the Future had arrived before we were ready for it.

It has just been reported that in liberated Ukraine, a girl combine-operator, Vera Panchonko, has received a Badge of Honour for harvesting two hundred and sixty acres in five days.

Let us consider exactly what this means.

There are few subjects harder to think *out* than this of machinery. An honest man will tend to be inconsistent. Even Gandhi, who decided to oppose with the whole force of his mighty spirit the entry of the machine into India, made an exception in favour of Madame Singer's sewing-machine. It is hard to be fully sensible on this subject. I shall tackle it here simply in relation to the land.

The farm labourer, I repeat once again, is a mechanic, always, from the word go, having to deal with nuts and screws and overcome difficulties without help from outside. A very bad mechanic, farmers may complain, lazy, stupid, and careless concerning machines, and needing specialist help in all serious problems. Perhaps; but my point is that mechanism starts on the land; however amateurishly, there we started to conquer nature with ever more ingenious weapons. There the machine is a natural growth, seen at once as the right thing in the right place, and the man who deals with it seen as fully a man – in staring contrast to the man at the conveyor-belt in a factory. The machines have evolved in the country almost as naturally as flowers. First the spade – then the plough. First the rake – then the harrow. First the broadcast of seed (father of the B.B.C.) – then the drill. First the flail – then the thresher. First arm-pitching – then the elevator. First the sickle, then the scythe, then the reaper, then the binder – now the combine.

Each in turn is felt to be grand by those concerned. I have described my first potato-planting and how I would have rejoiced to see a machine-planter and also a better method of unploughing them than the old usages. Both have come along – our attention being fixed, each time, on the matter in hand, without any principle being considered. And now we come to the combine. It has arisen as organically and inevitably as all the others. It is as natural an object as the picturesque thresher – and more admirable.

Yet here we pause. Here we reach a climax in our story. For though the combine has evolved as naturally as the other machines its effect is much greater upon the lives of the labourers. At one stroke it does away with harvesting – save for Vera Panchonko at the wheel. The age-long, centuries-old tradition of harvesting, of gathering up the year's work, is taken away from the labourers. In their place the one big machine. We look across the land for human beings, and we see – one engine. And in its wake the bare field: no ricks meet the eye, and no work for thatchers or threshers.

Gazing across, we try and take in the total situation, and we think it fair to ask – Is this fact a little thing, or is it a big thing? In the old, far away days, the whole village came out to take part in the haymaking and harvest. Bit by bit as wages went up and machinery came in, the villagers had to stay at home. Today the process nears completion, when the labourers themselves, the rick-makers, the thatchers, the general workers will stand afar off while Vera Panchonko alone performs, receiving the applause of the State and the Badge of Honour.

Does this constitute a problem? Hardly, in the eyes of the world, for it is not a utilitarian problem. It is a human concern. And though we are all human, and all seek happiness, we only regard problems in the light of utilitarianism, and to attempt otherwise is a battle lost in advance. The human problem here is simply that harvesting is one of the few really satisfying tasks in the world; it is a shared effort, communal work without being stressed as such, and enjoyed even though this may not be admitted. If it is knocked out, the agricultural profession will suffer on the human side. Gradually each man will come to work more and more on his own, neither able nor willing to take part at this, that, and the other tasks in company. There is something gloomy, to me, in the project.

Yet, eager to stick to the realities that will not be altered by such opinions, we must carry our inquiry further and ask again – Where are we then with our problem? And the answer is that, assuming the advent of the combine on a big scale, we see labour-saving carried a long step forward. So the real problem now turns out to be – *leisure*. We have reached the Leisure State. But the moment we say that, we know that it is purely theoretical, a mere theorem no more connected with the given situation than a conclusion by Euclid (who died mad). For we have done nothing to increase leisure while increasing the saving of labour. Some of the workers are simply exchanged for metal, while those who are not exchanged continue to work, as I have remarked in relation to the machine-milker, for exactly the same hours as before. I do not complain of this. I make no tirade against it. It is so much in the nature of things. To adjust matters of this kind, entangled as we all are in a thousand economic wires, will be frightfully difficult – on a par with establishing Justice herself in our midst. That's the first point. But there is a still more unfortunate one. It is, quite simply – that no one wants the Leisure State. All we want is work that suits us. Some of us have this. Nearly all farmers have it, and some labourers. These do not mind how long they work. The others want less long hours. But the idea of much leisure is something from which everyone turns in dismay. You can never make *that* a goal! We are quite unfit for it mentally. This was not always so everywhere. It was not so in the island of Typee before the West found and corrupted it. It is so here. We cannot bear idleness, we cannot fill that empty cup with happiness. Owing to the failure of intellectual leadership, the breakdown of religion, and the short-cuts to culture, our minds are now for the most part demoralized; in any true sense we know nothing, we understand nothing, we study nothing, we see nothing, we listen to nothing, we are incapable of reflection. Hence the hardest toil is a welcome refuge from the horror and tedium of leisure. We loathe a long holiday. We cannot endure pleasure for more than half an hour. Even picnics drive us mad. Agricultural labourers die six months after retiring. Unemployed middle-class people die slowly all their lives. Thus conditioned, where shall we find the *will* to create the Leisure State?

So, without less gloom than before, we turn again and look at the combine. It is splendid. But only from a utilitarian point of view; only for the employers of labour, for a few labourers, and for Vera Panchonko who harvests two hundred and sixty acres in five days.

44. Last Days of Harvest

Meanwhile we assembled on the field in order to cut and carry the remaining fifty acres. At 9 a.m. some clouds gathered in the distance. They spread; they came towards us; the entire sky blackened and it began to rain. There was no break to be seen in the sky anywhere, nor likelihood of one. We had come too late. All was lost. Several thousand pounds' worth would go up in smoke, so late was the hour, so lowly drooping were the ears – down nearly to the very ground. After one hour it cleared up completely and did not rain any more for a week. Worth mentioning, I think. It was like a human touch from above: a decision and then a withdrawal. Good luck like this is forgotten sooner than the bad.

I caught a chill just before we reached this last lap, and so had to do this final business for a week in that condition. Between 2 p.m. and 5.30 p.m. I knew exactly what constituted Paradise and could name its precise geographical position. It consisted in lying down in a sunny windless nook at the side of a copse which impinged upon this field. Unfortunately this knowledge was useless to me, since I couldn't go there.

Putting about twelve acres into each rick, we built four, and I began to feel that I knew what a barley sheaf looked like and could do without seeing another for some time. It was evening again when we were finishing and I had a good view of the big field. In the refreshing, sharp, evening air of autumn I compared the change that had taken place since the spring when I had been there drilling at the beginning of my experience at this farm. It seemed a long time ago since I had stood there feeding the oncoming drills, and I remembered how I had grappled with the horses and wagons and taken off the gate-post, and had had no time for dinner, and how 'E had laughed when I had spoken about the 'little pills of comfort'. How different the scene now, and how much I had experienced since then!

We began to get near the last sheaf. Finally we came to it and pitched it up (we were not using the elevator here), though it nearly fell down again. And as we approached this last sheaf, was there any sense of a grand climax? And when it was pitched up, did someone say – 'Ah, that's the one we've been looking for all this time?' And did 'E say cheerio and give thanks to all and sundry? No. It might have been the first sheaf.

45. Beginning with the Plough

The following day was our new year. We must hurry up now and get things ready for the next harvest.

There remained of course the harvesting of the root crops, swedes, mangolds (we didn't grow any sugar-beet), and above all potatoes. These are steady autumn and winter jobs; in the south of England it is often December before all the potatoes are up.

But my eye was on the plough. I was determined to get that into my hands now. And I did. There was an eleven-acre field of stubble, bounded on one side by a hundred-acre stretch of down which was about to be ploughed-up by Harold; and on the other by that field of kale where I had enjoyed working after haymaking – to which 'E now sent me with a tractor and a three-furrow plough. It was set properly for me in advance, for

I could not possibly do this myself. And without further instructions I set out with it to that far field, along the out-of-the-way lanes and through the gates, feeling pleased with life – for the plough fascinates me.

I reached my field and set to work. I had taken care to acquaint myself with the general practice in operation, and hoped it would work out for me. First I went round the field marking out a headland ten feet from the hedge, for without a headland you cannot have room to turn at the end of each row. Then I struck out a line across the field about twenty yards from the headland. It was an oblong field with a rise in the middle so that only the top half of the hedge was visible from one end. To assist my preliminary strikings-out I took a stick and put a white envelope on to it, went to the middle of the field, took a careful twenty paces out from the side and stuck in my stick, then went on to the end and hung a handkerchief high in the hedge after another careful measurement. This striking-out is an important business, for if your line wobbles or has a bad kink in it, you will find it hard not to continue along the same pattern subsequently. So I set the radiator-cap straight towards my flags and tried to keep it there as I advanced. It didn't keep straight, and when I got to the end I expected to find my line very bad. But to my surprise it wasn't too bad at all. How about the second striking-out when a parallel line is essential if there is to be neat workmanship? Again not bad. Indeed I was luckier in these first attempts than in some subsequent ones. All the same it was an error to have put up that guiding-stick in the middle. You need two sticks, Harold pointed out to me later, but not one in the middle – that is only a hindrance. You want one in the hedge and one just a few yards in front of it. Then if you keep those two, the one covering the other, in your eye from the far end, you can get a better line, and are much less likely to curve out or in as you go along.

This done it was only a question of going up and down my lines until I had come near to filling my parallelogram. Since the plough throws the turf over in one direction only you can't avoid working continually inwards on your figure; so when it became too narrow to turn in, I struck out a new line at another parallel of twenty paces, thus being able to go along the narrow lane in one direction only, while using my new line as the other route.

So much for the question of movement. At first I fumbled the question of depth. I went much too shallow. Then I went too deep and broke a share – that is, the end piece which does the spade-work. But I didn't notice this till I had reached the bottom and hitched-up. Luckily I had some extra shares with me – the kind that only need a piece of wood for a pin, plus a bit of cloth to stabilize it. When I broke another I spotted it before I finished the line, being very anxious about the possible wearing out of the stump. It was curious, this share-breaking, for I was not going really very deep at all, and in fact, later, I had to go less deep than 'E told me to, if I was to preserve my shares. It was not particularly stony ground; but I gathered that there are shares and shares, some given to breaking, some hardly ever breaking.

Apart from this I did not come to grief over anything, and began to feel in command of the situation. But I wondered how the closing up of my first parallelogram would work out. When it became a very narrow lane I saw how far from perfect my striking-out had been. There was a bulge in the middle of the field, and so I found myself finishing the other part before I had finished the middle. The next one was better, but there was room for improvement. My aim was the unbroken single trough which you see running down at given distances across all well-ploughed fields. At dinner-time, at every dinner-time, I walked to another higher field opposite and looked across to examine the work in progress. It looked grand! The troughs didn't seem at all too bad from there, while the furrows, though inclined to curve at the ends, presented a slice of ploughed land which looked on a par with other ploughed fields. I hoped that I wasn't kidding myself about this and that my turn-over was good enough – for I had by no means *buried* all the stubble completely. There was much green on top of the brown. It was not a clean turn-over. This plough had been left out in all weathers and had not been greased. Thus when I started, the blades were very rusty, and the earth stuck to them. This naturally militates against a clean overturn by the turn-furrow. So I got down at the end of every row and knocked away the clinging earth with a spade and then finished off with a long thin steel knife belonging to Victorian days. (By the way, this was the first time I had used a spade since working on a farm – fitting reply to friends who ask perfunctorily, 'How do you like digging?') It was a long time before the soil ceased to cling to my turn-furrows. But at last they began to brighten, then to shine, and at last to blaze like silver when on rising from the earth they caught the sun. When I knocked off for dinner I liked to have the plough in such a position that I could see it glittering in that way.

Soon 'E paid a visit and strode across with his famous strides to the portion that I had done. He had a good look at it, up and down, then said – 'That's good enough for I.' I tried not to look too surprised and pleased. He explained that he didn't want the weeds completely buried, because the couch and charlock could not then be so easily harrowed out.

My furrows were inclined to curve at the end for a very simple reason. When you reach the end of the line you must turn the tractor of course, and turn it quickly in order to avoid running into the hedge or getting so close to it that one wheel gets stuck. But just when this turning is necessary you must reach back and pull the rope that connects with the hitching-up apparatus which lifts the blades clear of the earth – and this latter must not be done until you have really reached the end of the line. But there is a strong tendency to start turning the wheel of the tractor too soon, and so you get your curve. Yet this can be overcome by going slow and not getting flustered. The moment I most enjoyed was when, after having swung round from the hedge and got the tractor's right wheel into the groove for going up the next line, I pulled the rope again so that the blades crashed down into the soil once more and immediately that solid substance turned into three fluid waves of earth that rose and fell, and having fallen, lay still again. It is most

unfortunate that one is placed in front of the plough with a
tractor, for one needs to watch the work for utilitarian reasons
and wants to watch it for aesthetic ones. And if you do this for
too long at a time while only the left hand guides the tractor, a
crook or a bad curve is the result. I did my best to *mend* such
curves by treatment each time I reached the place, but though
the spot looked obvious from the distance it disappeared as I
approached it, of course. On some occasions I threw down a
handkerchief to mark it. I should add that in this matter a
certain amount depends upon the tractor. A really steady one,
not too ancient, will go along with its right wheel in the furrow
without need of a guiding hand (especially uphill). Thus I often
observed Harold *walking* behind or beside his plough, while the
tractor quietly went ahead by itself. A cheering spectacle, I
always felt. Man is often the slave of machines, as also of cows
and of sheep. But not here.

It might be asked why there is so much fuss made about a
straight furrow. Apart from the initial necessity to strike out as
straight as possible and make your parallelogram true, why
should it matter if lines curve slightly here and there, or even
bulge badly at places, seeing that the furrows will presently be
knocked to pieces under the harrow? If you ask a farmer this
question he will give utilitarian answers: it makes for better
harrowing or it saves time. True enough, no doubt; but I think
the real reason is aesthetic. It is the tribute that Agriculture pays
to Art. It is felt that there is virtue in a straight line, not to be
found in one that wobbles even slightly. This calls for concentration and skill. Where there is skill there is art. Where
there is art there is passion for the absolute. The straight furrow
is the labourer's acknowledgement in the validity of art for art's
sake.

46. Horse Ploughing

These were the days! Now I never looked forward to dinner hour nor to knocking off in the evening. (Later, when ploughing in December, I was downright annoyed the way it got dark so soon, and I went on until I couldn't see what I was doing.) I recalled a remark made to me by Morgan at my first farm, when he was engaged in ploughing a pleasant six-acre field. 'I would rather be doing this than anything,' he said. 'I'd rather do this than go to any cinema.' Morgan was not an intellectual, not a man of ideas; he was a very level-headed, unpoetical sort of chap. He was just making a statement. There are some writers today who, with the cause of agriculture deeply at heart and worried by the very real problem of mechanization, tend to refer to tractor-drivers with a scarcely veiled sneer. Soulless fellows merely 'fiddling about with machines' seems to be their idea of such men. A justified view in some cases. I know a fair number of agricultural workers: for as a member of the Home Guard I met a lot more than those on this farm; some delightful men, but also, I admit, some tractor-drivers who were absolute louts who didn't see an inch further than their nuts and screws. But it is wrong to sneer at tractor-drivers as a body on that account. Anyway, it is not the tractor that is wrong. It is all a question of the attitude of mind brought to the work – it is the attitude of mind every time! The tractor-plough is a superb instrument to look at when stationary, and to manage when in action.

Yet at this very point I want to say a word about horse-ploughing. I have had experience of it also. At this stage in my narrative I cannot infringe upon the unity of place and time which I have imposed upon myself, by introducing any lengthy account of an experience elsewhere. But, with the reader's permission, I may say here that I have acted as horse-ploughman elsewhere for a season from September to December, which days were the happiest in my life. If I were asked the straight question whether I would prefer to plough, *always*, with horse or tractor, I might find it difficult to answer, since I very much enjoy working with a tractor and a three-furrow plough. Yet nothing can really compare with the simple, strenuous horse-work. For one thing there is no other physical work to compare with it: there is not a game in the world that can make you feel half so good. And, fascinating as the machine work is, you do not hold the plough. But it is just this *grasping* of the handles of the plough, both arms stretched out fully and often putting out full strength, that somehow is the very top-notch of satisfaction. Ah, I say, even as I write these lines, give me the plough-handles that I may grip them and strike out across the field! release me from this chair! (for it is so much easier to do a thing than write about it, so much easier to perform than to reveal). And to be able to see your work directly in front of you all the time, to watch your wave rise up and fall to silence in your wake – this you cannot get the other way. But again I say, it is the grasping of the handles for which there is no substitute, no compensation. Then your feet are upon the earth, your hands upon the plough. You seem to be holding more than the plough, and treading across more than this one field: you are holding together the life of mankind, you are walking through the fields of time. This work has always been done. Whatever happens this can be done. Machine-power may fail for fuel. This power will never fail. In the day of calamity, in the day of battle, all men must cease from work and rise to slay. All save the plough-man on the fields of Normandy. When D-Day came and battle raged upon the beaches; when the sky was filled with fighters and the land was lashed with fire, that Nameless Man took out his plough and did his work and turned his furrow in the midst of all. And when the brief hurricane of mortal men had passed, he was still there.

47. While Ploughing

Meanwhile the tractor-pulled plough is a very good second best. The exhilaration is not quite of the same kind, but it is exhilarating none the less. It is absurd to denigrate our own amazing creativity. To have a great metal horse in front of you, over which you have complete control, knowing that it will take that steep rise in the field in its stride, while you look back and watch the three waves falling on your ribbed and rolling beach – who could tire of that?

Ever since one memorable day, when standing on a rise in Devon, I saw in a field below the white leaves blowing round a ploughman, I have looked out for seagulls following a plough, for there are few more pleasing sights. I frequently saw them following Harold. Now they would come to me.

But this was anticipating. They did not seem keen on coming in my direction. Instead, I got numerous starlings, rooks, and crows, brown and black birds in whom I had no interest. However, one day the seagulls were kind enough to come over. They didn't do a great deal of swirling round me. But when I reached the end of my row on one occasion I looked back and saw the whole lot of them standing in the furrow right across the field, in perfect line, dressed by the right. I was satisfied with this parade.

Indeed I was well satisfied in every way on this work. The day was too short. Sometimes I had to attend to Harold and give him assistance, for he was ploughing-up the Down over the hedge, and occasionally went right into a hole and could not get out. I had to go over with my tractor and pull him out. Otherwise I carried on happily without any interruption. Here would I gladly remain, I said to myself, islanded from that world which is too much with us; let all men, all women, and all children, do what they like, I've got my tractor, my plough, my field, and am content. Having wandered in the realms of thought, I could bring the roving mind to rest; having journeyed between New York and Warsaw across the countries of the world, I could now discover one patch of ground at home; nor had I any need of games – for here my work was play, my play was work.

This field was on a considerable rise. I could see the village below and a long way across the land. We plan our habitations; we design; and the result is sometimes good. Yet how often one is struck by the beauties that are undesigned, where there was no prearranged pattern, yet all is pattern. We planned the position of the Manor House; but we could not have hoped to arrange matters so that the red creeper would climb just to catch that last sunset ray, nor so arrange the growth of yellow flowers that they would lean against the high green field beyond. We planned the position of the church, but now it is locked in Nature's arm. I looked down and saw the double beauty of man's deliberations clothed in all the careless forms of earth.

More often I looked upwards at the great cathedral piles of cloud that passed along the winter sky, extravagant and erring shapes radiantly rimmed or quite ensilvered by the sun. Once, a broad shaft of light, let out from the clouds, beamed down upon the distant land. It lit up the ground on which it fell and slowly moved from field to field, from hedge to hedge, as if looking for something – like a giant searchlight reversed. Then it went out suddenly, as if switched off. The clouds above increased in splendour. Ah, it is a land, a land up there, that does belong to us though raised so high! token of some great happiness that yet shall be fulfilled, the hope and promise written in every heart!

When the dusk fell and I could go on no longer, I often caught the sharp whiff of smell coming from the upturned earth. Scent is a mighty marvel. What it is I do not know. But I knew what this smell was, which is the most intoxicating of all. It was – Fertility: it was life itself coming across to me in pure sensation – the *odour* of eternal resurrection from the dead.

48. View of the Whole

The mornings were cold and dim now as I cycled through the village, past the copper-beech and the chestnut trees. Their way of life had fallen into the sere and yellow leaf, and then, obedient to the later ruling, no leaves at all. The clawing fingers of the ash, the bare pale branches of the beech, the high tracery of the elms, all spoke of winter. And for us this meant threshing, and lots of it. We must now take down the ricks again.

Put like that, by the way, it does make the combine seem rather obvious, doesn't it? The whole-hogging anti-combiner would have to say that the proper thing to do is to put up ricks in order to take them down. It is the actual logic of that view, I fear. We cannot say that the goal of life is work when the work is not necessary: otherwise, as I think Dr Maude Royden once remarked, instead of getting ten men to dig a trench with spades you could get a hundred to do so with spoons ... But let me not fall into further speculation on this, but discretely tiptoe, as Donald McCullough would say, on to the next.

There was certainly enough threshing for us to do, several months' work in fact, after all that harvesting. Thus again we assembled the famous rig-out and got going on the work of separation. Once more we unlocked the elaborate cupboard and took out the bread. Once more the untiring jaw was fed, and the bags bulged behind – ten, twenty, forty, eighty. When the actual day's threshing was over, it didn't mean that we had finished. The machine still went on for a long time dealing with the remaining bits, while we fiddled about clearing up, the lack of a definite thing to do being sometimes quite maddening. I was always glad when we got down to the formidable business of lifting the rows of sacks on to the lorry. As a solo sack-lifter I'm not only bad but a shirker: but in partnership with a mate I count myself as adept at it – and so never minded this heavy finish.

One morning I accompanied Jimmy in the lorry to the neighbouring town's railway station where we deposited a load of sacks. It was pleasant to find myself amongst the cheerful workers in the station yard and see the place from that inner angle. It was good to put the sacks in the truck. Where are they going? I asked. No one knew. Nor cared. Nor did I. But I was glad to connect them with the truck and have in my mind's eye the continuity from seed to truck and the number of operations that take place between that beginning and this ending when these sacks go away into the blue.

Robert, though rick-maker in general, was after all the shepherd, and it was not convenient for him to come out in the mornings if there was anyone else to do the work. So it happened that I started building the straw-ricks myself. Being an unpractical man, I am at intervals more practical than the practical, and I made a good job of it. Thus Robert didn't need to come out, and when he did late in the afternoon, he didn't interfere with me, but fed the thresher, subordinating the carter to string-cutter.

I was very pleased with this arrangement, of course. I had no assistant on the rick; but it is a fallacy to suppose that two are necessary for straw, just as it is an illusion to suppose that eleven men or even eight are really necessary for threshing. We started with the barley and finished it off first. Very short, light, slippery stuff, but I managed without mishap and without props. Robert, looking at one, said – 'No one could say you can't build a rick now, I allow.' A remark which he need not have made, and which endeared him to me. (Next summer he put no opposition in the way of my making a corn rick – and this time there was no question of failure from start to finish.)

There were some stoppages owing to something going wrong with the thresher. The chief members of the company went down on all fours under it, pushing and grappling with its inner mysteries, all quite beyond me. The good of being on the rick was that I didn't have to busy myself with something or pretend to look wise. Ejaculations would come up from below – 'Let it bide' or 'Leave very well alone' or 'That's some of it, I expect' – this last from 'E. 'That's some of it' was a favourite expression of his. In thus suggesting that *some* of the trouble had been located, he not only encouraged further research but showed a proper scepticism about it being all of it.

The barley finished, we went for the wheat. After a couple of ricks we began to use a trusser. The trusser is a machine which, placed between the thresher and the elevator, ties up the straw into fair-sized sheaves, after which they proceed up the elevator. You can sell straw better that way than loose – (and better still, I believe, when it is baled, that is, parcelled into two-hundredweight bricks). This called for a new technique and 'E expressed doubt as to whether I could do it properly. This put me on my mettle, and I soon got hold of the idea, found it in fact a good deal easier in the end than ricking loose wheat-straw, and up went my buildings, still unpropped. I derived what may seem a childish pleasure in looking round the fields and say-ing to myself – I put that there; and that; and that. It gave me particular pleasure to see them from the road on a bus when coming back from a visit to London and its vastly different scene. And I wondered whether those who journey up and down the roads notice how today there are two ricks on a field and tomorrow only one in a different place, larger and more light in colour. In days gone by I would not have noticed it. But from henceforth, wherever I go, through whatever land, I shall know what is going on beyond the hedge, beyond the railway line, and I shall realize the ardours that have been bestowed upon the silent scene by the unwitnessed workmen of the fields.

Again I rejoiced to rise on my pedestal and have a view of the whole. When I was fairly high up I could see over the greater portion of the farm. And as I gazed across, I realized that I had had dealings with every field: there I had harrowed and rolled, there couched, there hoed, there made hay, there drilled, there ploughed – and here now were my ricks. I did not feel a be-ginner or amateur any longer. I was well on the inside of the wall. I would no longer make idiotic mistakes: not now would I leave a prong lying on the ground or throw it down the wrong way up from a rick; nor walk on the wrong side of a horse and take a gate-post away; nor fail to examine the plugs of a tractor that wouldn't start; nor be absent-minded about implements I

was using; nor drop things as I went across the farm; nor try
and lift sacks in the wrong way and put them down untidily;
nor start hiling up and down instead of round the field – nor
wear shoes! Standing there with the straw waterfall well in
hand, I could look down on the company below feeling very
much part of the proceedings and by no means an outsider.

I could see from where I stood the changing scene of the
unchanging motion of the year. That hay rick over there, like a
great cake carefully sliced, had been already half-cut for the
cows. That straw-rick in the next field, left over from last year,
was steadily getting lower, and like a punctured balloon was
shrinking every month more and more until it was but a shadow
of its former self. The potatoes had been lifted and clamped
beside their field. The mangold field was half-pulled, the once
thin red roots were now bulging balls in tinted red and yellow
shades that no potter ever could come near. Beyond that hedge
the winter wheat was shining now, so fair, so green against the
dark leafless trees and the pale blue winter sky. And in a field of
stubble a crop of clover was rising fresh and strong. It was good
to see it there, bright witness of the rapid round – green youth
beside the stumped and paupered stalks of age; new life climbing on the knees of death; the never resting tireless toil of earth.
Down below me the sacks were filling fast. In my mind's eye it
was only yesterday that we had sown this field – then the green
light; then the yellow; then the brown; and so the fall. Now
seeds were pouring out, many times more numerous than those
which had been sown. Thus the Circle, thus the Order, confined
within the little space before me – type of all of Nature's vast,
relentless roll.

And as I stood upon my pile, this year, and the next year,
looking across the land, I looked also across the centuries. This
was the eternal tale. This did not alter and would not stop. The
historical tapestries hung across the streets of fame, figuring the
pride of kings, the frenzy of tyrants, the clash of nations, and
the fall of empires, held no meaning here. The same work went
on in each country regardless of whatever drama was being
staged by the men in cities. So it would continue as surely as

Nature continues to unfold in spite of all the roaring wrack beyond the fence. Those men below at work upon the thresher, whom I have not sought to glorify – yet are they not glorified in these natural tasks? – support the conditions for the theatre of history, but they work outside the drama. Civilizations rise, fluctuate, and fall, men reaching out for expression now in one direction, now in another; at one time, turning their gaze towards the perfect commonwealth, the greatest good, the glory of thought, and the rose of art, they raise a noble culture; and at another time riding recklessly on into the bitter darkness of their own night and the cold bleakness of massacre and crime, they are driven shamefully back along the fields of their pride. But here is the thing that remains constant. Here is the order that does not break, Here shall the husbandmen of all the world, using this device or that, this machine or another, remain obedient to the increase and faithful to the unfolding, from generation to generation and from age to age.

From this lofty stool on which I stood, I looked down upon the Great Highway that led from the cities to the sea. It ran beside our largest field for some distance. All day long and every day the Military dashed past in lorries, in jeeps, in tanks – ceaselessly every day. The clatter of the tanks was something awful. They passed in long lines, these the chariots of our day, their helmeted riders aloft in the turrets. I sometimes lifted my hand in friendly salute, but there was not much response. The division between us was too great for communication. Only a thin fence, but what a gulf! On this side was life everlasting: and over there – History roaring past. It simply passed us by. We were bound upon the field: and their only freedom was the hard, long, ribbon of road, their destiny and their doom. They could not possibly leap the fence and join us. They could not pause in their trampling nor turn aside from their path. They could not break from the bonds of history. They could not pass from that which was temporal to this which was eternal. On and on they clattered, making for the beaches and the sea, for danger, destruction, torment, death. From the field it seemed appalling, fantastic. But the charioteers were not appalled.

Truly we *are* such stuff as dreams are made on, entrancingly protected from the agony of truth! Already crowned with the laurels and the bays of sacrifice, they were lifted up into the realm of a dream, raised high above the material world and the earthly clods of care ... Marvelling at Mankind, I turned my gaze back to the Earth. And presently as often happened late in the afternoon, this traffic ceased. We worked on in the sudden silence. Militarism had faded out – as if it had never been.

BOOK II
DOWN TO EARTH

Reading through this book of mine, and subsequent ones of the same kind, I see that my approach has the merit of being highly unoriginal. This is a great asset for me. I need never go out of fashion. For I have never been in the fashion. I am always with it. I came upon the following only a few days ago by John de Dondis, a fourteenth-century sage, who after declaring that he was disinclined to attach too much importance to wholly explicable relationships, added:

I have learned from long experience that there is nothing that is not marvellous and that the saying of Aristotle is true – that in every natural phenomenon there is something wonderful, nay, in truth, many wonders. We are born and placed among wonders and surrounded by them, so that to whatever object the eye first turns, the same is wonderful and full of wonders, if only we will examine it for a while.

– JOHN STEWART COLLIS, 1973

PREFACE

The book of Nature lies closed before us. We look round, and everything seems more or less incomprehensible. At least that is my experience. I have come to the stage when, awake at last to the actual existence of the visible world, I also realize the shortness of life, and hasten to acquaint myself with a few of the facts before it is too late and I am dead before I have ever been alive.

The good of it is we can open the book if we choose. That company of devoted and gifted men, called scientific specialists, has placed a great many facts at our disposal. The time has come for me to take advantage of their labours. For many years my approach had been from the other end. For many years I sought for truth, or if you like, God. I did not find it. I found beauty instead. I then understood what was meant by the saying that beauty is truth and truth beauty. I had come to see the whole. Then I was ready to see the part. Now, today, I seek the part so as to enhance my vision of the whole. Facts have become my chief stimulus.

I never really got down to the facts until I got down to the earth. I date my resolve and my practice from the time when I became a labourer on the land. It cannot possibly be necessary for everyone, but for me it was essential to come in contact with a thing through work before I could actually see it! Finding myself confronted with the worm or the potato, with the ant or the seed, I was forced to ask myself how much I really knew of these mysteries. Not until I did ask this was I aware that I could hardly answer the simplest question. There may be some others in a like case. If so, they might care to join me.

But I must not pretend that facts are the chief thing about this book, either for myself or for the reader. Quite the contrary. As I have hinted above, facts are fascinating to me only because they heighten my sense of significance. I do not believe in 'the pursuit of knowledge for its own sake'. That phrase strikes me as silly. My pursuit of facts is for the sake of imagination. I always want to relate my physics with metaphysics. This is being very philosophical, you may say. Certainly, Philosophy is the only thing I am fundamentally interested in. For what is a philosopher? Only a man who likes to see the whole. Only a man who refuses to keep things in watertight compartments, and who seeks to relate his knowledge with a vision of life. If this is the poetic attitude also, let us not quarrel with words. There are many facts in this volume – but already I have forgotten most of them. I couldn't pass an examination on them. That doesn't worry me; it is merely a question of memory – which can be refreshed at any minute. The point is I have grasped the facts (and of course I do remember the chief ones). Having grasped them, then thought followed, and emotion followed, and I drew nearer to the mystery. Surely synthesis should be our aim now, and in the future. Only the specialists should specialize. There are now huge wads of knowledge about most things. We should learn to digest it. It is time we learnt to relate our knowledge organically and to see the significance of facts. Knowledge for its own sake is not more worth acquiring than bread for its own sake.

It will be seen from the above remarks and from all the pages that follow, that I stand a long way off from those mystics who declare, with Mr Aldous Huxley in his *Perennial Philosophy*, that it is only 'in imageless contemplation that the soul comes to knowledge of reality'. My position is at the side of the contemporary Indian seer, Sri Aurobindo, who claims that 'the touch of Earth is always invigorating to the son of earth, even when he seeks a supra-physical knowledge'. And he adds that perhaps the metaphysical can only be really mastered in its *fullness* 'when we keep our feet firmly on the physical'. I could not agree more. We are really lost if we fail to make these connections. There is nothing new about it; but today our minds should be freer to make the synthesis than when the great mystic Jakob Boehme wrote – 'View this world diligently and consider what manner of fruits, sprouts, and branches grow out of the Salitter of the earth, from trees, plants, herbs, roots, flowers, oil, wine, corn, and whatever else there is that thy heart can find out; all is a type of the heavenly pomp.'

Such is the trend of this volume. Nevertheless I have written up to no system – I hope. In setting out on my discoveries I have never aimed to say anything particular, and often have been well content to let the facts speak for themselves. When imagination has stirred and the same thought has flowered on several occasions from different stems, I have been glad to repeat myself, and thus support the view from more than one angle. Consequently there is a considerable degree of subjectivity even in Part One of this book. I can scarcely apologize for the very thing that gives me the necessary heat to pursue my studies and which is in fact my particular contribution. I must leave it to others to popularize science, they do it more thoroughly, and that is not my aim. In Part Two, when dealing with trees and forestry, my method is still more subjective and reflective. The inquiry called for a technique less taut than in Part One, for a slower pace, and an approach somewhat similar to that of *While Following the Plough.*

A word with regard to Authority. If I used jargon I could afford to be inaccurate, since no one could be quite sure what I had said. Since I like to make things clear, I have been careful to acquire my facts with all the thoroughness and conscientiousness of an ignorant man. This does not mean that sometimes I have not been compelled to choose between two schools of thought, or that the absolutely up-to-date finding is necessarily on my page. I can only claim that I have said nothing without authority, and indeed it will be obvious that many of the facts are too fantastic to have been invented. But when I have felt that a reference was called for, I have given it.

JOHN STEWART COLLIS

PART ONE

DOWN TO EARTH

---

1. The Potato

I am anxious to say a word about the potato. But will the Muse fail me? We sing the flower, we sing the leaf: we seldom sing the seed, the root, the tuber. Indeed the potato enters literature with no very marked success. True, William Cobbett abused it, and Lord Byron made it interesting by rhyming it with Plato; but for the most part it enters politics more easily and has done more to divide England from Ireland than Cromwell himself.

Yet if we praise the potato we praise ourselves, for it is an extreme example of artificiality. 'The Earth, in order that she might urge us to labour, the supreme law of life,' says Fabre, 'has been but a harsh stepmother. For the nestling bird she provides abundant food; to us she offers only the fruit of the Bramble and the Blackthorn.' Not everyone realizes this, he said. Some people even imagine that the grape is today just like that from which Noah obtained the juice that made him drunk; that the cauliflower, merely with the idea of being pleasant, has of its own accord evolved its creamy-white head; that turnips and carrots, being keenly interested in human affairs, have always of their own motion done their best for man; and that the potato, since the world was young, wishing to please us, has gone through its curious performance. The truth is far otherwise. They were all uneatable at first: it is we who have forced them to become what they now are. 'In its native countries,' says Fabre, 'on the mountains of Chili and Peru, the Potato, in its wild state, is a meagre tubercle, about the size of a Hazelnut. Man extends the hospitality of his garden to this sorry weed; he plants it in nourishing soil, tends it, waters it, and makes it fruitful with the sweat of his brow. And there from year to year, the Potato thrives and prospers; it gains in size and

219

nourishing properties, finally becoming a farinaceous tuber the size of our two fists.'

During my first year in the agricultural world I decided to have a good look at the potato and carefully watch its operations. I had never done this before. In fact I had little idea how potatoes actually arrive. With me it is always a question of either knowing a thing or not knowing it, of knowing it from A to Z or not at all; the man who knows a little about everything, from A to B, is incomprehensible to me. Thus I could approach the potato with the clear head of ignorance.

I took one in my hand and offered it my attention. It looked like a smooth stone; a shapeless shape; so dull in appearance that I found it hard to look at it without thinking of something else. I took a knife and cut it in two. It had white flesh extremely like an apple. But it had nothing in the middle, no seedbox, no seeds. How then can it produce more of itself? Well, the season had now come to put it down into the earth. So we planted them into the prepared field, at a distance of one foot from each other – plenty of space in which laboratory they could carry out any work they desired.

In about a fortnight's time I decided to dig up one and see if anything had happened. The first I came to had not changed in appearance at all. From the second, however, two white objects, about the length of a worm, were protruding. On a human face, I reflected, such protuberances would have seemed like some dreadful disease. One of them looked like a little white mouse trying to get out. I covered up these phenomena again and left them to it, wondering what they would do next.

After a few weeks I again visited this earthly laboratory to see how things were getting on. I found that the protuberances had become much longer and had curled round at their ends – now white snakes coming out of the humble solid. They had curly heads like purplish knots, and some of these knots had half opened into a series of green ears. And now there was another addition: at the place where these stems, as we may now call them, came out of the potato, a network had been set up, of strings, as it were, connecting the outfit with the soil. These, the roots, went downwards seeking the darkness of the earth, while every stem rose up to seek the light. But as yet there was no indication where or how new potatoes could appear.

During these early weeks the surface of the field showed no sign that anything was going on underneath. Later the whole brown surface began to change into rows of green – the light-seeking stalks had risen into the air and unfurled their leaves. As the weeks passed, and the months, these little green bushes grew in size and complexity until in late July they were all flowering – and a very pretty field it then looked. As all flowers have fruit, so had these – potato fruits, of course. But not the ones we eat.

Even after the green rows had appeared above-board and I made a further examination below I still did not see where the crop of potatoes was going to come from. Eventually the problem cleared itself up. I found them forming at the end of the network of roots. A few of the roots began to swell at their extremity – first about the size of a bird's egg, then a baby's shoe, getting larger and larger until some of them were four times the size of the original potato planted in the ground. And here we come to the curious thing about potatoes. The substance which grows at the end of the root is not itself a root. It is a *branch*. It is not a root, the botanists say, because roots do not bear buds and do not bear leaves, while this, the potato, does have buds and does have leaves (in the shape of scales). It is a subterranean branch, swollen and misshapen, storing up food for its buds; and botanists, no longer having the courage to call it a branch, call it a tuber. So when we plant a potato we are not planting a seed, we are not planting a root; we are planting a branch from whose gateways, called 'eyes', roots reach down and stalks reach up.

To complete the circle, what happens to the original potato? It conforms to the rule of eternal return by virtue of which the invisible becomes visible, and the visible takes on invisibility. It darkens, it softens, it becomes a squashy brown mash, and finally is seen no more. I used to enjoy taking it up in my hand when I saw it lying on the ground looking like an old leather purse. It had performed a remarkable act. Now its work was done. All the virtue had gone out of it. It had given its life to the green stalks above and the tubers below. Here I seemed to see a familiar sight in nature; many things coming from one thing, much from little, even something out of nothing. This is what we seem to see. Yet it is not so. True, the original potato started the business going, sending down those roots and sending up those stalks; but they in their turn built the building. The earth is not a solid; it is chiefly gas. The air is not thin; it is massed with food. Those roots sucked gases from the earth, those leaves sucked gases from the sky, and the result was the visible, hard, concrete potato. When we eat a potato we eat the earth, and we eat the sky. It is the law of nature that all things are all things. That which does not appear to exist today is tomorrow hewn down and cast into the oven. Nature carries on by taking in her own washing. That is Nature's economy, contrary to political economy; so that he who cries 'Wolf! Wolf!' is numbered amongst the infidels. 'A mouse,' said Walt Whitman, 'is enough to stagger sextillions of infidels.' Or a potato. What is an infidel? One who lacks faith. What creates faith? A miracle. How then can there be a faithless man found in the world? Because many men have cut off the nervous communication between the eye and the brain. In the madness of blindness they are at the mercy of intellectual nay-sayers, theorists, theologians, and other enemies of God. But it doesn't matter; in spite of them, faith is reborn whenever anyone chooses to take a good look at anything – even a potato.

2. The Worm

I have heard it said more than once that the reason why there are now more wire-worms afflicting the crops than in the past is because there are more tractors. The idea being that since the tractor-driven plough turns over three or four furrows at a time as against the horse-plough's one furrow, the result is that the birds get far fewer troughs in which to find worms. Thus more worms are left in the soil.

It is an attractive theory. There is something cheering in the knowledge that Nature always hits back. It is metaphysically inspiring, if physically discouraging. Everything in nature has a meaning and a purpose. Everything is necessary to the universal scheme, every germ, every microbe, every pest. When anything ceases to serve the harmony it dies out. When man threatens the harmony he is attacked in one way or another. Those who dislike the advent of tractors see the multiplication of the wire-worm as an example of Nature's revenge.

Unfortunately there is a difficulty about this latter case. We cannot suppose that the seagulls and other birds who eat the worms are always agriculturally-minded. We cannot count on their patriotism in eating only wire-worms and leaving all the earth-worms. And if wire-worms do harm to the soil, earth-worms do a great deal of good. In so far as the birds have less chance to eat them we could argue with equal plausibility that the soil thereby gains by the tractor.

Eyeless, legless, faceless, earless, voiceless, the earth-worm is not much to look at – a mere squirming piece of flesh. Yet with its powerful muscles, its two stomachs (one inside and one outside), and its false teeth, it is able to carry out remarkable works.

These worms are the only creatures that eat the earth. They eat clay. They do not digest it neat like a piece of chocolate. As it passes through they extract from it organic matter in the shape of ova, larvae, spores of cryptogamic plants, and micrococci. That is the first reason why they swallow earth. They swallow it also in order to make their underground passages, their burrows – casting the material upwards into delicate little towers. This continuous mining has prodigious results. Charles Darwin estimated that fifty thousand worms often inhabit an acre of ground, and subsequent counts have put the figure at a million or more in rich soil. Since each worm ejects from twelve to twenty ounces a year, we find that from seven to eighteen tons

of earth are frequently thrown up every year on an acre. Thus
stones lying about on an uncultivated field will sink at the rate
of two inches a year, so that in thirty years you can gallop a
horse over what was once stony ground without its hoofs striking a single stone. Sometimes there are so many worms at work
that a narrow stone path across a lawn will sink so quickly that
a gardener cannot control it. Some of the slabs of Stonehenge
have already gone down a good way, though it will take time
before the rest of the ruins disappear from sight.

The worm is a friend to archaeologists who owe to it the
preservation of many ancient objects. Coins, gold ornaments,
stone implements are buried and stored for future inspection.
Not long ago a neglected field near Shrewsbury which was
ploughed-up revealed arrow-heads used at the Battle of Shrewsbury. The war-time ploughing-up has brought to light many
new objects – a bomb which fell near my neighbour's house
blew a Roman knife into his bedroom window. But that is only
the minor museum-work of worms: villas, abbeys, pavements,
walls, even towns have been carefully preserved by them. The
remains of a large Roman villa at Chedworth, found under a
wood by a gamekeeper digging for rabbits in 1877, with coins
lying about dated A.D. 350; the tessellated pavement of Beaulieu
Abbey; eighteen chambers of a Roman house at Brading in the
Isle of Wight, with coins dated A.D. 337; the walls, tesserae,
pottery, and coins of Roman Emperors from A.D. 133 to 361 dug
up at Abinger marking another villa deserted fifteen hundred
years ago; the town of Silchester with a wall eighteen feet high
extending a mile and a half round a space of a hundred acres –
all these, according to established authority, had been let down
into the earth by the action of worms.

Another by-product of their activities consists in lowering
the hills and widening the valleys of the land. Wherever there is
a tumulus, an embankment, a hill, a slope, a valley which is not
made of gravel or pure sand, worm castings will be thrown up,
and then through the action of rain and wind their towers of
earth will roll to the bottom so that gradually the mound is
lessened. Small effects have vast results in the calendar of

nature, and the eye that could keep watch across the passage of centuries might see the Sussex Downs and the Dorset slopes vanishing through the movement of worms.

Their general work is more ambitious. They create soil. Everyone knows that rock is really solid soil. When it becomes broken up and mixed with vegetable ash it is called clay. Worms, by means of acids and salts which they digestively generate, carry on a steady decomposition of rock. They go further; they wear down the small particles of rock which other agencies can do little to diminish, by grinding them in their gizzards with beads of glass and angular fragments of bricks or tiles which they employ as millstones or artificial teeth in order to crush the earth that they so largely consume. At the same time they add to the organic matter in the soil by the astonishing number of half-decayed leaves which they draw into their burrows to a depth of two or three inches. These leaves are moistened, torn into shreds, partially digested, and intimately mingled with earth – thus giving vegetable mould its uniform dark tint. This mould differs from subsoil by the absence of fragments and particles of stone which are larger than a worm can swallow.

It is pleasant to reflect when we look out upon an expanse of land with a fine superficial mould that it has all been swallowed by worms, that it has all passed and will pass again through the bodies of worms. For during the course of this journey the finer particles are sifted from the coarser, the whole mixed with vegetable debris, and saturated with intestinal secretions, so that the ground is prepared as by a gardener for the growth of fibrous-rooted plants and seedlings of all sorts. The soil is turned over and over, it is in perpetual motion. Thus the worms plough, and thus they harrow. They drain the land also; their burrows which often penetrate to a depth of five or six feet provide a vast drainage system. And yet another thing: they make way for aerial penetration, and they greatly facilitate the downward passage of moderate roots. They go further: they specially nourish those roots with the humus that lines their burrows like a cemented tunnel.

It would seem that before we proclaim that it is a bad thing for tractors to aid the preservation of wire-worms, we should consider whether it is not a good thing that they should aid the preservation of earth-worms. But it is possible that some people are uninstructed concerning this monarch among animals. I have not observed golfers flinch at the spectacle of thousands of dead worms on the fairway poisoned for their pleasure. Some people know nothing of the worm save that it 'will turn' under certain unspecified circumstances. Others, when they have cut one in half, honestly feel that they have performed an act of creation, making two creatures proceed where there had been only one before. There are no songs in its name. True, the poet who bent the most concentrated gaze upon the tiger, and saw that in it the fire of life burned brightest, was also he who, looking down into the damp, dark earth, perceived the worm and said – 'Art thou a worm? Image of weakness, art thou but a worm? I see thee like an Infant wrappèd in the Lily's leaf.' Yet even he may not have known that the worm is more powerful than the tiger, that by its vast operations in ploughing, in harrowing, in levelling, in draining, in airing, in manuring, and even in creating soil, it adds to the wealth of nations and governs the destiny of man; and that given time and condition it could remove a mountain and cause a city to vanish from the face of the earth.

3. Contemplation upon Ants

I took a horse and cart and a good sharp spade and went across to a field that had to be ploughed up. It had been neglected for many years and now contained a large number of ant-hills. To promote easier ploughing the removal of these hillocks was ne- cessary, and this was my task. My method was simple: first a hard blow downwards with the perpendicular blade through the centre of the mound; then a similar thrust at right angles across that cut; after which a few digs at the base enabled me to take out large slices and throw them on to the cart. When it was full

I drove it away and dumped the lot into a pit. It took me some weeks, working all day, before I had cleared that field of ants.

And the odd thing is that I can say this, I can write it down here, and it will be accepted by the reader as a perfectly ordinary proceeding, a normal and rather tedious piece of agricultural work. That is all it is, provided we do not pause to think. I do not advocate that we should thus pause: for how could Man face reality, the reality of what he daily does, and yet pursue his way? When I did pause, sometimes, to consider what I was doing on that field I could not fail to feel the enormity of my act. The shining blade crashed down through the centre of a city built up with skill and labour; the inhabitants were thrown into confusion; then another flash and crash of the blade, and another, till bits of the home were flying through the air – thus my work for hour after hour and day after day.

Sometimes I stooped down to watch the effect of this spade-work, and saw the ants hurrying about desperately in every direction, most of them carrying white parcels considerably larger than themselves, going a little way in one direction then turning back at an obstruction and trying another route. Then my spade got to work again, sometimes neatly taking up a whole hill and chucking it into the cart. My power of destruction over this ant-world was really prodigious, as if a giant with legs the height of Snowdon and arms as long as the Sussex Downs, were to throw London away in an hour or so. I wondered whether even the ant-specialists (who I now began to study) could really imagine just how these ants would begin to restore order upon the heterogeneous conglomeration into which their planned cities had been thrown.

Mankind has often been depressed and sometimes alarmed by ants. Schopenhauer, never notable for excessive cheerfulness, was much pained by contemplation of the Australian bull-dog ant. For if it is cut in two it fights with itself, a battle begins between the head and the tail. The head seizes the tail with its teeth, and the tail defends itself ferociously by stinging the head. Such battles have been known to last for half an hour, until the combatants died or were dragged away by other ants, themselves perhaps appalled by the spectacle. Still, Schopenhauer might have been cheered by the thought that at any rate here pain, as we know it, was absent, just as it was surely absent in that spider reported by Forel to have made a meal of its own leg amputated by itself, and in those caterpillars who occasionally devour their own tails.

Yet a creature like that Australian ant which can be increased by division is phenomenal, since animals differ from plants precisely in the fact that when you divide plants you multiply them, but when you divide animals you destroy them. That bull-dog ant was behaving like a curious kind of plant; but of course its double life was as brief as it was brutal. It is true that the head of an ant does not represent its capital in the same way as our heads do, and that decapitation need not always imply death. Dr C. P. Haskins mentions an ant which carried on a fairly normal life for forty days without its head, but he does not suggest that this was a good thing for it, or that such a mode could be encouraged and developed. In a battle, a complete ant may be seen engaged in combat with a number of still ferocious heads, but those heads have no future.

An average specimen of the species, when it has all its limbs intact, presents a formidable design. What it lacks in beauty it gains in function. When we contemplate its two stomachs, one social and the other personal; its sting and poison bag; its four pumps; its brush and comb; its teeth that serve in turn as a battle axe, a pair of shears, a flour mill, and even a leg; its two elongated and movable noses with which it speaks, and with which it sees the shapes of things, and which serve it as a compass when far from home – we feel that personal functionalism could go no further. Yet its individual equipment is enhanced by its resource in composition; for not only can a single ant become a bottle, a door or a carriage when necessary, but a company of ants can turn themselves into a boat, a bridge, a tent, a ladder, a tunnel, or a covered road according to the needs of the hour.

The strength of their muscles in proportion to their size is such that we must compare it with that of a man who could easily lift his motor car over a fence, while their speed at getting about should be compared with a man going at twenty-five miles an hour on foot. Their endurance is so great that some can live without food for three months. They can do without air for a week, or if drowned, come to life again. Their energy seems indefatigable. This very morning, one having arrived on my book and run across it, I turned the book round so that it ran up again. I kept turning it round every time the ant reached the end. It never paused for breath. A long time passed and still I turned my book presenting it with an everlasting hill, and still it ran at a tremendous rate without need of rest or fuel, and making no distinction between the flat and perpendicular. In the end I grew weary of my role and anxious at its anxiety.

This Form in which life has been able to express itself, has been found so suitable – or so necessary to the economy of the world – that there are now over three thousand five hundred different species of ants, none of which can inter-breed. Their history is of immense length, disappearing into the misty millions of years that preceded the arrival of man. Thus by now their variations are many and extreme; especially in terms of size, for in this matter they differ so monstrously that some are a thousand times larger than others living in the same nest, the difference being truly as great as if one kind of man could walk about in the palm of another man's hand, or climb the Everest of his brow. Their adaptability and their expeditionary zeal are so pronounced that they can be found everywhere (except in Iceland, for some strange unreason). In regions of perpetual snow; in the burning sands of the desert; on the loneliest islands of the ocean; in the thick of the massive vegetation of jungles; on ships sailing in every direction – wherever we choose to look, there we shall find colonies of ants adapting themselves to their circumstance, displaying bright colours in warm climates, black and grey in cold countries, and discarding their eyes when, like the *Stigmatomma*, they live wholly beneath the soil in coniferous forests or seek to set up their galleries in the fastnesses beneath mighty rocks. The celerity and thoroughness of their movement in colonial expansion finds the best exemplar in the *Iridomyrmex* which in fifty years had spread from Argentina to England, and from England to Asia.

The number of the different species is immense, but of course some lines are more famous than others, commanding the astonishment and sometimes the fear of their human spectators. We think of the terrible carnivorous Siafu ants who, though blind, nose their way on vast expeditions, attacking any creature they come across, large or small, with insatiable savagery and blind impassioned gluttony. All living creatures, including man, fly before the holocaust of the locust-like tempestuous plague. Fowls, horses, and donkeys are dispatched by them in a single night; the skeletons of mules and monkeys, of parrots, rats, and mice are left in their wake; the largest serpent in Africa does not escape them; while at Tanga it is said that the natives found them killing a leopard. We think of the Legionary Ants, the nomads who find no rest, doomed for ever to scurry in long marching columns across the forest floors in search of flesh and blood, never able to stay and colonize but condemned to march onward in unappeasable hunger. These are they who bivouack in tents composed of their own living bodies, who conduct their nymphs through roads arched by themselves when the sun is too hot, who again use their bodies in the composition of a bridge when they come to streams, and who, rolling themselves into a compact ball, float down rivers to new destinations.

These have been called the Visiting Ants, and they are fighters. But many more of the species fight, and indeed carry on wars in a deliberate scientific manner. These wars have engaged the notice of mankind perhaps more than any other of their activities, for on this subject we are glad to find other species as bad as ourselves. And it is true that war, as opposed to jungle-fighting, is the correct word. For it is cold-blooded and planned. They do not fight for the immediate satisfaction of hunger, but for theft. One species will attack the fortress of another with the sole object of carrying off the larvae for future food or slaves. Thus the militant *Polyesgus* captures every year forty thousand cocoons from the *Fusca* or the *Rufibarbis*, while

one Amazon colony has been known to carry out forty-four
raiding expeditions, squadrons and cohorts deployed in strategic
formations carrying out concerted movements of attack bearing an extraordinary resemblance to the warfare of mankind.
Unlike men, they are their own weapons. Just as they grow
tools upon their bodies for civil life so they are their own sabres
and their own flame-throwers. A quick thrust from the battle-
axed mandible of a soldier-ant and the head of another is
pierced to the brain. An enlarged picture of an ant squirting its
poison-jet at the advancing foe is almost an illustration of the
terrible flame-throwers that scattered the Germans in 1944 (a
weapon so ghastly in conception no less than execution that we
pretended not to know about it). Battles between ants provide
many strange scenes. It is then that we can see a giant ant
overcome by a company of small ones running along its legs,
climbing upon its head, and sawing off its limbs. Then we may
witness a victorious ant, minus a few limbs, with the severed
heads of its attackers still biting, and fastening upon it like the
gargoyles on a cathedral. We may even see the heads of two
enemies, after decapitation, carrying on the combat. The fury
of some of their battles has been known to continue without
cessation for as long as a month and a half.

We pass, and we pass willingly, from these scenes to the contemplation of their peaceful pursuits. They live in what might
almost be called cities. The nests in the shape of little hills such
as I have been digging out and carting away, provide but one
example of their architecture. They make them in earth in
Europe, on trees in forests, in sand in the desert; they may raise
them dome-shaped or dig below the surface making a crater or
rampart above; they build round the stems of grass so that the
stalks make a pillared hall of many compartments; they get
beneath stones, employing the slab as a ready-made dome; they
use marshes and peat bogs, the crevices of rocks, the cavities of
certain tropical leaves, the caves of oak-galls, even the perpendicular tunnels of dry stalks; they sculpture their homes out
of the trunks of rotten trees and beneath the barks of sound
ones; they find room for their communities in the beams of

houses, chalets, and bridges, sometimes causing them to fall; they make carton nests by using their glandular secretions to consolidate wood-rot, sand, or fungus; they cultivate gardens in the forks of trees, planting the epiphytes of the genus *Cordin*, the resultant roots giving them the framework for their arboreal habitations; and many of the nests to be seen upon the trees by the astonished traveller in Eastern lands are made of leaves and the finest silk woven by means of the thread of their own larvae which serve as shuttles.

Equally various is the interior arrangement of galleries, corridors, storerooms, nurseries, and dormitories. Here, then, they live their lives, many hundreds of them together on the basis of mutual service. In short, they are societies. That is how we see them: as individuals working together deliberately for the good of all. But *they* do not see it like that. They do not see it at all. They have no conceptions. And if occasionally the glimmering of intelligence seems to inform their actions it is generally when they do something foolish and in vain. They are not held together as we are held together, by an economic nexus and by conscious motives. Invisible wires draw them together as if they were a whole giving an illusion of parts. We cannot fathom this. We may utter the word *instinct*, but can we understand, can we conceive life lived under the command and in the keeping of a directing force not consciously obeyed? Can we, even with a mighty effort, imagine living for a single day when nearly all our actions are *done for us* as some of our actions, notably the movements of our stomachs, are done for us without thought and without reprieve?

It is too difficult, and more profitable, to contemplate their economy and exchange. Their distribution of labour is based upon a scheme of bodily structure. They act according to their speciality. The females can lay eggs and rear their young; the males can fertilize the females after which they cast themselves aside, now useless, and therefore unworthy to live. The remainder, wingless workers, carry on according to the tools they display. Thus he who has a jaw like a battle-axe will act as soldier; he who has mandibles like clippers will cut leaves; he who has grain-grinding jaws will serve as miller and make flour; he who has a head like a wall will live the life of a door; he who has a head like a bucket will be a wheelbarrow; and, above all, he who has a good communal stomach will be a barrel. This last has been celebrated by all myrmecologists. In order to be prepared against barren days when food is scarce, a considerable number of worker-ants suffer their social stomachs to be filled with a great amount of liquid food until they swell so much as to look like barrels with a few handles in the shape of claws. These sacks of skin are hung in rows along the ceiling of the storerooms in the nest; and there they can be seen, living honey-jars, ant-bottles, awaiting the day when they shall be tapped for the benefit of the community. They are never thrown away as empties, but are continually refilled by their fellows. They remain where they are; that is their life now, they know no other; they hang from the roof until they die. This is intolerable! we say. It must be torture, such an existence. They can have no feelings, they can have no thoughts. They cannot really be individuals, for no separate being could be capable of so total an obedience, or so great a sacrifice.

Thus ants are specialized in activity, but they all share common destinies and dooms. All, for instance, are without ears, and live in a world dedicated to silence. Here again we cannot easily conceive this life. There is silence along their streets, and even on the field of battle there is no sound. And since they are deaf it seems certain that they are also voiceless. It may be that we have not the ears to hear the utterances of insects even as we have not the eyes to see the tiniest of their brothers. Anyway the fact is that we don't hear anything and it is probable that the silence is absolute. Just as we can watch a spider attack a fly caught in its web and see it slowly eat its living meal without a sound being heard, so also, however close we might bend down upon cohorts of embattled ants, we will hear no shout of insectual command, no cry of triumph, no moans of the dying, and even when a head is sawn off or a severed limb falls to the ground, no shriek of pain will human-ize the scene.

Ants also share the possession of remarkable antennae. Their sensitivity to smell is perhaps their salient characteristic. They are able to detect objects from a long way off by their antennae, which can best be described as extended noses. These serve the ants as a far more reliable guide for finding their way about than their eyes, when they have any. By smell alone they are able to sense the *shape* of things – which is as good as seeing them. And since they are movable, the ants can use them for other purposes as well. They can wave them as flags, thus signalling directions to each other. They can apply them as whips to urge sluggards to action or awaken them to danger. Most important, these antennae are their chief means of speech. They hold antennal conversation, expressing their feelings, their discoveries, their anxieties, and their intentions with the aid of signs which they read as easily as we read the book or the tongue.

Each species of ant has a different smell and thus the formicaries are consolidated by a brotherhood of smell. By this means one species is able to spot the vicinity of another species that will supply them with slaves. For though ants support each other in their nests and formicaries on the basis of mutual exchange even to the extent of feeding one another by process of regurgitation, they raid other species for extra labour. Foremost amongst these are the Amazon Ants who advance in strategic formation upon a suitable alien fortress in order to carry away the larvae and subsequently train up this progeny. Larvae are used by ants as a form of food. They often eat their own larvae. But since this practice is as unsatisfactory for them as it would be for hens to live on their own eggs, they seek to procure the larvae of other species. Thus there is an evolution here from food to slavery. Certain ants began by raiding other nests for larvae as food. But sometimes they didn't eat them all and the larvae hatched out and grew into workers perfectly ready to serve their masters, since naturally they were unaware that those 'parents' were really masters and they were slaves. The process continued until gradually the habit of procuring larvae for slaves as well as for food became established. This developed until the slave workers did practically everything for their owners who at last could not even eat without assistance, and if neglected, starved in the midst of plenty: for here, as elsewhere, we see the end of all slavery, which is the turning of the tables, the revolution of the wheel, when the masters become slaves and the slaves masters.

In fact the host becomes parasitic upon the guest. But there are also a number of genuine parasites who are tolerated by their hosts. One of the most pleasing characteristics of ants is their cleanliness, and to this end they grow upon their bodies a brush and comb. But they can have their ablutions thoroughly attended to by certain parasites who like nothing better than to lick them for hours: hence we find a large species such as the *Myrmica* suffering the attentions of a small spieces, the *Leptothorax*, who ride about upon them and perpetually lick them, receiving in turn abundance of food. The parasites by no means always belong to the species of ant. In all, three thousand species of insects are harboured by ants for reasons clear or obscure. The most familiar to us are the aphids, the leafhoppers, and other sap-sucking insects who are kept for the sweet secretions which they exude. In fact they are domesticated animals like cows, and the ants keep them apart in stables to promote regular milking. The secretions of the parasite-beetles, the *Lomechusa*, are particularly popular amongst ants, but we can hardly speak of these beetles in terms of cattle because their hosts regard the delicacy which they receive from them with such favour that they look after and bring up the beetle-grubs with greater care than their own offspring – even allowing them to eat the ant-grubs!

When we think of ants we generally visualize extreme order and efficiency, but the oddity of the parasitic intrusion undermines this idea. If we ourselves were to sit down to table with porcupines, alligators and lobsters, and to feed them at the expense of our own children; if we were indifferent to crickets nearly as large as ourselves; if our houses were inhabited, against our wills, by cockroaches the size of wolves, and flies the size of hens; if we fed monstrous animals with our babies because they exuded whisky, we could hardly stress the efficient ordering of our lives. Yet that is a fair comparison, according to Wheeler and Huxley, with the habits of ants. Moreover, there are many parasites who climb, creep, and intrude into the fold on false pretences, and by virtue of mimicry deceive their hosts with all the cunning of certified hysterical swindlers. These are often beetles who slip about undetected, ready to devour the helpless, to steal from the unwary, or to ride upon ants while sucking their blood. Some specialize in intercepting the morsel of food in its passage from one ant to another at the moment of regurgitation – a disappearing trick which bewilders the authors of this amiable practice. The highly individual tricks of the *Clythra* command our respect; this is a small beetle who builds itself into a little barrel of damp earth and walks about in this condition on its front legs. On the approach of an ant it stops and draws its legs under the barrel, thus presenting the ant with a convenient place in which to lay eggs: and when the eggs are deposited the little truck moves on, and the *Clythra* enjoys a good meal. More sinister is the species *Phorid* who attacks a big worker of the large *Camponotus pennsylvanicus* until it has succeeded in laying an egg in its neck between the head and the pronotum. This is the ant's death sentence, because once the egg is laid the subsequent larva creeps right into the head where it devours the muscles and brain, the ant meanwhile wandering about in a state of increasing stupefaction until at last, becoming motionless, it hangs down its ever emptying head. When everything possible has been eaten in this interior the parasite cuts the last ligaments that join the head to the body of the ant, which then falls to the ground, thus providing a safe and comfortable cocoon in which the larva can turn into a nymph. Not less grim in execution and more extraordinary in result is the action of the female parasite aptly called *Bothriomyrmex décapitans* who having got into a formicary, seeks out the queen, considerably larger than herself, mounts upon her back and spends a few days sawing off her head: and no sooner has the head dropped than the parasite is adopted by the community she has invaded and whose queen she has murdered.

236

It will be observed from all the foregoing that appetite and great hunger are salient characteristics of ants. We have noted some of the ways by which they satisfy their desires. But they are highly ingenious creatures, and besides feeding upon nectar, meat, and eggs they send out foraging parties to carry in grain from the harvests of mankind. Their nests contain elaborate cellars and storerooms underground, rather like those familiar shelters of our own which we must now number as the fourth necessity of Man. Here they store up their wheat grains, keeping them so dry that they seldom germinate – for actual grain-growing does not enter into their economy. Then the corn-grinding ants, with the special jaws, get to work and mash up the grain to a paste which hardens into little loaves of bread. (Forel speaks of ant-butchers also who prepare joints.) So considerable is this agricultural activity, so far-reaching the carrying of harvests, that their granaries have become the cause of litigation amongst farmers, and the object of certain clauses in the Talmudic Rules of the Jews. Even so we can hardly call these harvesting ants actual agriculturalists; but it would be a most proper term to apply to the Attiine ants who grow vegetables and live on them entirely. They cultivate a species of fungus with such continuity that it has become extinct in the wild state no less than the grasses cultivated by mankind. These ants, who sometimes have nests the size of cottages, reserve deep galleries for their fungus gardens which they not only keep clear of any sort of weed by assiduous *hoeing*, but send out the workers who possess leaf-cutting mandibles to bring in leaves, which they then chew into a compost for the fungi, as if in conformity with the requirements of Sir Albert Howard. Elaborate columns of these leaf-clippers leave the formicary, ascend trees in a body, cut down the leaves, and return home with them. 'It is an experience never to be forgotten,' says Dr C. P. Haskins, 'when, returning tired and hungry through the misty jungle at eventide, one first stumbles across the foraging columns of the parasol ants, their course marked by a line of waving banners, vivid green against the rain-soaked earth, as they return laden homeward.'

Thus the ants live. Thus they work and eat and fight and forage, sometimes unbending in relaxation to indulge in mimic warfare, gymnastic jousting, or caterpillar-riding. But for the most part there is little time for these relaxations, and they attend without pause at the great task of eating to live and bringing up their young. The workers are as tireless inside the nest as outside, carrying out, with unfailing obedience to the forces that govern them, the complicated business of midwifery when they liberate the nymphs from their silken shrouds and usher them into the world. These neutralized workers are wingless and work for the present; but new formicaries must be established, more eggs laid, and foundations placed for the continuance of their ancient line. This is the task of the males and females. At a given hour, in a given locality, when the temperature is just right, there is a great stir amongst all the nests of a locality. The ants assemble outside their nests, male, female, and workers. The males and females spread their wings in the midst of the now excited assembly of workers and fly away, and even as they fly they perform the act of fertilization, the females sometimes carrying upon their backs three or four males who in turn are granted their brief instant of pleasure which is also their sentence of death. Their work is done and they must die: and the real work of the female begins. She descends to the earth and there burrows or seeks out a hole which shall serve as the beginnings of a new nest. In the darkness of her chamber she *takes off* her wings and throws them down into the earth, and by the aid of her salivary ducts converts them into a fatty substance which alone serves as food for the nourishment of her first brood. She herself either eats nothing or eats some of her own eggs; then lays some more, then eats some more, then lays some more. If she belongs to the genus *Atta* she will carry with her on her nuptial flight, in a special pocket, the hyphae of the fungi to which she is accustomed. She will deposit them in her chamber when they will speedily flourish under her care, receiving manure in the form of larvae and wings, after which the mushrooms can be eaten by this queen and her daughters. And there we will leave her, brooding: a strange sight; nothing stranger than this in nature, a creature whose young are fed and whose fungi are nourished by virtue of her own body and her own eggs – a little circle within the great Circle of Life.

When instructed, I still remove ant-hills, throwing them in pieces on to a cart, in order that men may have fields to themselves. But as I raise the spade in spoliation of their temples I must let my mind play with humility upon the scenes of these lowly children of the earth. For it is the destiny of man that he should seek to take upon himself the burden of understanding, and to move in the comprehension of his works and the consciousness of his crimes. I gaze down upon these ants. I have looked into their houses, and passed along their ways, and sat beside their cradles – and yet I destroy them still! I do not know how much I really care about them; and am I not also fatally bound and driven by the laws of life, my brain and my heart as yet but tiny lanterns in the windy darkness of the world?

I give them my attention. I pass in review the singularity of their works. I sing their long and venerable history and rehearse the resourcefulness of their economy no less than the architectural versatility of their designs; and I would apologize to them if I could. But what I cannot do is to join with Solomon and say – Go to the ant. That was an unfortunate remark. To compare men with ants, as if there was significance in the comparison, is ridiculous. In its context, Solomon's remark may not have been so foolish as it sounds. Perhaps he was observing the tireless labouring of the harvesting ants over against the slackness of his own people, and in a moment of exuberance, said – Go to the ant, thou sluggard. After which, for generations to come, this supreme absurdity was canonized by the repetitions of unthinking publicists. For the wisdom of the wise is continually turned into the folly of the fool.

In saying this I would not wish it to be thought that all who have played with the idea are fools, least of all the great Forel, who, being very concerned about the League of Nations, could not refrain from using the ant to further that cause. But these loose comparisons will not do, and in the most recent book about ants (1946) they have reached an altitude of silliness beyond which other specialists will probably not easily ascend; a book wherein the regurgitation of ants is compared to an author writing books, their nests to the city of Athens, and the parasitic success of interlopers to the Chinese introduction of Buddhism among the people of Inner Mongolia. We may smile; but the general idea is equally absurd. There are similarities between the ways of ants and of men; comparisons can be made; but they should only be given a passing glance or as a joking reference.

There are many ants and there are many men – we can't get much out of that, especially as there are thousands of species of ants and only one of men. Ants live together and so do men, but many other animals live in nests and flocks and family groups, while the tight societies of ants bear no resemblance to the vast interconnections of men. Ants go in for a species of agriculture – but how silly to make a serious comparison with men. Ants wage war; and there you can truly make your comparison – but what of it? We may note with interest that slavery turns out as badly for them as for us. They keep domestic animals but are not quite so much their slaves as we are to ours, calling some of our own species not men, but *cow*-men. My point is that we can make comparisons for fun, and make jokes about them if we choose, but that is all. We cannot learn from them, nor be forewarned by them. Our ways are not their ways, neither is our destination theirs. Between us and the animals there is a great gulf fixed. The most important thing about man is that he is *not* an animal. He is different, and in this difference lies his ultimate hope and promise. A miracle happened to man when he was an animal. That miracle was the *birth of language*. This has made his life incomparable with any animal. We are not concerned merely with the difference *to* him which this miraculous event has made in the ordering of his life. It is the difference *in* him that is crucial. For this was the sign of the birth of consciousness. Not of intelligence, but of consciousness. Something *broke in* on man. It may have evolved, but it is not strictly a question of evolution. It is something outside evolution. Something to which the animals are not evolving. Life goes on, evolution goes on, but never does there come a time when any animal attains the miracle of language (which is not the same as capacity to communicate). Animals can do all sorts of things and become subdued to us in a hundred ways, but this obstinate difference remains. It does not matter how 'human' a dog is, how much it feels or understands, how dear it is to us; dogs can go on changing and evolving, but never will there come a time when they will be *spectators* and attain consciousness and use the instrument of consciousness, speech: no matter how extraordinary may be the tricks of a dog, we can never convey a Thought, as a thought, to it, never see it evolve to the point of our being able to say – 'I'll be back on Sunday night.' Consciousness is the miracle of man. That is his whole significance, and the meaning of his imperfection, and his promise. Because it has broken in, because he does possess it, then it will evolve in him as it has already done, it will go on evolving; this burden of apartness and semi-understanding which he often feels too heavy to bear, will be lifted; he will attain a higher state of consciousness and enter again into the unity that he has lost. He should not turn to the animals for directions. He should not go to the ant. He should fix his gaze steadily upon this human gift that makes him unique, and see in it, and the evolution of it, the key to all his set-backs and the meaning of all his suffering.

4. While Standing on a Dunghill

Good farmyard manure. I take large spadefuls of the stuff, like great slabs of chocolate cake, and throw them into a cart. As we open up the dunghill it begins to steam and its excellent odour becomes somewhat stronger. Various insects alight upon it. I cannot see the very small ones, of course, but would like to know the full insectitude activity. I observe one that always seems to be sharpening his forceps like a man in front of a joint – he of the brown wings. Also he of the beaked and vampire

241

face. He of the dumb-bell body. He of the sleek and jet-black mail. I lift up their mountain of food into the cart, drive it off, and then throw it on the field. After which I climb on to another huge dunghill and fill up the cart again. And I must say I never felt better employed.

Not long ago the subject of manure and dunghills was regarded as low. There has been a great change. Today it is considered almost a test of man's intelligence how much he appreciates manure. Throughout the land, people who formerly thought it only proper to show off their herbaceous borders now call on their neighbours to admire their compost heaps. A housewife gathering up the droppings from the milkman's horse in the suburbs is a normal sight. Nearly everyone has already grasped that there is no such thing as *rubbish*. Some go as far as to declare, with Lord Northbourne, that a man who burns an old pair of trousers is committing murder.

Let me see if I can make farmyard manure slightly more intelligible to myself than hitherto. Where begin? It starts with the grass and the roots and the corn upon which stock feed. These things are burned in the furnaces of their stomachs. The ashes are passed out. Mixed with the straw of the stable they are piled up every day into a dunghill. As it stands it is no use. It would be strange if the grass having been eaten could then be immediately eaten again by grass. Yet this does occur after a time, and grass and other plants do eat this which has been already eaten. But it must first be treated. By whom? Not by man: he couldn't manage it. By whole empires of creatures visible only to the microscope, called bacteria. Though small they belong to the organic world and have their own special problems, not least of which is vigilance against gigantic enemies, also invisible to us, called protozoa who gobble them up.

These bacteria, minute and unhonoured, labour ceaselessly for the good of all mankind. Or, rather, of all life upon the earth. For without them not only would the manure-heap never be usable as food, but the soil itself would fail to serve, its chemicals would not coordinate, and the great sun itself would administer its blows of light in vain. Let their labour cease and all vegetation would be choked and the earth would become a wilderness, ugly and silent.

In order to carry out their great work they need above all things numbers; vast battalions of them must be on the job. Thus not the least interesting thing about them is their rate of birth. Within the compass of twenty-four hours one bacterium is capable of producing an offspring of one hundred and seventy thousand times as numerous as the present population of the world. They multiply by division, and that division occurring every half hour, a single individual can become within the course of one day the ancestor of 280,000,000,000 bacteria. This is an adequate rate of birth, and therefore when we say that empires of them get to work on manure heaps and in the soil, we are making an understatement.

And what are the offices they perform? I confine myself to their work on the manure. In an ounce of soil there may be about 150,000,000 bacteria, but in a similar amount of manure there may be about 30,000,000,000. Broadly their labour consists in breaking down complex substances and in building up inert constituents into energetic bodies. Farmyard manure consists of excreta, urine, and the litter of the stable. The first movement in the bacterial symphony is the destruction of the litter and its conversion into a dark brown moist substance, humus, which finally retains none of the structure of the original straw. The manure proper contains a great variety of carbon compounds, with also phosphates and potash, which can be summed up as nitrogenous material, the nitrogen of which is not yet in a position to serve as food. So the next task of the bacteria is to bestow such order as may be necessary to release the vital potentials.

The hill heats. It is burning. It is shrinking. Could we watch what is happening we would perceive the waxing and waning of different armies of bacteria, each handling the material in turn. The first army seizes upon the nitrogen, tears it from its complex grouping, and splits off ammonia from its protein. We cannot see this operation, but we can smell it all right. That is the work of

243

the first army; they then hand their product over to a second corps which immediately sets to work to change the ammonia into nitrate. This done the division of labour continues and a third army takes control turning the article finally into the soluble form of calcium nitrate.

Not that these operations always go through as smoothly as this. Too much oxygen may get in owing to a loosely piled hill, or unharmonious bacteria may undo the good work and denitrify the nitrate expelling it out in gases, until another body of bacteria comes forward, the gallant Azotobacters who, rising to the occasion, re-nitrify the de-nitrified and unburn the burnt – if I may be said to have followed the proceedings rightly.*

Anyway there is no place where I am more content to stand than here upon this dunghill, where that which is invisible is found to be mightier than the monumental mockeries of men – nay, where the things that are not, are raised above the things that are.

5. The Mystery of Clouds

While harrowing one afternoon I saw a cloud looking like a cloud-capped tower itself. (I was pleased with it for this, for it did something to make up for the annoyance at having once seen a cloud like a grand-piano before ever I heard Trigorin report the same thing.) Then, as is my way, I asked myself, with resolute candour, how much I knew about clouds. Did I know what a cloud is? And as usual I found only a few bits and pieces of ill-related and undigested fact strewn about somewhere in the upper floor of my head. So, again according to practice, I threw the lot away and started from scratch.

First, as to the different kinds of cloud (for Nature seldom goes in for one sample of anything). They have been classified, of course, and named. It is amusing to read academic writers

*See *Agricultural Bacteriology*, by John Percival. *Johnstone's Elements of Agricultural Chemistry. The Soil*, by F. H. King. *The Spirit of the Soil*, by G. D. Knox.

when they get going on the classification business. Studying
such authorities one would really think that the clouds had been
classified and named at the Beginning; whereas it is we who
classify them in a frantic attempt to bestow order amongst them
so that we may be able to see them better and grapple with
them. Speaking for myself, however, I find that the exhaustive
classification, including the inevitable sub-divisions to cover the
numerous border cases, only makes the thing more mixed than
ever, and I am content to acknowledge just three classes. First,
the upper or Cirrus clouds often small and in vast droves of
celestial sheep, wispy and frail – 'flocks of Admetus under
Apollo's keeping. Who else could shepherd such? He by day,
dog Sirius by night; or huntress Diana herself – her bright
arrows driving away the clouds of prey that would ravage her
fair flocks'. They are often as high as thirty thousand feet and
are not seen low. Second, the Rain clouds which are the lowest
of all and are seen as wide films of grey and dark. Third, between these two lots there are seen accumulated heaps which
are gathered under the general head of Cumulus. It is these last
that hold our attention most.

What is a cloud? It is invisible water made visible. The
atmosphere is full of water, but we cannot see it until too much
of it gets up there. Then it suddenly becomes visible, like a
magic flower growing out of nothing in the sky. The heat of the
sun is constantly evaporating water from land and sea, and
taking it up into the air until saturation point is reached – as
declared by the clouds. I make that statement because it is
'authoritative' and I must be authoritative; but I do not understand it, since on that showing one might expect more clouds on
a hot day than on a cold one. But let it pass.

Clouds are water, and they have weight – we know that
much. Then why do they not sink to the ground? They should
be continually falling at our feet. Yet they stay up there, though
they are not supported from below nor held from above.
These are simple questions; but the greatest descriptive writer
of all time – he confined himself to the sea – acknowledged that
he always found these simple problems 'the knottiest of all'.

When I seek an answer to such questions to whom do I turn? Not to the schoolmasters, not to the academicians, not to the authorities. I turn always to the Masters, to the Stylists – to a Fabre, to a Melville, to a Ruskin. Is Ruskin puzzled by this? Of course. And his answer? He hasn't one. He says he can't make it out. 'I believe we do not know what makes clouds float. Clouds are water in some fine form or other: but water is heavier than air, and the finest form you can give a heavy thing will not make it float in a light thing. *On* it, yes; as a boat: but *in* it, no. Clouds are not boats, nor boat-shaped, and they float in the air, not on top of it.'

Yet perhaps the solution is provided in a book I have beside me on clouds by G. A. Clarke, F.R.P.S., F.R.MET.SOC. He does not raise this specific question deliberately or clearly, of course; but if I can pierce through the language in which such books are written, I think he says that clouds continually evaporate at the bottom and renew themselves at the top – so that our given cloud which should be falling at our feet does not do so because it is always ceasing to exist and always being rebuilt. But maybe he hasn't really said that, or wouldn't hold that he had said it – for the minor scientist, like the minor philosopher and the minor statesman, never likes to say anything definite.

Another question. How is it that clouds are so complete, so sharp in their outline? We look up into the sky and see these chiselled leviathans swimming through the ocean of air at the bottom of which we walk, these drastic shapes each margined against the blue with a termination as clean as the Cliffs of Moher; but they are not solids, and the last thing we should expect is this firm binding of the unboundaried moisture in the airy wastes.

I turn again to Ruskin, and again he does not know the answer. 'What hews it into a heap, or spins it into a web?' he asks. 'Cold is usually shapeless, I suppose, extending over large spaces equally, or with gradual diminution. You can't have, in the open air, angles and wedges, and coils, and cliffs of cold. Yet the vapour stops suddenly, sharp and steep as a rock, or thrusts itself across the gates of heaven in likeness of a brazen bar; or braids itself in and out, and across and across, like a tissue of tapestry; or falls into ripples, like sand; or into waving shreds and tongues, as fire. On what anvils and wheels is the vapour pointed, twisted, hammered, whirled as the potter's clay? By what hands is the incense of the sea built up into domes of marble?'

No doubt there are up-to-date answers to such questions; but personally I would just as soon leave it there. Certainly there is nothing in Nature more mysterious than clouds. And nothing stirs the imagination more than those creatures that are not alive; those buildings not made of brick; those domed and daring palaces in which there reigns no king; those vast foundries flaming without fire; those mountain ranges upon which no feet may ever walk; those radiant prospects of a far country belonging to the paradise lost regions of the heart. They stir us; but they do not calm, they cannot soothe. 'We all look up into the blue sky for comfort,' said Coleridge, 'but nothing appears there, nothing comforts, nothing answers us, and so we die.' And if we see therein some clouds, vessels made of water, journeying to nowhere and appearing out of nothing, they do not answer us, they bring no comfort. Indeed we have to be strong in spirit to bear looking at them at all. We must not be depressed. We must not be ill. We must not be worried. We must not be in debt. We must not be in prison: there is real agony of Wilde's forever haunting lines on the wistful look cast 'Upon that little tent of blue We prisoners called the sky, And at every careless cloud that passed In happy freedom by'. We must not be feeling futile – for then they will seem infuriatingly futile and drive us mad. It must not be Sunday afternoon in a town; we know what Franz Kafka meant when, feeling miserable on a Sunday afternoon, he was 'astonished sometimes by the almost unending senseless passing of the dull clouds'. It must not be in time of war. We cannot cloud-gaze today (1943). The time is not yet, but even as I write the time draws near when many who saw them only as the phantoms of their fears, shall hail them as the messengers of joy and peace.

6. The Books of Stone

One day, while ploughing the chalky Dorset down, my share threw up many stones. When, at the headland, I stopped my horse and lifted the turn-furrow clear of the soil, I saw that a number of attractive-looking flints lay at my feet. I picked up a few of them. They were all much alike: flat on one side, and on the other shaped like a little hill; and upon that hill a graceful design was traced: a star with five wings, some deeply engraved – embanked railway-tracks with sleepers the size of ribs on a nail-file.

They were the flint-casts of sea-urchins belonging to the Chalk Age of the earth in the Mesozoic Era. One hundred million years ago those creatures had made their likeness, had traced their death-masks on the flowing flint. One hundred million years ago these very things I looked at were existing! Was it Time made visible? Did I hold Eternity in the palm of my hand? Standing there in that lonely and lovely place, on that bare ocean-moulded hill, in November 1944, I pressed my mind back through the bottomless abysses of time, back beyond the dawn of man, beyond the Tertiary, beyond the Eocene, back to the Cretacean shore.

Then Australia and New Zealand, joining with Africa and South America, made a single mass. The north of England and Ireland were one with America and with Norway. The Mediterranean flowed across the Sahara Desert. Italy lay buried in the deep. Some of France emerged, but Paris was the centre of a deep basin. Holland, Belgium, Denmark, and the regions of the Rhine were all part of a sea that stretched to the Carpathians. The south of England was submerged. Such is the general picture; but we are dealing with unmeasured immensities of time – this given period covering over fifty million years itself – and during that age the site of London alone, for instance, seems to have been above and below water several times. Today we think of the long, wild washing of the Atlantic waves and of the depth of that water: it is hard indeed to think of it ever as land – still less of becoming land again, as may happen, when the enfossilled wrecks of ships will reveal their tale of violence and death. It is hard to think of an enthroned mountain peak or sheep-grazed valley as folded in the arms of the sea. Yet thus it has been. Many parts of the earth have been widely flooded, and then have risen again, only to sink once more. But the rate of rising and sinking, according to the measurements to be read from the rocks, is in the nature of one foot in ten thousand years. At the moment we might be pardoned for considering this stationary. But there are no stations upon earth: not one single thing is fixed; and though I may stand today upon the hill, deciphering the tablets of stone, I must learn that the cold waves flowed here before, smoothing out these rounded hills, and that they may flow again and wash away our chronicle ... Not quite, though; future fossils too will make their script, and the mighty Mind, exalted above all time, will read the pages of the flinty books.

Between the end of the Jurassic and the beginning of the Tertiary Era a great amount of chalk was formed. It was such a striking episode that the whole period has been called the Cretaceous Age. Minute and innumerable oceanic animals, called foraminifera, floating about near the surface of the sea, sunk to the bottom when dead, and then accumulated in a slowly solidifying ooze. We call the resultant accumulation Chalk. If we examine a handful of it under a microscope we find that it consists of the casing of the foraminifera – really shells of the most delicate and beautiful design, six thousand to a square inch. In view of the fact that such deposits are only found today at a depth of about twelve thousand feet, it would seem that this Dorset hill was once in the abysses of the sea whose surface flowed where the low flying clouds float now ... We approach the white cliffs of Dover, and gaze upward at the seeming solid shows of earth and rock. It is well to realize the reality, that this too is water or chiefly water in another style, and that upon the backs of innumerable urchins of the sea our history is stayed.

The era that is called Chalk is given a span of some sixty-five million years, and is said to have ended roughly one hundred

million years ago – (though we can hardly suppose that foraminifera were absent from the seas in either Jurassic, Triassic,
or Tertiary times). It is proper to call the Cretaceous Age
modern if we are willing to think realistically of Time: for the
earth had already rolled for two thousand million years. We can
call it modern, also, because some of the trees and flora familiar
today began to appear. Man was not to arrive on earth for
another hundred million years; and yet the scene would not
seem wholly strange to us even now. Ferns, sedges, and reeds in
marshes and swampy places; a grove of poplars against a
winter's sky; willows and alders by a river bank; laurels, magnolias, and vines on the hillside; elms, oaks, conifers, maples,
palms and eucalyptus trees: all these things, so familiar to us,
had ancestors rooted at that time. 'No man knows' said Walter
de la Mare, 'through what wild centuries Roves back the rose.'
Flowering plants do reach back to the Cretacean lands, while
the ancestry of trees breaks the boundaries of our conception.
To this day we can see, on the shore of the Isle of Wight, a
Chalk Age conifer which had been swept down a river and
buried with silt, a twenty-foot length of fossilled trunk,
indifferent to the assault of centuries. The leafy arbour, the
climbing ivy on the bended trunk, reel back in time beyond our
power to pass in thought; that is why, seated in such a place on
a summer's day, we lose ambition, and hardly claim identity,
made languid by an air that joins us with the immeasurable
wastes of the Mesozoic.

Some of the animals of that time are also familiar to us, and
have sent representatives down to our day. Then, as now, the
crocodile lay on the shore like a log of wood; that slippery rope
of life we call the snake was there; the four-legged footstool of
stone named turtle had his place. In those days they had the
whole earth as their playground. But they did not rule it, they
were not the lords of life. There were other creatures, more
formidable, who have sent us no messengers. These were the
Dinosaurs. They were the supreme beings of that world –
though called by us monsters. They ruled throughout the Jurassic and lasted until the end of the Cretaceous Era. There

were many of them – in Britain alone at least one hundred and twenty-one different kinds. They have given us no descendants but they have left us some of their skeletons, by which documents we can tell what they looked like. Anyone in London can gaze upon the erected figure of the Iguanodon. In 1822 it was dug up in Kent. After a hundred million years it has risen from the grave. Assisted by men's hands and surviving men's bombs, it stands on its hind legs at South Kensington, a twenty-five foot skeleton (others have been found twice the size), untarnished by time, and ready to march on through the years, its extravagant and appalling aspect a silent and perpetual admonition to bewildered man.

With the neck of a giraffe, the tail of a sea-serpent, the body of a kangaroo, the head of a horse, and the brain of a hen, the Iguanodon hopped on land and swam in the swamps. Possessing multiple rows of grinding teeth it fed upon plants. The amount of herbs eaten in those days is suggested by the equipment of the Trachadon who had two thousand and seventy-two teeth. Indeed the turning of vegetation into flesh was on such a scale that it promoted the growth of the Atlantosaurus who roamed in those regions now lost to the waves. It was nearly eighty feet in length – a territory too extensive to be governed by a single brain. Since the controlling nerves from the head would have had to traverse too many feet of neck before reaching the limbs or establishing communication with the tail, the Atlantosaurus, in common with the some other Dinosaurs, evolved a second brain in a cavity within the hinder part of its body.* This was the largest of the herbivorous monsters, but the Brontosaurus who made a noise like the advance of thunder was sixty feet long, its footprint covered a square yard of ground, and it weighed as much as thirty-eight tons. The Diplodocus was built nearly on the same scale and looked like an elephant whose nose was its neck and whose tail was a snake. These Dinosaurs, including the Morosaurus of forty feet, and many others were amphibious and may have had some peaceful times in the water when nothing of them could be seen save the neck – a pole

* See *The World in the Past*, by B. Webster Smith.

giving little hint of the island of flesh below. There they were safe from the carnivorous Dinosaurs on land. But they must have had to face the sea-dragons or fish-lizards. The Ichthyosaurus had a fish-like body without a neck: its limbs were paddles, its nose a sword, its jaws an armoury of teeth, while its eyes, the size of arc-lamps, enabled it to explore the darkness of the depths where it could see for long distances. It dwelt, amongst other places, at Lyme Regis, in company with the Plesiosaurus, or Sea Dragon, one of which found at Ely, had a swimming paddle seven feet long, a jaw of six feet, and a tooth of fifteen inches. These and others, of which there were over fifty varieties, were all air-breathing. So were the Sea Serpents, of which there were more than forty different kinds, varying in length up to seventy-five feet, abounding in North America and at what is now the mouth of the Thames. Though they had teeth in columns of fours along the roofs of their mouths they swallowed their prey whole. They were very like snakes, with arrow-shaped heads. Such was the Elasmosaur whose neck rose twenty feet out of the water while its body was forty feet below the surface.

There may have been birds during this era. At least one is known to us – the Archaeopteryx. It was feathered, and about the size of a rook. There were plenty of flying reptiles. They certainly were not birds, and we may be sure that they sang no songs. They had no feathers, just as the earth-bound Dinosaurs had no fur. They pertained to the condition of super-bats. These were the Flying Lizards, the Pterodactyls, whose beaks, about the length of a rifle, were set with teeth, and whose outspread wings in some instances covered as much air as a small aeroplane.

These sea and airborne carriages could keep out of reach of the carnivorous Dinosaurs. Those who remained on dry land had to fight it out amongst themselves. The ferocity of the battles between Dinosaur and Dinosaur is sufficiently signified by the frightfulness of their armour. The Stegosaurus carried upon its back a series of enormous plates resembling a double

252

row of tombstones. Formidable indeed must have been the foes that caused the evolution of such defence. Who could take this fortress? Who enter in at this gate? The Polacanthus Foxi was a walking wall with barbs; the Triceratops was a twenty-five foot boulder; the Scolosaurus, with its cuirass and armoured cape, its ruff of plate, its spiked nose, and its mace-like tail was fit to face the Tyrannosaurus whose teeth were nearly the size of bayonets, and was a match for the Struthiominus who was one hundred and thirteen feet long. Some of the eggs of these plated reptiles have come down to us. The age of mammals had not yet arrived, and these immensities of bone and flesh, these armoured engines of destruction, at first lay confined within the circle of an egg, which was about the size of a super hand-grenade – though informed with a greater potential.

In spite of the fact that the Brontosaurus and others used one brain at headquarters and another at hindquarters, it was yet too little. They could not adapt themselves permanently to the world. But their kingship lasted for what may have been close on ninety million years. We marvel, not at their ultimate extinction, but at the enormous length of their reign. All that time they roamed in the swamps and battled on the plains. They do not belong to history. There is no record of their wrongs. No human eyes saw them, no human mind was confronted by the riddle and the paradox of this clash of life with life for life's sake. From the Jurassic to the end of the Cretacean day they were the highest beings, the boldest expression of Energy organized in earthly envelopes. Then they went down. These vessels perished. The soft garment of silence fell around their fate.

Standing on my hill in Dorset in the pure clear air of the winter's eve, while the clouds, unsanctified by history and living to tell no story, passed to their empty destination, I gazed upon the fossils in my hand, the books of stone, and sought to realize the actual existence of that monstrous age to which they joined me. The Dinosaurs did really exist, they did truly trample across the world for ninety million years; but when they passed from the surface of the earth and were seen no more, Man did not yet arise. Not for a long time; not in the Eocene, not in the Oligocene, not in the Miocene, not in the Pliocene, not for another hundred million years, in the Pleistocene, did earliest Homo appear.

I tried to grasp this reality, this great *fact* of Time. I did not succeed. Once, in the middle of the Atlantic, looking at the horizon, I tried to imagine the space beyond it. For a second I had a true glimpse of that space, and of the space beyond that space. And perhaps for as much as a second now I saw the reality of a hundred million years, and realized how Man, having only had one million years at most, has only just begun his career. But this knowledge soon slipped from me and became merely intellectual. It did not remain organic with me, as is the fact of gravitation or the roundness of the earth. That is our general trouble. The findings of geology are too recent to be as yet incorporated in our consciousness. This weakens the sensibility of our thought. We can be weak in economics; we can be weak in human history; we can be weak in doctrine; we can be weak in literature; we can be weak in many branches of science – and no great harm be done. We must not be weak in anthropology. We must not be weak in geology. The old cosmologies have gone. And because they have gone men have lost faiths and beliefs. They are inclined to despair. There is no need to despair. The message of geology is so inspiring. Our hope and faith should be increased. Consider the main fact. Man has lived a million years: that is all. He may live another hundred million, perhaps a thousand million. We do not spontaneously think in these terms when we speak of posterity; we think of a few hundred years hence – of 2346, not of 22346 or 2222346. And when we think of the past we feel that the civilizations of Greece and of Rome were a long time ago. Yet in the eye of geology a thousand years hence is as tomorrow, and the age of Socrates as yesterday. These are necessary facts to incorporate into our daily consciousness. Then we should have patience. Then we should have room for hope. We should think sensibly. We should believe in progress – even that! Take our main fact again. A million years ago the ray of consciousness broke in on

Man. He stood back, he saw, he became detached. That was a rudimentary ray. There is nothing more obvious than the evolution of our awareness. We are not wiser than Socrates. We are wiser than Neanderthal Man. We are not more ethically inclined than Confucius. We are more ethically inclined than Neanderthal Man. We are not more aesthetically developed than Shakespeare. We are more aesthetically developed than Neanderthal Man. If this is true, it is a tremendous truth: for if the aesthetic sense alone is developing it means that love and peace and beauty and worship and reverence are growing. This has grown – backslidings or not. Another million years will show as much difference again. We may call this faith – it is close to fact. Facts move us, they have much emotional effect, and these facts should inspire us. Our development is attended with sorrow, it is woven with tragedy, it is dedicated to perennial disasters – but it goes on, it does climb upwards. All the arts tell us this. Listen to the symphony! Are we not swept up into the windy mountain passes of the soul? Do we not hear the choir of angels that unspeakably proclaim the unwritten truth?

7. The Unfolding of the Seed

The corn is rising. The orchards are in bloom. Before the movement goes a step further I am determined to grasp in detail the process of the unfolding. This has gone on year after year around me, and I have admired the performance and paid lip-homage to the mystery of growth. The time has now come for me to follow the workings of the miracle. Anyone in the same state of mind is invited to join me.

The seed – it must serve here as the exemplar of all seeds – arrives in the earth by the agency of man or nature. There it is, ready to start the great work. It is an envelope; or rather two envelopes, in which is confined – a *new birth*. We cannot see this living Principle. It is invisible. It never comes to light, it can never be touched, though it is the hardest of all facts. But we can see the machinery it employs; and having seen it we are satisfied, for we seek no more than the certainty of purpose and design. Within the envelopes are two store-rooms (sometimes only one) containing food to start off with, which we call the cotyledons or perisperm – and this is the nearest we can get to the nascent embryo. At the base is a tiny prominence, the radicle, the beginning of the root. At the top, so incredibly packed that Nature would seem to make zero contain infinity, is a bundle of leaves. And somewhere betwixt and between is another minute prominence, the tigellus, from which the stem sprouts.

Thus seeds are portable dormitories in which repose unborn generations, provided with food when they wake from their sleep. If no moisture gets near them they can remain in their cradles for years, even for centuries, still retaining their power to rise up. Seeds of the kidney bean have been known to sprout after sixty years of rest, while cornflower and raspberry seeds dug from the dry darkness of Celtic sepulchres have grown and flowered like seeds of yesterday.

So we take a seed from its dry place and put it in the earth. If the soil is good various chemical agents therein will immediately begin to act upon the seed, chief of which is water. The moisture softens the envelopes and soaks into the embryo, and straightaway the hoarded provisions are set in motion. One of these rations is a substance called starch. As it stands it is no good, for water will not solve it, and an unliquefied substance cannot travel and penetrate. But there is another substance in the store-room called diastase which, when water acts upon it, acts upon the starch, turning it into glucose in an excellent state of solution. It is this liquid which now sets the whole outfit in motion, digging and building, so that soon a root is sent down from the radicle and a stem up from the tigellus.

They have most definite and determined natures, these two things, the root and the stem. One seeks the darkness, the other the light. We cannot alter their characters by interference. If we take a seed after the above process of germination has been set going, and twist it upside down so that the root points upwards and the stem downwards, then the root will turn in its course

256

and descend, the stem will turn and ascend. Do this many times, and still the creatures (as we feel them to be) will not alter their determined direction, and will die rather than abandon their cause. Put an acorn in a vertical tube full of earth; let it germinate; let the root seek to explore the darkness and the stem steal up towards the sun – and then reverse the tube. Do it many times, and each time the root and stem will turn right round in their tracks.

The composition of these vegetable parts is not simple like a shaft of steel. There is a complicated but very definite arrangement of fibres, tissues, veins, vessels, channels, and spiral threads all held in place by innumerable bricks called cells which are so small that a host could find comfortable lodging-place on the point of a needle. They are much more than bricks and have many tasks. They are neither solid nor empty; they are bags holding precious properties in a solution which, like blood, is thicker than water.

The root, then, a porous membrane with the above composition, plunges down into the moist earth. It is not alive quite like an animal or part of an animal, not like a claw that grasps or a mouth that sucks – yet very nearly so. Water, which is a thin or weak solution, will always percolate through a porous membrane filled with a thicker solution – this in physics is called Endosmosis. It will also do another thing: it will go upwards, anti-gravitation-wise, by a law of suction if it enters a tube so narrow as to be comparable to a hair; such a tube if placed in a pond will suck the water upwards higher than the level of the pond – this in physics is called Capillary Action. The tube need not be straight, it can be curved, it can be a dense complexity of channels, so dense as to seem like a lump of sugar or the wick of a lamp; yet the water or oil will, on entering a low portion of the sugar or wick, rise to the top. A root provides the conditions for the process of endosmosis and the action of capillarity, and as soon as it is in the moist earth it sucks up water by these two means.

This water which rises upwards against gravitation is called the Ascending Sap.

It is not pure water. For the food of plants must contain in solution some if not all of the following chemicals – carbon, hydrogen, nitrogen, oxygen, phosphorus, and sulphur, plus a modicum of potassium, calcium, iron, magnesium, and sodium. With the exception of carbon, roots can carry up any or all of these preparations from a good soil; and, either through their own intelligence or someone else's, they do gather up precisely these ingredients which they need, rejecting those which are useless or harmful. Yet on examination sap is found to be little more than pure water, the other quantities being incredibly minute in spite of their importance.

Thus we may regard the roots as a colossal network of water-pipes and hoses pumping up tons of water from the soil. I say colossal network, for the aggregate of the ramifications of the roots belonging to one single average stalk of corn is said to be about a quarter of a mile. And I say tons of water, for an acre of corn will on average lift up two hundred and fifty tons a fortnight, while a single elm will in its season raise enough water to fill a tank thirty feet long, three feet deep, and three feet wide.

And yet in spite of all this the plant is not getting enough to eat, and the food which it is getting is not adequately prepared to promote full growth. It cannot go on like this. The stored provisions and the soil's contribution are enough to raise it above the earth; but that done, the part of the building above the ground must help. Brick buildings are built with hands: leaf buildings are built by the leaves themselves.

Since the soil cannot supply all the nutriment, the atmosphere must make up the deficiency. You cannot make things out of thin air, people say. There is no such thing as thin air, if by that is meant something empty. It is really very thick and powerful, and from it all things are made that are made, or without it cannot be made, whether tree, plant, person, or army tank.

What is the atmosphere? It is an air ocean. We walk at the bottom of an air ocean at a depth of from two hundred to five hundred miles. We cannot see it, we cannot touch it, and yet it presses down upon us with a pressure of a ton to every square foot. Each acre of land sustains forty-six thousand tons of air. It is possible to carry this surprising weight on our heads owing to the way it equalizes the pressure all around us. This atmosphere is composed, as everything is composed, of small items called molecules. They are not all of the same kind. Some contain oxygen, others carbon dioxide; some nitrogen, others argon; some ozone, others nitric acid; some water vapour, others ammonia. In quantity nitrogen heads the list and oxygen seconds it, while in importance the carbon dioxide is second to none. When we grasp that water, carbon, nitrogen, nitric acid, and ammonia contribute ninety per cent of all the materials that are built into the tissues of plants, it is easy to see how necessary it is that they should have roots in the air as well as roots in the soil.

The leaves are these upper roots or mouths – plants are pretty well all mouth. Their first appearance in Spring is in the form of knotty bundles, buds – looking like the claws of a dormouse on plum trees, as thin and sharp as toothpicks on beeches, and like half-buried beetles on the twigs of apple trees. In due course they change and open up and throw out what seems a new material altogether, as surprising as if tiny silk handkerchiefs began to grow from one's finger-nails; yet they are wood – thin, pliant, waving wood. The pressure behind this production is the Ascending Sap which, quietly but with great strength, slowly with unperturbed pace like the Hound of Heaven, advances throwing open the green fans. It receives some help from the sunshine, without which in any case nothing could be set in motion; but only when the leaves are fully open can we say that the plant is working from above as well as from below, that leaves are building leaves, and the bars of bough enshaded by their own exertions.

The leaves appear on the twigs in so carefully planned an order that not one overshadows another. Each must get as much sunshine as possible, and their co-operation to this end is such that one leaf never gets in the light of another, but each aims by spiral arrangement at the goal of the greatest sunshine for the greatest number. As one side only is fitted to receive the rays with maximum advantage that side alone is turned towards the sun, and if deliberately twisted over by us, will turn round again with the same unfaltering determination as the root and the stem when treated in a similar manner.

The surface of a leaf consists of a fine shred of stuff like green varnish, which is thus spread with a view to checking too swift an evaporation of moisture. This is the epidermis, consisting of cells each of which harbours two million globular corpuscles called chlorophyll whose green colouring is responsible for the verdant foliage around us, and whose work lays the foundations of the world. The whole epidermis is shot through with tiny holes smaller than the prick of a needle and numbering twenty-five thousand to a square centimetre. These are the stomata, doorways for entrance and exit: of entrance for the atmospheric effects; of exit for the ascending sap after it has deposited its cargo of chemical goods in the ante-chamber of the epidermis to await further instructions.

The blade of the epidermis is supported by a girder called the petiole which rises from the twig. After it enters the blade of the leaf it sends out more ramifications called nervures, they themselves branching out into still more fibres until a beautiful scaffolding is set up. Their task is more than that of a scaffolding; they serve as corridors up which is channelled the ascending sap and down which flows the descending sap after the great operation in the parenchyma. This last consists of a certain tissue of cells in the epidermis which constitutes the supreme laboratory where labour is performed upon which rests the life of the world and the destiny of nations.

Let us consider that labour. The primordial elements of all living things can be reduced to the basic materials of carbon, hydrogen, oxygen, and nitrogen – or even more simply to carbon, air, and water. 'Animals,' says Fabre, 'whether wolves or men, who are not wholly unlike wolves, both as regards food and other things as well, eat their carbon in combination, in the shape of mutton; while the sheep that gives us mutton absorbs

its carbon in the form of grass ... It is this wonderful transformation which enthrones a vegetable cell as monarch of the
world, with men and wolves and sheep as its subjects.'

How does the plant that builds up the flesh of sheep as the
sheep goes to build up the flesh of man, consume its portion of
carbon? It takes it in the raw. The digestion of its cell is such
that it can take carbon neat. Everything living, every one of us
must take carbon, for it is combustible, and if we do not burn
we die. In order to keep alight our torch of life we breathe, that
is we take in oxygen which burns the carbon which we have
synthetically eaten – then we breathe out, we expel the oxygen
in combination with the consumed carbon, and the gas is now
carbon dioxide or carbon acid. It is a poison gas. We breathe in
pure air: we breathe out poison gas at the rate of a hundred gal-
lons a day. All animals do likewise to a certain extent. The air
might eventually become hopelessly vitiated and we would perish
in our own poison were it not for the vegetable cell which feeds
upon this gas, this deadly gas, and purifies the air for us. It is the
chief and essential food of the plant, this poison; the cell, that
astonishing stomach, exulting in the products of putrefaction,
recreates life from the poisonous relics of death.

The leaf, through its myriad mouths of stomata, breathes in
this carbon acid gas, selecting it in preference to oxygen, absorbing it into the tissues of the cells, and conducting it into the
laboratory where the labourers immediately set to work to
break it up. By some incomprehensible means, under the
influence of sunlight, they decompose, the composition separating the oxygen and at once sending it forth into the air
again. It entered the orifices of the leaves as an unbreathable
gas, it departs purged and changed into a life-giving elixir – a
lily, for example, exhaling five hundred pints of oxygen in a
summer's day. It will return again with a fresh cargo of carbon
to be again purified before once more resuming its aerial wan-
derings. We, the animals and man, by eating plants and eating
ourselves, manufacture carbon dioxide, the poison gas that
would choke us even if we used a gas-mask; they, the plants,

gladly receive the poison as food and give us in exchange pure oxygen to breathe, while also treating the carbon in such a way that we can eat it.

For what happens to the carbon that is left behind when the oxygen is expelled? Just as the cells of chlorophyll set to work upon it when it came in, so when it is separated they instantly combine it with the ingredients brought up the ascending sap and awaiting treatment in the ante-chambers. The cavity of that wonderful cell not only decomposes carbon dioxide, it composes new compounds. The carbon is immediately transformed. By combining with the other ingredients gathered from the soil it instantly becomes the raw material of sugar, starch, wood, flowers, and fruit. In this state it is known as the Descending Sap. The ascending sap carried up certain properties. Combined with what has been taken from the atmosphere, those properties, forged in the cellular furnace, have gone to make a final substance which flows down the plant distributing largesse as it goes – leaf-tissue for the leaves; colour and scent for the flowers; starch, sugar, and jelly for the fruit; fibres for the wood; cork for the bark; and gossamer for the roots.

Thus the sap's circle is completed.

By mentioning 'flowers' above I have anticipated our story. The buds do not always open into green leaves which set at work those masters in the art of chemistry, the cells of chlorophyll, that weave the wood and build the twigs and feed the whole concern. These work unceasingly for a prosperous present. They care nothing for the future. But the buds also open into other leaves that do not toil and do not spin in that way, and yet are clothed, not in modest green, but in a softer raiment, embellished and perfumed, the admiration of the world. These are flowers. They also work of course – beauty is always incidental – but their work looks to the future.

These flowers are made from the same materials, based on the same architecture, and raised by the same labourers as the other buds. This is the more surprising when we observe how different their instruments are. The following must serve as a general example. Passing our eyes from without inwards we see first a few lovely soft leaves called petals, the total of which is well crowned by the name corolla. Next stand in a circle half a dozen little pillars called stamens, each terminating with a head called the anther, and full of dust called pollen. In the centre is another pillar like a walking stick with a good knob-handle and a sheath at the bottom – this is the pistil, the knob being the stigma, the shaft the style, and the sheath the ovary, which is full of rudimentary seeds called ovules. We should add that the whole flower may be protected by some green tongues called in sum the calyx.

Such is a full flower. Any flower can get on with less than this, with only stamens and pistil if necessary. Thus some plants, lacking the gorgeous paraphernalia of petals, may give the impression that they have no flowers, though all plants have flowers, all plants have fruit, and to talk about flowers as if they appear on some plants and not on others, and to talk of fruit trees as if any tree or shrub could fail to bear fruit, is to suggest that Nature moves with a view to man's aesthetic tastes and gastronomic desires.

The purpose of the erection is to work for the future – to make seeds. Given the above instruments, how is it done? Briefly, by an exchange between the stamens and the pistil: more accurately, by the pollen reaching the ovules and striking up with them the spark of life – which we call the moment of fertilization. Inside the anthers of the stamens the pollen is found in the shape of countless grains each consisting of a single cell with a double envelope harbouring a viscous liquid in which float numbers of minute granulations called the fovilla – for, as we are constantly finding out, Nature delights in the utterly and increasingly minute no less than in the gigantic.

One thing more we should observe since it bears so much upon the pleasure we get from looking at flowers. At various places in the interior of the corolla there are pockets or pouches of nectar in order to attract insects who shall come and disperse the pollen, should the wind fail to do so. And in order to signify the presence of these tempting morsels the petals serve as painted flags.

When the flower is fully blown and the anthers have let loose the dusty pollen to be scattered by the wind or carried by the insects, then the stigma proceeds to exude a liquid slightly thinner than the liquid held within the grains of pollen, so that when the latter falls upon it, it sticks, and while it sticks there the action of endosmosis is again set going so that the liquid of the stigma passing into the grains of pollen pushes out the fovilla, handsomely packed in a painted tube, which, penetrating the stigma and passing down the style, enters the ovary and reaches the chamber of ovules. And then – how is the vivifying influence brought about, by what means is the flame of life enkindled? At this point all great scientists are silent and give up the chase, declaring – 'No one knows. Before these mysteries of life reason bows, helpless, and abandons itself to an impulse of adoration to the Author of these ineffable miracles.'

Once the ovules have been given life and have achieved the status of seeds, then the life of the flower is over; the beautiful petals that advertised the pollen, the stamens that pillared it, the pistil that received it, fall to the ground, disregarded now in their withered and scarred disgrace of ruin. But the ovary, at first so thin, swells with increasing pride of colour and shape, until it seems to us as we gaze upon the astounding apple, that the petiole cannot possibly bear such a weight without breaking. Finally the seed is loosened and leaves the parent plant, and is dispersed by a hundred different methods across the land.

8. The Plant: Apostrophe to an Urban Gentleman

It is past five-thirty in the afternoon. For us on the land work is over. We can rest. But when we have gone home, the workshop we have left behind does not close down. We can go home and leave Nature to it, knowing that she will not rest, she will not take off.

Recently I heard a man who was visiting his wife in the country, say – 'Give me the plant at home any day.' He was a progressive man with far more use for a piston than a pistil. By the plant he meant the factory, and it was clear that for him factories constituted the only plants worthy of the name.

If Nature were not so silent he might have changed his opinion. There is nothing like noise for suggesting importance. Had we a finer sense of sound we might be able to hear the natural movements. Could he have heard all that was going on around him that man might have been impressed.

Even so, without hearing anything, could such a man contrive to gaze upon the work in progress here with concentrated attention over a period of time, looking down upon it from the Hill of Knowledge, as it were; could he cast his eyes from above the earth to beneath the surface of the soil and attend at the first movement after the seed is sown and see the approach of the water, the cracking of the envelopes, the swelling of the perisperm, the awakening of the embryos from their slumber in the dormitories of the seeds; could he see the translation of the hoarded starch into the magic liquid of glucose from which proceed stems that press up to the light and roots that dig down in the dark; could he see the roots select from the great storehouse of chemical foods flowing within the soil those which they need while rejecting those which they do not, and then under the pressure of endosmosis and by the power of capillarity raise up whole reservoirs of water to the skies; could he see that sap ascend creating as its fluid flows the extra limbs and mouths that soon shall feed the whole; could he see those leaves open out their blades to embrace the sunshine's beaming blows and seek the air for gases while the roots explore the darkness of the earth for liquids; could he see the stomata on the leaves spraying forth to heaven the tented tons of water which have carried up the chemicals into the ante-chambers of the epidermis; could he see those same stomata taking in the carbon acid gas so that the leaves may pasture on our poison; could he draw closer and observe the operations carried out by those master miracle workers, the cells of chlorophyll, in the laboratory of the parenchyma where oxygen is separated from carbon and restored to the atmosphere, where carbon is compounded with other elements and turned into other things, where the hard branches reaching up to the loftiest brightness are first boiled together in this burning cauldron of creation; could he see that sap after its ascension being thus combined and treated then descending through the ribbed corridors of the nervures on the leaves, through the green-paved passages of the petioles, through the fluted pillars and the twisted towers of the stems, down into the roots, distributing good as it goes; could he see these toilers for the present erecting those toilers for the future whose coloured petals and glorious perfumes are the delight of all mankind; could he, still standing on his Hill, still standing there, making use of the divine gift that has been bestowed upon men, the gift to learn, to see, to comprehend something of the Mystery and the Law, could he now turn his gaze upon those flowers in their maturity and see the clouds of pollen borne from the anthers on the wings of the wind or the backs of bees, throw down their fovilla on to the receiving stigmas; could he see the penetration of the pollinic tubes as they pierce the sticky surface of the pistil and then pass down the style into the ovary at the base; could he see this final act, more powerful than that which happens within the perisperm of the grain, more wonderful even than the elaborations in the laboratory of the parenchyma, the final act or the First Act, the moment when the ovule in the ovary becomes a seed, when the spark of a new life is kindled and the Wheel revolves again; could he gaze upon this Plant tirelessly toiling for us and spinning for us, it might happen that he would come to think that it compares not unfavourably with his factory at home.

9. The Imperialism of the Plants

One July day while hoeing in a bean-field which had become badly overrun with thistles, I was surprised to find myself suddenly caught in a blizzard. The flakes whirled about, very thick, not falling from above but rising from below. It was thistle-seed, of course, which had become suddenly airborne in a gust of wind. A very remarkable sight all the same; and it set me thinking of the various ways by which plants disperse themselves throughout the world.

The great aim of any given plant, it would seem, is not only continuation of the species, but colonization and empire. Few are content with local habitation. They wish to spread themselves across the world. To this end they employ many means of transport. They charter the birds to chariot them across continents and seas. They engage animals and insects to transfer them from place to place. They use floating driftwood and logs and barges on river and lake. They harness the wind and become their own aeroplanes. They surrender to the currents of the ocean and become their own ships. They encourage mankind to administer to their imperial needs. Some even move along the ground unaided.

Let us imagine an island somewhere in the ocean – in the Pacific, say – which has been let down from the sky for our benefit. We will suppose that it had no plants on it. And there we stand, awaiting the arrival of seeds. They will come; for if Nature hates a vacuum, she detests a piece of soil with nothing on it.

Looking out to sea we soon catch sight of a swimmer, making for the beach – evidently a shipwrecked native. His brown head is clearly seen. But when it reaches shore we find that this brown head is really a coconut. The nut contains a large seed packed in oakum and so protected by the strong hard shell that it is safe from the violence of the waves for long periods, voyaging from one island to another, landing and germinating.

Following the coconut many other seeds will make port, their germs protected by every kind of impermeable apparatus, their envelopes turned into boats by pockets of air. Some can sail for over a year and still germinate. Some have been known to cover three thousand miles before their pilgrimage was completed. Others will be shipped to our island on rafts of dead bamboo and sugar-cane, logs and other vegetable remains which glide along in the currents that encircle the seas and wash the shores. It is known that on rafts like these, rats and lizards, snails and slugs and ants have reached remote islands; and it is certain that such Arks likewise lend hospitality to seeds.

So much we might expect, and a good deal more, from the ocean as a means of transport for seeds. At the same time, while they have thus been arriving by sea, others will have confided their dissemination to the winds. For many kinds of plants send their fruits round the world by parachute. We have all seen the dandelion sailing off – its seed ballasting the most delicate aeronautical appliances. Such seeds many go a few yards or a few miles or hundreds of miles. There is no reason why we on our island might not expect a visit from that famous little creeping composite, *Chevreulia stolonifera*, which has been known to carry its message across five thousand five hundred miles from Montevideo to the island of Tristan da Cunha.

Many grasses would also arrive by air. I would hope to see the *Spinifex squarrosus* coming along. Its fruit looks like a porcupine. It can travel by air over four hundred miles, and if necessary cover part of its journey by sea – for the porcupine is so buoyant that it floats very lightly and spreads some of its spikes for sails. Such airborne arrivals would doubtless be followed or accompanied by various spores of mosses and ferns and orchids, travelling from fifty to nine hundred miles to join us.

Thus already our island has been considerably recruited with seeds arriving by water and air. A third service will also be employed, perhaps the most popular – namely, carriage by bird. The procedure is well known. First of all the seeds are introduced into the crop of the bird. To ensure this the plants hold up flags, called berries, to attract attention both as to presence and ripeness of fruit – the red flags being the most popular, though yellow, white, black, blue, and pink are used as the occasion demands. The bird eats the fruit but cannot digest the seed, which in due course will be passed out intact. Meanwhile, safely cabined, it can be charioted across ranges of mountains and arms of the sea. Since over forty different kinds of birds are said to eat any one species of fruit, this bird-mail, however irregular and haphazard in the delivery of its envelopes of seed, can and does make a vast distribution throughout the world. Plants anxious to promote colonization in far distant realms charter birds that fly up to two thousand four hundred miles. But in this case the seeds do not reside inside but outside their vehicles. They adhere to the feathers by means of hooks and brackets and claws. Or they reside within clods of earth carried away by the birds – a ball of earth which had stuck in the feet of a bird, on being examined by Charles Darwin, was found to contain eighty-two seeds of five different species.

There is one bird which seems to specialize in its planting to such an extent that one might think it deliberate! This is the Eichelhäher in Germany – the name meaning acorn-carrier. It is a famous planter of oak-trees. According to Herr Johannes W. E. Schmoll, it likes nothing better than to carry an acorn in its goitre and subsequently spit it out. It is said that wherever the Eichelhäher plants an acorn it flourishes, though foresters planting in the same area must risk the destruction of the seed by mice or boars: for the Eichelhäher's acorn appears to be distasteful to all acorn-eating animals. The soil of the Grune-wald in the Potsdam district was found to be poor for the cultivation of all but pine-trees, and the forestry commission planted only pine; but if you take a walk through the wood you sometimes come across lonely but mighty oaks, which were all planted, according to the foresters, by the Eichelhäher – whose call can often be heard in the district.

After about twenty years our island will have begun to display considerable vegetation in the shape of grasses, shrubs and even trees. It is not a particularly small island; it is over two hundred square miles, containing mountains, rivers, and plains. There is no feasible spot on this land which the vegetation will not attempt to inhabit; no fertile cranny or crevice into which it will not creep. Thus we must be prepared to see many more devices for transit.

If at any season of the year there are fields of ice or glaciers, then certain seeds like poppy, willow, and saxifrage will *skate* to a further place propelled on the wings of the wind. And plenty of others, with the wind behind them, will be blown across the plains, scattering seeds as they go and by stages of colonization carry their empire to the confines of the land.

Meanwhile the rivers and the floods will carry on the work of dispersal. At least ninety species will travel by water. Some will drift by themselves. Others, brought on to logs by ants, will be ferried for long distances. But there is one plant which is singular in the execution of its designs – the Lotus Lily. Growing by the side of a river, it creates a wooden basin on the top of its stalk in which the nuts reside. When the nuts are ripe the wooden cradle breaks off from the stalk and sails downstream. And as it travels the nuts germinate and the boat becomes a navigating nursery, a floating flower-pot.

We are assuming that by now this attractive island is by no means devoid of animals. Here is another means of plant distribution. According to the number of animals, we may count additional vehicles for seed. And again it is as if we saw determination, intelligence, will, deliberate contrivance to ensure means of transportation. We are all familiar with the simple burr that clings to our clothes in an embrace impossible to shake off. The burdock growing by the wayside or the goose-grass in the hedges fasten their fruits to anything that brushes against them, be it fur, feather, or cloth. There is a frightful plant called the Grapne which has harpoon-like spikes several inches long so that any animal lying on one will be driven frantic with pain and will gallop wildly about until it gets rid of it. Certain seeds exude a viscid or glutinous liquid so that they stick to an animal as with gum – to such an extent that a bird gorging on the species *aculeata* can be found lying helpless with its wings stuck together. And of course a sticky seed may adhere to a dead leaf and ride the wind as on a magic carpet.

A considerable number of animals are employed one way or another. The elephant, the alligator, the rhinoceros, the lizard, if handy, will serve; the grasshopper, the termite, and the ant are extremely useful; while the dormouse, the fieldmouse, and the squirrel are inveterate tree-planters, having a convenient habit of storing seed in the ground and then forgetting all about them. When the sky rains flesh and blood with a plague of locusts there will be another highly favoured means of migration. And, again, birds discharge their duty for short as well as long distances, sometimes whisking seeds from one spot to another at three hundred miles an hour. At the same time, more pedestrian-minded plants, such as the Cacti, may be seen to go by tortoise – perhaps winning the race in the end against another fruit mounted on a hare. The spores of fungi make their excursion by slug, changing later to toad, when they progress faster. Geraniums, stocks, and strawberries may employ the snail, advancing at the rate of one mile in twenty-two days. Some prefer to go by fish. Perch, eels, and cat-fish eat waterside plants and migrate down rivers – often changing from one river or lake to another. Any seed engaging this submarine service must be prepared to complete its expedition by air – that is, if in company with its vessel, it passes down the throat of an eagle, a stock, or a pelican. In the same way an orchid, starting its Odyssey by earth-worm, will frequently continue by blackbird or thrush.

All the plants already mentioned use exterior means for locomotion. But there is one plant which is a pedestrian – the Loranthus. It actually uses its radicle, not as a root, or not wholly so, but as a prop, a leg, a pedestal by which it levers itself to another place. And there are plants which, anticipating the gun and the bomb, *explode* when ripe. The Squirting Cucumber goes off with a bang if you touch it, throwing out its seeds as far as seven yards – while some of these plant-catapults can fire their shot about twenty yards. But let us not forget our well known, well loved, common trees. The twiddling sheath of the Ash rotates sideways to the ground at a reasonable distance from the parent. And no sight in the world is more compelling than a Sycamore seed horsed on the gale, a pair of wings without a bird, a propeller without an aeroplane.

Finally, one last important means by which our island would be fed with seeds – namely by Man himself. When he comes to it he will carry all sorts of seeds attached precariously to the objects of his commercial activity, while he will also bring others deliberately in the pursuit of agriculture.

And so – looking at our island now, with its rich vegetation and smiling fields, what a change is there since we first saw it!

Washed by the waves, conducted by the wind, piloted by the birds, seeds have been delivered from all points of the compass. And, having come, they have again charged the wind and the birds to carry on the work of dispersal. They have used the ice and the rivers and the floods. They have enlisted in their service the beasts and the insects and the fishes. They have enrolled mankind to speed their empire and spread their story.*

10. The Turning of the Wheel

The painter has a start on the writer in dealing with landscape and fieldscape. He can frame his picture, isolate it, and hang it in front of our eyes so that we have to look at it. But the painter can only show us the static picture, he cannot present the seasonal unfolding, the turning of the Wheel. This is where the pen comes in. Painting exists only in space, music only in time: literature commands both time and space.

The harvest is nearly gathered in. I have been passing in review the developing spectacle since March. Beginning with wheat in March, what do we see? The refreshing sight of a brown cultivated field. In April a gleaming green comes on it. There is little to be seen from close quarters; but from a distance, in the morning and the evening sun slanting as it comes and as it goes, that green gleam is like a light, giving rather than receiving rays. This is our second vision, perhaps the best. In May where are we? That illuminated carpet has gone, and a forest of stalks, small pillars of a darker green, have arisen, each culminating in a ribbon – a sort of plume, a pennant, a flag. In June the portion of the pillar immediately below the pennant, looking like a lovely green pencil or fountain pen, begins to swell. It becomes fat. It is not hollow as below that point. It is filled with something which is trying to burst out. And soon a rigging of seeds, no longer enveloped, now develops and rises above the plume, above the pennant which ceases to point upwards and bends

*See H. N. Ridley's monumental work, *The Dispersal of Plants Throughout the World*.

over, so that as June turns to July we no longer watch the dark green ribbons on the surface of the corn waving in the wind, for every pennant has been lowered, all those plumes have been cast down, and in their place we see the military, speared, and massed formation of the upright ears. From then onwards until they fall before the knife, the parade is constant, and there is no change save colour: the surface passes from green to grey, from grey to light brown, then to a brown as dark as Hovis crust, even a touch of black at last; the stalks directly beneath the ears being sometimes enlightened by an unacknowledged blue, while farther down the colours become rainbowed in their richness, the charactery in the columns making an evening contrast to the spring-tide shoots at birth, for in a few months they have taken on the weather-beaten beauty of stone besieged and yellowed by the stains of Time.

In the same way the equally disciplined rye stands up presenting the unbending blades in their phalanx on the fields. There is rectitude: there is uprightness. And here is grace; here in the field of oats are seeds as delicately displayed as ear-rings, and when the movement is completed we find imaginary miniature fir trees as alluring as the grassy forests of yorkshire fog. The wheat, the rye, the oats – these, when they have lowered their pennants, thrown down their flags, stand upright, till the end. Not so the barley. From the tip of each barley seed a hair grows out and up looking extraordinarily like the antenna of an insect. Wheat and rye sometimes have 'beards' also, but you have to look close. The barley beards are numerous and long. They give the impression of being intensely alive, positive feelers, real antennae, reaching up with the utmost determination to scrape the sky. Thus for May and June. But as the pointed caskets of seed become ripe then the necks of the stalks upon which they are displayed begin to bend, and the antennae cease to pierce upwards. It is at this time that a field of barley shines with that silky sheen that captures and holds our attention beyond all the other exhibitors. The necks give way still more, with swan-like grace bending right round now until at last the antennae point downwards to the earth as if to find the

273

darkness of the grave as surely as before they sought the light of heaven. This is the sign that the hour of the binder is at hand.

I do not understand it. Why does the barley alone need these whiskers? What is their search, and what their prize? If they pick from the air minute portions of life-giving gas, how comes it that the others do without that gas, or do not have to employ such suckers? And why, if the stalks of wheat are strong enough to bear the burden of the ripened ears without bending at all, does the stalk of barley fail to do so, or for what reason does it bow the head? Altogether lost in an ocean of ignorance, I abandon the quest. I am content, though, to stand before these buildings, cap in hand. I could gaze for some time at those wheat stalks alone. Think of the weight of the ears. Nearly half a hundred-weight in an armful. How are the tons in the field thus held aloft by those slender columns of green stalk? Because, we are told, not only is the stem rounded and hollow as with the bones of animals and the pinions of birds, not only is it strongly notched at intervals, but it is impregnated with silicon which is the material that an ordinary pebble is made of. Thus the tons of corn are held as safely on their columns as Nelson on his – for those stalks are made of stone.

Which sight in this unfolding is the best? The first sign of the shoots above ground – at least from the labourer's point of view. As the season advances we become accustomed to the bounty of Nature, we are inured to miracles, and get anxious about the harvest. But the first green uprising on the brown field makes itself felt with the same force as the first warm rays of the sunshine. We have ploughed, manured, cultivated, harrowed, rolled and sown the field. We have done everything possible. We can do no more. Unless we are mistaken we have now set a vast machinery in motion. For several months we need do nothing to the field except roll it; it will do everything for itself until the last moment.

In April those green shoots appear. I do not know whether there are many men, or any at all, who can observe that arrival without surprise. I am not amazed when I see it; but I might well be, and my furthest fathers were. Sometimes when regarding some out-and-out city man who seems capable of taking such a sight for granted, I tell myself that he is not really capable of this, that he also is part of the human race with forefathers who knew nothing of cities. If the sight of the green appearance gives him no stimulus, it must, if dimly, call up some comfort. In the voyages of discovery and invention there can have been no greater moment than when the first man sowed the first seed as an experiment in the earthly laboratory. What can we know of wonder beside that Wonder which was the companion of Fear? We may not know that wonder as we cannot know that fear – nor that hunger, nor that relief. We can imagine; we can recall; we can still stand beside Hiawatha, in a true sense partakers of his wrestling and sharers in his triumph.

11. The Plough

The field lies before me. What is a field? I take a piece of it up in my hand. It is not a substance made of one thing like a lump of cheese. It is a mass of small pieces. These are the ruins of rocks: by the play of the atmosphere, by the heat of the sun, by earthquakes and volcanic outbursts, by the motion of the wind, by the rush of rivers, by the action of rain, by the melting of snow, by the scraping of glaciers, by changes of temperature the rocky places of the earth have been laid low and crushed so small that we can hardly see the fragments. Here I tread upon the ancient mountains of the world; beneath my feet lie the solemn peaks that once only to the stars were known, and the cold lunar beams.

In this guise they are remarkably active; for, being informed with chemical properties they throw off gases and acids and liquids – the first foods. From them grew the first plants. As century pursued century the plants let fall their residuum, spread deep their ashes still holding and multiplying the chemical energies from which the Phoenix of Life rises up renewed and increased in glory and power. This field is a laboratory; it is a store-house of food; it is a reservoir; it is the nursery of battalions of bacteria in ceaseless chase; it is the habitation of countless worms who swallow it. It is a vast potential.

Yet this field will not realize its potentialities without the help of man – who adds so immeasurably to the beauty of the world. It will lie there, barren and dull. Like many a human being it will remain sterile, ugly, and sad, all its powers stuck and cramped and closed, unless it is released by some liberator. Open it up, let the sun beam down its blows, the water penetrate, the chemicals stir, the molecules move; fertilize it further; impregnate it with seed – and in due season that bare stretch of earth will wave and glitter with so much beauty and intention that the scene will be utterly transformed. So we come to the instrument of liberation, the spade, the moving spade – the Plough.

For the first thing that we must do is to turn over the top of the soil. Then it can be broken up by the harrow. This is the first thing which must be done, which has been done ever since man ceased from simply hunting for food like the animals, and, stepping outside the fatal flow, channelled the force of life to serve his own ends. Thus the Plough holds up the clearest symbol known to man, and is woven into the memory of the race. For this reason the Emperors of China held the plough once a year. The respect paid to it is based on the firmest of all foundations – *need*; at bottom we respect only what we need. Here is a thing we shall always need. It outlasts the marble monuments of princes and even the loftiest rhyme; palaces, temples, towers; factories and foundries; creeds and philosophies; systems of government; great Mars himself in his triumphant car – these hold their day of ascendancy in greater glory, but they fail and fall at last, and are ploughed in.

I was eager to get the plough into my hands – especially the horse-plough. And at length the time came when I stood on the field with a plough and two horses. It lay on its side, for it was extremely like a ship out of water – a ship with a great fish's fin for keel. And awkward hulk to handle until it was launched into its proper element, the earth. The launching and guiding with two horses is of course not easy for the beginner. Yet I got into

this extraordinarily quickly and surprised approval was regis-
tered on the faces of those who had shaken their heads in scepticism. My striking-out lines were even a success. My main
difficulty at first was at the turnings. I began by losing the share,
and failing to observe that I had done so – the most reprehensible and amateurish of all mistakes. And it was some time
before I could get the horses to turn without stepping over the
traces, and prevent the plough from falling on its side. I still felt
the need of four hands in order to deal with reins and handles at
the same moment.

It was worth any difficulty involved in turning at the ends, if
only to see the blade of the turn-furrow come up from the soil
flashing in the light, clean as a sword. If we did not 'know' that
this happens we might scarcely expect it – that a rusty blade
dipped into the darkness of the earth should rise up glittering
and burnished! It is always a great moment when the wave of
earth falls away from the prow. In a second everything has
come into place; the big wheel and the little wheel in front are
holding a level; the coulter cuts; the share digs; the turn-furrow
tosses over the slice. Given level ground and not too many large
buried stones, there is no occupation more pleasant and less
boring than this. All the body is engaged, and all the mind,
while eye keeps watch on the horses and the plough, fascinated
by the way the solid soil leaps up into a seeming fluid wave to
fall immediately into stillness again in your wake – a green
wave rising when on ley, light-brown on stubble, grey on stony
ground. It falls and falls away, this little earthy breaker, until
quite soon you see that a section of your field has turned colour
completely, and you say to yourself – 'I've ploughed that
much.' The eye is severely engaged indeed, and yet there is time,
and a great inclination, to glance round at the scene as a whole –
at the seagulls snow-flakingly following, at the cloud figures, at
the sunset as the day closes. I could look down from a certain
high field in Dorset into a deep vale which was often filled with
sparkling light while we were in shadow. One late afternoon
the clouds so gathered that one field below alone received the
sun: one lanterned ray enlightened it, filled it completely, not

going over the hedges but just down upon that green field only –
as if the finger of God were pointing to one page which I must
con for truth. I could not con it, being otherwise engaged, but
was glad to see the print was there; and glad also, many a time,
to glance up as the cold winter day closed down, and see the
sunset blooming like a rose, and the tree-top tracery write its
hieroglyphics on the lofty scroll.

PART TWO
THE WOOD

1. The Wood and the Work

My task was to clear and thin an Ash wood. It was situated between Iwerne Minster and Tarrant Gunville in Dorset, and belonged to Rolf Gardiner of Springhead, amongst other things a Forester of no mean knowledge and activity. My debt of gratitude to him for commissioning me to do this work and to reap its reward, is outside calculation: I can but dedicate these pages to him.

The last time this wood had been touched was eighteen years previously. It was chiefly composed of ash, though it also contained a considerable amount of hazel, and also some spruce, larch, and oak. In addition there was the eighteen years' worth of undergrowth in the shape of privet and bramble and a great deal of the clinging, climbing, thottling ropes of that hangman's noose called honeysuckle. I could not see into the thickness for more than a short distance, nor advance a single yard unimpeded. As for the ash itself, the trees were of all sizes. There were some very fine single ones, now nearly full grown; but often a clump of five or six rose from one stool, interfering with each other.

My job was to introduce the idea of freedom into this tangle – freedom for the ash. Not for all the ash; only for the best, the straightest, never allowing more than one to remain out of any single clump and cutting down even good ones if they were too close to others. Darwin said that in Nature the fittest survive. In fact, he only showed that those survive who do survive. It is only when Nature is acted upon by Man that the best, the fittest survive. When Man acts upon Man the same principle is not applied. The Spartans alone seem to have pruned our species on principle. We do not do so now, for no one can foretell how great a mind or skilful a hand may belong to a fragile body.

Thus I started clearing and thinning the wood, which covered some fourteen acres. I advanced upon the tangle with an axe, a bill-hook, an ordinary hook, a slasher, a saw, and a pole-saw. Though my chief tools were axe and bill-hook, I used each of the other instruments at intervals, rather like a golfer selecting a suitable club for each new occasion. I put my head down (quite literally) and slashed my way through the undergrowth, brushing up the clinging thorn, the entangling and infuriating privet, and hacking down the honeysuckle's parasitic climbers until I had free play to deal with the trees themselves. Some of them were in very poor shape and it was a relief to get rid of them. But there were many good ones which I had to take down only because they were too close to one another. This sort of thing goes against the grain even when singling mangolds, and in the case of trees it is hard to realize how much room a single tree eventually demands if it is to be a fine specimen. Yet it is a fact that in the first stage of a plantation as many as fifty to a hundred plants may occupy the space taken up in the end by a single mature tree.

The beauty of this job lay from the beginning in the fact that there was so much to show for it. In quite a short time I had made a distinct impression, a definite clearing – the jumble of brambles and shrubs and misshapen trees had vanished from the space I had worked upon, and now just a few straight ash trees stood up clear and free. People speak of 'not being able to see the wood for the trees'. This phrase actually does mean something – (though it might quite easily mean nothing and yet be repeated twice daily by our publicists). It means that a too careful dwelling upon many particulars blinds us from a vision of the whole: you cannot catch sight of the wood as a totality if entangled in the trees. Many botanists are in this unfortunate position. But often the opposite of this is meant. The man who mechanically trots out the phrase that he cannot see the wood for the trees, often means that the confused bulk and muddle of facts confronting him make it impossible to see where his own particular problem stands. He cannot see the trees for the wood.

Now that I had already made a beginning, a neat clearing in the wood, I could for the first time see the individual trees.

And as I made a clearing in the wood so also I made a clearing in my mind with regard to timber. As I began to bestow order and tidy up the confusion in front of me, so I began to sort out my odd bits of knowledge about forestry. That is generally my method of advance in matters of this kind. I cannot see, I cannot actualize for myself any department of work unless I have taken part in it myself. I do not possess the politician's and the sociologist's imagination to grasp the actuality without participation. I have to get in touch with it first through work. For me it is first the tool, then the book. I could not take down the word Forestry from its hiding-place in my head and relate it to the world I know.

My first question was naturally very relevant to the work in hand – What is ash used for by man? The answer is that it supplied the material for most of the instruments of husbandry. Perhaps slightly less so now than formerly. An early nineteenth-century farmer declared, 'We could not well have a wagon, a cart, a coach, a wheelbarrow, a plough, a harrow, a spade, an axe or a hammer if we had no *ash*. It gives us poles for our hops; hurdle gates wherewith to pen in our sheep; and hoops for our washing tubs.' Today neither harrows nor ploughs owe much to wood, but we still need it for the other things.

So already an ash ceased to be 'only' an ash-tree in my eyes. And henceforth, when I look across any wood like this I shall see more than trees, I shall see their translation into the familiar objects of the farm and the garden. I shall also see tennis-rackets, golf-sticks, and cricket-bats. Above all – walking-sticks. During some days I had a craze for making walking-sticks myself. The method was so pleasant. Having cut down a tree and observing that it possessed some nice straight branches not too thick for a walking-stick, I cut one off just above the junction of a tributary branch and then cut off the latter a few inches below the terminus. That gave me my handle. Then I measured the stick in my hand against my thigh and made a final cut at the bottom according to my needs – and there was my stick.

When I had finished off with a penknife I often had an excellent stick.

2. The Floor of Flowers

Apart from any utilitarian considerations, I have always been particularly attracted by the ash whose witch-like fingers with black nails claw the winter sky, and by the aristocratic manner in which the leaves are the last to come and the first to go. The larch, the sycamore, and the horse-chestnut will be in rich leaf without the slightest sign from the ash; the maple, the white-beam, the hazel, and even the elm, the beech, and the oak are often well away while still the ash remains quite bare as if there were nothing doing this year.

An eighteenth-century forester named Gilpin called the ash 'the Venus of the Woods'. Few would subscribe to this if we think in terms of leaves, since it cannot compare with the glories of the beech or the chestnut; but if we are thinking of a naked winter tree then the ash may well claim to be the Venus of the woods. Its branches are at the top of the tree – a crown – in marked contrast with the oak or the chestnut. Thus you can see a long way into an ash plantation and be fascinated by the beauty of the barks. This lack of low branches and late arrival of leaves provided a further advantage for me – a very import-ant one. I could work in the sun till well into May. Further-more, the amount of light which ash-trees let into a wood promotes a fine floor of flowers. How vastly different is the other extreme! – a pinewood floor. I used to take a walk oc-casionally to a little pine wood a short distance away, and look into its daily darkness where nothing grew and no bird sang. In my ash wood the common wild flowers were abundant. They arrived punctually according to the well-known schedule. First the primroses in March – when I began work. Then the violets, soon to be overtaken by the anemones who in turn gave way to the bluebells, while the ground-ivy and bugle also appeared, though dog's mercury provided almost the main floor of the entire wood.

We call wild flowers common because of their quantity. But this is just where we strike the great difference between the productions of Nature and the productions of Man. When we produce many samples of the same thing they are of poor quality and we speak of them as mass-produced. The mass-productions of Nature do not fail at all in terms of quality. Take the bluebell. There indeed is quantity. Yet every single year we are freshly struck by their quality. Only a flower-snob could fail to see that any one of those bells on the uplifted belfry is as delicate a construction as any tulip or any rose. I will not say more beautiful, or less, for in this realm of flowers we actually are in the presence of abundant examples of – *perfection*. I think that perfection is the key to the emotion that flowers cause in us. When a thing is perfect the problem of its existence is solved. Gazing at flowers in a wood an unexpected signal seems to go up; we feel a movement of happiness and hope about everything; there is a suggestion that all is really well, all is right with the world, regardless of the geographical situation of the Deity. It is because of this that all men, even ruffians, feel attracted to flowers. For they do intimate to us that, in spite of everything, all is well. Undoubtedly that is what they 'say' to us, and why it cheers us up to look at them. Philosophers say that all the ultimate problems – freedom, immortality, beauty, development – are presented and solved in plants. 'The flora does not only raise, but also answers, all the problems which the human spirit may propound,' said Count Keyserling. 'For anyone who could understand plants perfectly, life would no longer hold any secrets. And the plants surrender themselves so ingenuously to man. No being could be more sincere than they are, more truthful, more genuine. They perhaps of all the world's creatures represent themselves precisely as they are ... these blessed, pure creatures are never subject to evil moods, and always mirror the very core of their beings.'

Maybe it was because of this that the Sage who sat under the Bo-tree wanted to make plants of men: and we must admit that a Buddha resembles a plant more than anything else. Certainly flowers inspire us: they hold up before us the image of the

Ideal. What we would be, could we be true, they are. Ripeness is all. We know that. We see it in the flowers, they are the mirror in which is glassed that goal. But our greatest problem is our unfolding: in nearly every case something goes wrong at one stage or another. We fall. There is no fall of flowers.

3. The Tree-shed and the Tools

Every day before I went home I put my tools away in my shed. It had been built for me solely by Nature. I discovered a fairly full-grown ash-tree whose trunk was hollow inside at the base for about four feet upwards. There was an opening large enough for me to put my tools through it. Here I placed them every evening, knowing they would remain dry and quite safe since it would be hard to imagine a better camouflage for a tool-house.

In spite of being rotten inside, this tree was in fairly good condition. A tree is not useful to man, of course, as timber, if internally decayed either by disease or the tooth of time; but its own health is not affected if the outer sheaths of the trunk are all right, because the life of a tree resides in and receives reinforcement at its circumference and not its centre. Thus many an Old Village Tree while presenting a magnificent foliage in summer, also provides a huge hollow at the base of its trunk, equally fit as a shelter from storms or a tryst for lovers. Once I saw Mount Etna in full volcanic eruption. It was a sight which held my attention. But at the bottom of the mountain there was another manifestation almost as fascinating – the Chestnut Tree of the Hundred Horses which is said to be the largest tree in the world. Thirty men holding hands do not quite succeed in surrounding it, while a hundred horsemen can find ample room beneath its foliage, as indeed was actually proved when Joan, Queen of Aragon, was caught in a storm nearby and took shelter there with her enormous retinue. And at the bottom of this tree a hole runs straight through, wide enough to admit two carriages abreast. It still yields a good crop of chestnuts.

284

On my arrival in the wood I took out what tools I needed for the day from this tree-shed of mine. Very often I contented myself simply with the axe and the bill-hook. These are two delightful instruments. There are not many agricultural implements one would speak of in such terms – certainly not of the hoe or the saw. But all good men love an axe; and all Prime Ministers and Literary Prophets in their old age are discovered by the visitor using an axe in the garden. Tolstoy regarded axe-work as a religious discipline. Bernard Shaw declares that it keeps him sane. And it was the axe that inspired Gladstone to say to the messenger who came with the news of his recall to office – 'My mission is to solve the Irish Problem.'

I do not know whether there is any absolutely official method of handling the axe. I have no doubt that my own methods leave room for improvement, but I think I must have done the obvious things since in the end my results were good. In cutting down a tree you need to cut low on the stool and to cut clean. A battered, slashed-up stump not only looks unsightly but promotes arboreal disease. Experience taught me to strike down and then strike up, never horizontal, thus carving out a $<$ shape. When I was nearly through I very often went to the other side and with one blow finished the job, or administered a second while the tree was falling over. If the stump then displayed any ragged edges I cleaned it up with my bill-hook. After sufficient practice my wood presented clean stumps and stools instead of a series of wooden clefts and cliffs such as are found whenever a company of schoolboys have been on a job of this kind. I soon learnt not to dash at the thing with undue speed and not to hurl the whole force of my body at the tree, as it were. My technique was somewhat golfer-like. I kept my eye steadfastly on the spot I intended to strike, kept my left arm straight, did not lurch after the axe with my body and only exerted full force at the last minute when also I did some good wrist-work. (Thus I grandly write about my method, and should have done it that way, and possibly, on occasion, even did do so.) I certainly think that the secret of a good cut, especially when dealing with a medium-sized hazel-bush, is in that last golfer-flick of the wrist. I was once held up for a considerable time by a ticket-collector at South Kensington Underground Station who explained to me that his particular and striking ability as a boxer was due to the fact that he didn't put out his strength till the final second of a blow. He was not a big man and he insisted the success in boxing went to the most intelligent, to men like himself who realized that force should be reserved till the last second. 'I box from here,' he kept repeating, and tapped his forehead to indicate the seat of his weightiest weapon in the ring. This unexpected pugilistic tutorial stuck in my mind, and I carried it over with some degree of success into the realm of forestry.

The great thing is to keep the axe sharp. Much depends upon the strength of mind to do this, for it saves much expense of body and spirit. I found out before it was too late (though late enough), that it is an illusion to suppose that one must take an axe to a grindstone with wheel and water complete. The ordinary hand-stone will serve if applied frequently and with a level pressure that does not merely grind the edge but the space before the edge. I used to tell myself to aim at never touching the very edge at all with the stone, but to grind down the rise behind. Given a big stone – not one broken in half – one can sharpen an axe all right and be independent of the elaborate wheel which requires two people to be on the job. For comfort with axe-work, then, I beg to prescribe a sharp edge. And secondly a good axe. That is to say an axe that is neither too heavy nor too light. This is not so simple as it sounds. There are many absurdly balanced axes about: axes with monstrously heavy blades and handles that do not balance them. I bought an axe with a fair-sized blade and a well-balanced shaft, and used it with pleasure for some time, till I was offered the use of a heavier axe. At first I thought the latter much better, and when I took up my own it seemed ridiculously light, and on using it I completely missed my aim. But I found that I couldn't possibly keep the heavy one sharp and it became temper-losingly blunt. So I went back to my old axe, and soon it gained in the weight it seemed to have lost, and I never changed again. (Have I any hint regarding a method of sharpening with the stone? Yes, take a stick, lay it on the ground, kneel down and grind away at the blade the edge of which is kept free of the ground by means of the stick.)

Here as in all these matters, to do your job properly and get pleasure from it, you need the good tool. This is equally true of the bill-hook. For a long time I was content with a light, blunt, rattling affair – thinking it all right. But one day I went out and bought a heavier one, a beauty – the gain in speed of work, cleanness of cut, and pleasure in execution being far in excess of the cash value. I generally learn this sort of thing too late, and I learnt this too late since two-thirds of my job was done before I got rid of the old bill-hook. I hadn't realized the difference it would make. The fact is we have in the bill-hook an even more delightful tool than the axe. Especially if you are thinning. You cut down a tree, after which it is necessary to clean it, that is knock off the branches and thus produce a clear pole to be taken away for firewood or any of the other purposes. This is the time when a sharp bill-hook is a joy: a single back-handed slash will generally sever the small branches, while with one or two strokes you can dispatch the larger branches; and if your pole is not too thick and you wish to cut it in half, you can still use your bill-hook for this if it is good and sharp, holding the pole in the left hand and coming down with a back-hand stroke with the right hand. This is an exercise that engages the whole body. It is difficult to think of a more delightful job than this, stripped to the waist in the sun, and thus enabled for a few too briefly passing hours to step aside from the inanities of our repellent civilization. I am writing this account while finishing off this forestry work, and since I am very near the end of the wood the thought of possibly never using a bill-hook again in a big way is very depressing. No doubt I shall be able to use an axe from time to time, and even a plough; but when shall I ever again have a whole wood to thin?

But before passing on I must mention one peculiarity about bill-hooks. They have a way of disappearing. This experience is shared by all woodmen. You are always changing over from axe to bill-hook and vice versa. You put the bill-hook down, take up the axe, and having done what you want it for, reach for the bill-hook again. It has disappeared. Often it is impossible to find it without an irritating search. True, one gets wary at last about this peculiarity and one automatically plans a conspicuous place for putting it down. But, once a more than usually strange disappearance trick was played on me. Near the end of the day's work a shower came on, and leaving my bill-hook I went a certain distance away where there was good shelter. On returning I could not find my bill-hook. In this case there were only ten square yards where it could be, an area not overgrown with anything. I searched minutely and scientifically within that given area. To no avail. It was not there. At last I went home, hoping that on the morrow it would have returned. And sure enough there it was in the morning in the middle of the space I had gone over again and again while searching for it.

4. Meditation on the Struggle for Life

During my work of clearing there was one thing which gave me particular satisfaction. This was the cutting away of the honeysuckle. Belonging to the parasitic company of plants that engage trees for climbing up instead of rising on their own accord, they often provide grim spectacles in the woods of merciless throttling and strangulation. Ascending from the bottom of the trunk they spiral their way upwards, clinging tightly to the bark. This hinders the sap, the tree's circulation, and after a year or two the young trunk itself becomes a spiral-shaded pole, bulging out in a remarkable manner as if an erect rubber tube full of air had been tightly wound with cord in spiral formation so that it bulged out between the cord (though in the case of the victimized tree or branch the bulge appears *at* the cord of honeysuckle). The tree struggles to live in spite of the stranglehold, but generally in vain. It is apt to die and rot and bend over, a parched ruin upon which the honeysuckle thrives, spurning the base degrees by which it did ascend. I have come upon portions of the wood where honeysuckle had practically taken over: the captive, the twisted, the mutilated, the dying, the dead ash-trees stood hopelessly entangled in the network of ropes, pulleys, nooses, loops, ligatures, lassos which outwardly appeared as lifeless themselves as pieces of cord, but were centrally bursting with life and power, ready and willing to pull down the wood.

Mr Aldous Huxley once suggested that if Wordsworth had lived in the tropics he would not have written about Nature in the way he did. This is pretty obvious. Such speculations are not very fruitful; we cannot move in these hypothetical fields with any profundity. In the tropics Wordsworth would not have written his known work, and perhaps none at all; but that does not mean that men who are native to that clime may not find an approach to a total vision of the Absolute. It also begs the question that if Wordsworth had not been capable of total truth, Nature, in England, as elsewhere, provides ample opportunity for the half-truth. The king of the half-vision is that other lordly and everlasting bard, Thomas Hardy. In one of his forest descriptions in *The Woodlanders*, after speaking of Nature's merciless battles, he adds – 'Here, as everywhere, the Unfulfilled Intention, which makes life what it is, was as obvious as it could be among the depraved crowds of a city slum. The leaf was deformed, the curve was crippled, the taper was interrupted; the lichen ate the vigour of the stalk, and the ivy slowly strangled to death the promising sapling.' I came across the same sort of thing every day in my wood. It could make me silent and it could make me sad, but personally I cannot see the spectacle in terms of unfulfilled intention save superficially. What I see is – an almost liquid surging up of life. I see that life as a massive unity, moving and flowering under the influence of Fire – the air itself taking visible shape in the plants. Some of it does not get up, all of it cannot get up. But if one tree succeeds, one baby survives, I applaud.

Thus, even when we are feeling gloomy, philosophy will keep breaking in, with its happy, glancing gleam.

The spectacle in my wood which fascinated me most, and

encouraged me most, was – decomposition. As I hacked my way through the undergrowth I came upon many fallen trees which had been lying on the ground for years. They lay there presenting every variety of rotting trunk and bough, in every stage of transition as they slowly burnt their way back into the ashes from which the Phoenix of Life rises up again. I would take my bill-hook and cut into a trunk lying covered with moss. It would go in deep as easily as into a lump of cake, until it struck abruptly the inner part not yet decayed. I would take out slices, letting them crumble in my hand and fall to the ground – as *humus*. Once a seed, then a sapling, then a great hard tree, now softly turning into *earth*. I found them, I say, in every shape and style, lying in the silent shades in a melancholy mightier than beauty. At a touch a branch would fall, already dust. Under my feet a weeping clod of wood damply squelched like wet paper. Deep, soft, dark green moss covered nearly every limb, like velvet on old discarded furniture. Age or storm had laid these low, but there were also stumps where full-grown trees had once been sawn off. I was never tired of testing their present status with my boots. Some were still hard as a table, with perhaps a large fungus growing on them, nearly the size, colour, and shape of an elephant's ear. Others, enmossed inches deep, were as springy to stand or sit on as an armchair. Some had almost wholly conformed to the law of return and scarcely differed in appearance or material from the earth around. Others made magnificent portals and main entrances to rabbits' burrows.

Sometimes I knelt down beside one of the most ancient trunks, and peered under the bark and into the caves and recesses and cups that marked the erosion of time; and there I found colonies of insects building their Jerusalem in these countries of decay which must represent for them the acme of perfection. And there also fungi, like jellyfish, like sponges, like rubber flowers, took life-giving elixir from the burning bark. And as I sat and leaned and looked upon these lands it seemed to me that here too was blessedness and peace, and glory though it did not shine, and innocence untainted as the new-born babe.

Here might the weary and the sick come and lay them down; and without anguish, and without misgiving, fall back and return to the ashes that never die.

5. The Virtues of Hazel

As I advanced, the terms 'hard-wood' and 'soft-wood' began to mean something definite to me now, for the difference in resistance to the axe was decisive. There were a few spruce-trees at the edge and my axe sank into that wood very easily. The extreme softness of young oak surprised me. The hazel was by no means as hard as the ash. All the same I was puzzled by these terms; for we all know how hard the oak is when seasoned, and the spruce becomes excellent, I understand, for rafters and boarding, ladders, props, and packing-cases. That miserable tree, the elder, which occasionally I came across, can be cut without effort, but seems to become harder even than any of the others. The axe makes a different sound against each species of tree, and a skilled woodman ought to be able to tell from a distance whether, say, an ash or a hazel is being cut down.

It is easier to get your axe into a hazel than an ash; but it is much harder to get at the hazel. It gave me little pleasure to come upon a row of hazel-bushes to be cut down and laid. The hazel does not aspire. A dozen shoots from an ash-stool will seek the perpendicular, and the most favourably placed amongst them will stand up straight and high. But the shoots, fifty or more sometimes, from the hazel-stool, while they *start* straight, later begin to fan out, and even the one at the centre makes no attempt to grow straight, and all the branches intertwine tremendously. In short the hazel is a bush, not a tree; and a bush is a tree whose shoots thrive in concert and together make the unit. The hazels' quick growth, abundance, flexibility, and thinness make them one of the most valuable of all timber crops, since they can be twisted so easily into fences and hurdles, while their tributary twigs are the very thing for beanstakes.

I imagine that they are also excellent for fishing-rods. I do not know whether this is officially right but I think it must be, because certain branches that I handled *were* fishing-rods. While at work I caught fish with them in my own peculiar way. When you cut down hazel you do not clean it for firewood or poles (unless the bush is hugely overgrown with shoots the size of small trees). You lay the branches on the ground all facing one way, placing each branch behind and half over the previous one, so that when you are dealing with many bushes you make a long line of sloping hazel branches like a kind of hedge which is called a drift. It is pleasant to transform the tangle into drifts running parallel through the cleaned-up wood. But to lay them thus is not very easy. The numerous tributary twigs of hazel-bushes are so intertwined that when you start to extract the branch you have just cut off, it is no easy matter getting it free from the main clump; and if you have left anything within reach on the ground, say a coat or a hat or a handkerchief, then often the terminal twigs of the extracted branch, bending down, will tend to scoop up your property. Once when struggling to lay a long flexible rod beside the other branches on the ground, I hooked up my hat exactly as if it were a special kind of fish. I mention this trivia because it is my only fishing story, and it would seem to suggest that here is the perfect material for the complete fisherman's rod.

It serves another purpose which also may not be official. It is splendid for the amateur chimney-sweep. Nowadays if one wants anything done one must do it oneself. To be my own plumber is quite beyond me, and when my only tap – a short one from the rain-tub to the copper – split in a frost, I never had even that one tap to use. But having once set my chimney on fire I saw that in future I must keep it swept. So taking a tip from a countryman who is full of ways and wiles, I did my own sweeping. The tip was to select a long hazel-rod of fair strength and much flexibility and take it home. Then tie a number of sprigs of holly round the thin end. This was the sweeping-brush. It was too long to fit into the room, so one just let it in from the door or window and then curved it up the chimney. Such a rod easily reached to the top of my chimney. As I cleaned lower and lower I cut the rod, thus greatly facilitating the thoroughness of the brushing. By this means the soot came down perfectly. Half-an-hour's job. And having taken the precaution of wearing gloves, an old hat, and mackintosh, I did not emerge from it in the least grimed. I do not say that this would work in a big house, but it is the chimney-sweeping solution for anyone with a cottage in the country; and so I think we must definitely give such brushes a prominent place on the list of the hazel-tree's gifts to mankind.

6. In the Primeval Chase

The atmosphere of the wood was entirely altered by my intervention. It became a different place: not the same place altered, but as different as if on going down a lane to see a certain wood in a given country, you came upon another landscape. There was now no disorder; the trees were visible, and (before I had done) you could look for a long way in all directions through a small forest, whereas before you could only see a few yards. Space and light and orderliness had been introduced. It now seemed more alive, happy, and beautiful – from the view-point of man (who sticks on the labels). And since we do stick on labels it is a sad ineptitude to suppose that Nature cannot be improved upon from a 'beauty' point of view, by man. The idea that 'every prospect pleases, while only man is vile' is not the whole truth. Man has added to the beauty of Nature in as measurable a degree as, say, between an area of uneven, tufted, coarse grass and a well-tended lawn margined by geraniums.

I often used to think of this when I strayed beyond my wood into further forest-land, especially one portion which seemed to have been neglected for centuries. It was a gloomy place at most times of the year. The trees were chiefly oak with some silver birch. It was like walking at the bottom of the ocean and continually finding some wrecked vessel. Or again, like coming upon the scene of a battle waged long ago: huge corpses of tree-trunks sprawled on the ground, their limbs like the broken arms of giant men lying where they fell. From some ancient oaks, a great branch, through weight of years, violence of storm, or stroke of lightning, had cracked at the fork and the branch leaned to the ground – a giant arm with fingers gripping the earth. Often it seemed as if I had visited the place of some terrible calamity long since closed in the withered page of history, and now made ghostly by the ever-reigning silence which I dared not break. I could see little of the greenery above, but walked submerged down there amongst the dereliction and dismay of lost causes and abandoned hope. How different all this would look, I pondered, if it were taken in hand by man.

The silver birch were not doing well amongst the oak trees. Many of them were dead – blasted poles erect in the foliage of other trees. Some, still in feeble leaf, had begun to fall over, and remained on the slant, upheld by surrounding branches, looking as if they had fainted but were just caught in time. A number of trunks lay about on the ground, short pieces nearly covered over by the dog's mercury. One of these had a hole in it which ramified in several directions, at the entrance of which was a damp, round fungus; or so I thought, till I noticed it was breathing, and saw it was a large slug. This old trunk lay at the foot of an erect log – I cannot call it a tree for the trunk had broken off about ten feet from the ground. There it stood now, immensely lichened and mossed, a shaky column with one exceptional feature – it had steps placed in spiral-shaped form going up. They were small steps but very attractive in their wonderful colour congruity with the weather-washed, old, white-patched bark of the birch. Had they been firm enough they would have served me admirably for climbing up to examine the top of the column. But they could hardly hold me since they were made of fungus. Nevertheless I have never seen more definite and attractive steps than those upon that tottering tower.

It is not surprising that there was an ancient atmosphere about this place, for I was working in the middle of Cranbourne Chase. At one time it had a perimeter of over eighty miles, from

Shaftesbury to Salisbury on the North, and encircled by the Stour and the Avon at the other sides. Now it is shrunk to a small oasis of wild country. But that oasis has changed little in the course of centuries. It remains, as Thomas Hardy has written, 'a truly venerable track of forest land, one of the few remaining woodlands in England of undoubted primeval date, wherein Druidical mistletoe is still found on aged oaks, and where enormous yew trees, not planted by the hand of man, grow as they had grown when they were pollarded for bows'. Wandering here I could well feel that if the world is too much with my fellows it was not too much with me. In the strange days in which we live I could actually say farewell to the world far more effectually among these shades and natural debris than on any island in the Pacific Ocean.

I decided that if ever I were a fugitive from the Law this is where I would hide. But I learn that this decision of mine is not strikingly original. In fact, before 1830, the Chase had become so popular as a smuggler resort, and so sought after by thieves, murderers, and criminals of every grade no less than by poachers, blackmailers, tramps, and vagabonds, that in the end it was treated as a covert for crime, and was disafforested.

7. Bracken

You have to keep your eyes open in the country if you want to see the spring before it is all over. This is borne in on me every year. The whole affair is so swift and so variegated that unless we are careful we miss half of it. During some months of summer and some of winter the casual eye sees little change, but during April and May the speed of appearance and disappearance is almost on a par with the cinema. One wants to see the show through again at once, and get the order of things right. Nothing requires more deliberate intellectual exertion than to follow the unfolding closely, nothing more time-eating. I found it much easier just to get on with my job of thinning, and I often put off looking at something until 'later' – by which time it was gone. Luckily the flowers do not all appear quite at once. The primrose path has time to make an impression before it becomes the property of bugle and ground-ivy; the celandines, the anemones, and the violets have fallen before the bluebells rise to spread their gospel and then yield to the aristocracy of the foxglove.

In this wood it always seemed to me at one period, near the end of May, that everything would have to give way to the empire of dog's mercury. But of course this was reckoning without the bracken which steps in and takes control from June onwards. Here indeed is a case in which you must keep awake if you are not to be surprised at almost an apparition. For the unfurling of these fern-flags from their unnoticed beginnings to great thickness and height is one of the swiftest of all the transactions. The leaves are packed in a roll very much like those things you find in Christmas crackers and blow out. And they unroll so swiftly that their internal chemical apparatus might seem to have the force of steam. Unlike ordinary ferns and all the other plants around, they continue to grow higher and higher until six or eight feet is not uncommon. A miniature forest has suddenly appeared in which a child might get lost.

Farmers can very seldom enjoy aesthetically what they deplore agriculturally, and since bracken has a very bad reputation as a particularly injurious weed, we seldom hear anything good of it. But a philosophic mind, uninstructed in the claims of agriculture, might well conceive the frond in a favourable light. For it is a direct descendant of those Tree-Ferns that once covered the whole land of Europe before bird, quadruped, or man appeared. The atmosphere was then unbreathable, containing in suspension in the state of poisonous gas, the huge mass of carbon which has since become coal. The tree-ferns cleansed it. They subtracted the carbon, storing it in their leaves and stems. They continued this atmospheric purification for generations, and when at last they died their buried remnants became coal in which even today we can find many leaves and stems wonderfully preserved, archives in which we may read 'the history of this ancient vegetation which has given us an atmosphere that we can breathe and has stored up for us in the bowels of the earth those strata of coal which are the wealth of nations'. Fabre, from whom I quote those words, traces bracken as descending from that noble line, and states that 'the stem of our common Bracken reproduces in its bundles of blackish, lignous tissue, the rather sketchy design of a two-headed, heraldic eagle as though to blazen the nobility of its ancient race.'

And should the man of philosophic mind, while contemplating these things, fall into a less elevated mood and inquire whether it was really worth while for the ferns to cleanse the air of carbon poison gas if we, the inheritors of their bounty, prepare a poison gas of our own to destroy ourselves, he may still reflect that Necessity, so aptly called the mother of invention and discovery, has in these latter days found uses for bracken unsuspected by our ancestors. Thus the Glasgow Research Station finds that silage can be made from it. Mr Ronald Duncan cooks it as a kind of asparagus. Dr Krebs of Sheffield University claims that yeast can be made out of it. The Germans make petrol from it. Silage for stock, petrol for machines, yeast and salad for men – not bad for a weed.

Not bad; and a hopeful sign of the times with regard to the future. A new principle is beginning to be advanced – that of each country making use of its own resources before dashing off to the ends of the earth for new materials. Hitherto we have tapped our own resources only to a small extent, and when we saw something in a far country we built a ship and went and got it from there. Other nations have followed suit, all trying at once to procure the rare substance from the far place, and claiming 'equal right' to do so. That was called Imperialism. Today a new possibility opens. Science steps forward demonstrating in a remarkably concrete way that since all things are all things, almost anything can be made from anything. Before our astonished gaze they turn wood into jumpers, milk into buttons, maize into mud-guards, glass into shirts, bracken into petrol. The dream of the old alchemists is surpassed and transmutation becomes the order of the day. No longer shall Imperialism be necessary. No longer shall men, in the name of trade, in the name of religion, in the name of civilization go to Persia, to India, to Honolulu in order to steal away some local treasure. They shall stoop down and find it at their feet.

In the meanwhile I am more content to regard bracken as bracken, and not as petrol or anything else. Indeed I fear that if I am right about future developments, men will look at phenomena even less than they do today. To *look at* the object, at any object, and see it in its own right is the key to a fuller apprehension of the mystery and significance of life. But there is no money in this, and so people do not bother to use their eyes in that way. Perhaps in the future they may look at the object more closely – but only with the motive of turning it into something else.

Let me look at my bracken here, I said to myself, without ulterior motive or agricultural disgust, and watch it spring up mushroom-like before my very eyes. Most of the flowers have already faded and now they are disappearing beneath the ferns, and the great kingdom of dog's mercury no longer usurps the scene. And as I gaze at it I gaze back across the years of my life and see again the tall bracken in the lonely glen on the Wicklow Mountains through which deer and stags leap with amazing speed.

8. Old and New Attitude to Trees

This wood had been neglected so long that I came upon great waste of potential timber. Here and there a full-grown tree had evidently crashed down upon surrounding shoots. I occasionally found a trunk or a big branch lying right across a stool from which ten shoots were growing. All would be twisted, none worth keeping there. Many of these young ash-trees had thereby assumed the strangest shapes, for they had had to twist themselves as if they were made of rubber. Sometimes they looked like the neck plus the head of a swan, and I saw one that reminded me of that queer flamingo that Alice used as a croquet-mallet in Wonderland. Some had twisted their way up snake-wise in order to pass the obstructions. Some were link-ed in close embrace and one had grown in such an extraordinary way that it now *ran through* a larger stem. I could do nothing in such places but get rid of all the twisters and leave an open space.

At other times I came upon three or four excellent trees, all straight, all doing well, all big and high. But since they were too near to one another, only one could be left standing, and I had to select the best. I was often in a real quandary in deciding which was the best, for just as at once place I would find three to five twisters closer together, at another I would find an equal number of champions.

When it was thus necessary to axe a beautiful ash-tree for no better reason than that it was too close to another one, I felt extremely apologetic. For trees do exert a strong personality. It is said that in certain parts of Austria there are still to be found peasants who beg the pardon of a tree before felling it. Sir James Frazer told how the inhabitants of Sumatra used to lay the blame at the door of the Dutch authorities. A native would go to a tree which he had to cut down in order to make a road, and would pretend to pick up a letter which he then read aloud to the effect that the Dutch authorities enjoined him to fell the trees ... 'You hear that, Spirits,' he would cry, 'I must begin clearing at once, or I shall be hanged.' The seriousness of tree-worship in ancient Germany brought ferocious penalties upon anyone who peeled the bark of a standing tree: his navel was cut and nailed to the tree, and he was driven round and round it until his guts were twisted about the trunk. Plutarch relates how the withering of a sacred fig-tree in Athens or Rome was re-garded with consternation; while if a tree was observed by someone to be drooping, a hue and cry was set up and people rushed to its assistance with buckets of water as if to put out a fire. At many times and places it was considered essential to make sacrifices to trees sometimes with fowls, and sometimes with human beings. If we bear in mind the many beneficent qualities ascribed to trees in the past, it is easy to understand why a custom like the May-tree or the May-pole prevailed. In

Spring a tree was brought into the village amidst applause and rejoicing, the intention being to bring home to the village and to each house the blessings which the tree-spirit had the power to bestow.

Mankind dominates the world today. It is certain that trees once did so. It is not possible for us even to imagine the immense forests that existed at the dawn of history – when clearings were but tiny islands in the atlantic stretches of wood. In the first century the Hercynian Forest stretched eastward from the Rhine farther than any man knew: men, questioned by Caesar, had travelled for two months without reaching the end. I like to think how the Weald of Kent, Surrey, and Sussex are remnants of the great forest of Anderida that once clothed the whole of the south-eastern portion of the island, joining another (older than the Chase or father of it) from Hampshire to Devon – and how in the reign of Henry II the citizens of London hunted the wild boar and bull in the woods of Hampstead.

However, since the days of tree-domination and tree-worship we have progressed so much that we now can see them in terms of £ s. d. When I cut down a tree I had levelled a piece of 'timber' valued at so much a foot. During many a five minutes I have knocked out about a shilling's worth a minute. I stacked the poles neatly in piles of a hundred – (my own pay being so much a 'lug'). One day a timber-merchant came to the woods to decide what he wanted to buy. He was accompanied by the foreman of the estate. Together they arrived at the just price. Then the timber-merchant inspected a portion of the wood not yet tackled by me, marking specially straight trees that he fancied. I said in an aside to the foreman that not all the ones the man was marking could rightly come down, and the foreman said to the merchant at intervals – 'But we must look after our own interests.' The man took no notice and continued marking trees while we looked on disapprovingly, the foreman repeating – 'Of course we must look after our own interests.'

When the timber-merchant had gone, the foreman, an unexuberant personality, looked round at the wood, appraising it. 'There baint nothing in trees,' he said. I made some kind of commercial remark. He looked round at the wood again and finally dismissed the whole prospect with two weighty words – 'It's *dead money*,' he said. Having brought forth this gem of ages-old wisdom he gazed over the wood sourly and mournfully as if filled with sorrow at the sight of so much dead money.

9. Clothes and Sanity

It was not until the bracken had started to appear that the roof was put on the wood. Since the ash does not send out its branches till near the top, we do get this effect of a roof in any reasonable ash wood. Visualize a larch, a chestnut-tree, and many a beech and oak, and then remember the tall, bare trunks of the ash branching only at their crowns, and you will grant that it is indeed the placing on of a high roofing that we witness in May and June. It was pleasant to look through an acreage of bare trunks that I had disentangled from the press of competition, and then up at the intermingling greenery enlightened by the sun. You can seldom get this effect from other trees growing together. The chestnut branches out very low, and while beeches do often present a high, lone stem they often do not, and you see beautiful leafy branches sweeping the ground; while the oak, though also capable of the long clean trunk, goes in for great thick limbs sprawling out parallel with the ground or twisting upwards from a low fork. However, I must not run my image of columns upholding a roof too far in connection with my ash, for there were many gaps of course between the crowns, and also a number of blanks owing to lack of trees.

I welcomed these gaps and blanks, for otherwise I had to work in the shade far too often. And when the sun is shining I do not take kindly to working in the shade. Give me heat every time, I do not mind how much. I can do twice the amount of work in the sun than when away from it, or clothed off from it. This is partly due to my attitude towards clothes. I like to wear the right thing in the right place, and am no advocate of unconventional attire. But the right thing, at certain times, in certain places, for many people, is often a pair of shorts and nothing more except for the feet. For many agricultural jobs that is not the right thing at all, but for some it is. As for axe-work in the summer, and bill-hook work while cleaning your fallen tree, it certainly is right when the weather is hot or muggy or showery. Thus unencumbered I can do, and like doing, a week's work in two days. The hotter I get the harder I work, perspiration making me almost cold and the sun not hot enough to make me even feel its heat then. The sheer freedom of the limbs with the breeze on the body gives a pleasure not easily excelled; one could justifiably enthuse about it; I content myself with saying that though this is not the only way of feeling happy and alive, it is one way. To use the mind at full concentration is one of the most manly things we can do, since this capacity happens to be the special gift of man; but we are also animals, and we experience great joy when, in primitive surroundings, we are not dolled up and tied down with artificial skins. Thus with me anyway; I cannot exaggerate the satisfaction I get from becoming a 'savage' – even in colour. And I fear that many a Lancashire young man – need I say 'lad'? – having come home from the Far East, will miss, at intervals throughout his life, sometimes quite savagely, his shirtless army days in the jungle.

There exists a strange crowd of people called Nudists. It might be thought that here we have sane people in an over-civilized world. But this is not so. They are misled. They imagine that by simply taking off their clothes they can side-step the sophistications of metropolitanism. Yet of course they can do nothing of the sort, they merely become unclothed and in their wrong minds. Once I turned off a main street in London, and having paid a fee of two shillings, was admitted into a large house in which a nudist gathering was in progress. When standing in the porch and glancing round at the pavemented vistas of the metropolis, I felt surprise at the assumption that inside this house it would be possible to 'return to nature' by the mere removal of clothes. And having entered I did not find the scene or the proceedings in any degree inspiring. There was one room reserved for games, though no particular games were being played and people were wandering about in it aimlessly since there was no possibility of exercise of an exacting sort. Most of the members were in the next room – having tea and cakes. No one wore anything. This looked incongruous in the electric-lit room with its tea and cakes and the people sitting in rows – idiotic might be a better word. And should anyone have come along, I reflected, with an erotic *arrière pensée*, he or she would quickly have found that nudism is the enemy of eroticism (though possibly not if everyone wore a mask). As I had entered fairly unnoticed it was easy to slip away without offence, and I was glad indeed to regain the comparative sanity of the city streets.

The point is that these nudists run a principle – no clothes: (and this insistence upon none at all is an indignity). It is just a thoughtless principle with no sense in it, seen in practice to be far the most unnatural and unsane affair in the whole city – a sort of climax of absurdity. The more reasonable, open-air nudists do at least enjoy the sun. Unfortunately they sun-bathe. That is to say they *lie about* doing nothing. In moderation that is all right, of course, but done in company and as a great thing in itself, it is pretty miserable. The whole thing is done too seriously and too thoroughly. One should avoid thoroughness in such fields. My own principle concerning the whole matter is simply this – that the way to enjoy the sun is through working in it or playing a game in it, and that there should never be the raising of an eyelid if a shirt is removed in any congruous setting. But today we still have crazy people who think nothing of a bather approaching the sea in bathing-shorts, but would stare at a cyclist going up a steep hill on a hot day in shorts only. And then over against this we have the lunacy of a whole-hogging nakedness carried even into a city mansion during a winter evening!

In my wood it was unnecessary to consider the existence of either sort of person. I could do the natural thing without the slightest botheration. Much of the work was really strenuous. There were trees to cut down large enough to merit two men

with a saw; and when I had axed them down, and cleaned them
up, and then chopped them into poles short enough to load on a
lorry, I arranged them in piles of a hundred. All this was wonderful exercise, the axing and the hauling about requiring full
strength, while the branch-clearing with the bill-hook as I held
up the heavier branch with one hand, engaged every muscle in
the body. It gave me unbounded pleasure to go at this furiously
for hours on end if the sun was blazing down on me. It didn't
matter how hot it was, the hotter the better, for then I became
very wet with perspiration and needed the warmth of the sun as
one coming out of water, while if it rained the drops melted at
once. Thus dressed I often felt that I could go on all day without exhaustion, whereas in the winter I couldn't do a third of
the work in the time. I used to smile sometimes at the thought
that I was being paid to enjoy myself thus, in a world where a
boss who says – 'I'm not paying you to enjoy yourself, my boy!'
is considered a particularly reasonable and high-minded pillar
of society.

10. The Garden of Eden

That was one peak of pleasure. But I got as much out of sitting
down for my breaks. To be tired enough to make the act of
sitting down a sensation of real relief is a pleasure which has
much to be said for it. And provided that you are not over-
exhausted but just physically in need of a rest – then the mind
often functions at its very best. After some food, hot tea
from the thermos, and a cigarette, it is quite remarkable how
freely the brain can move, and how favourable the conditions
are for unpremeditated meditation.

There is one more proviso for me – the perfect seat in a sunny
spot: or in a shady spot at those hours on certain summer days
when the sun is actually too hot to sit in. I was expert at finding
such places. I kept finding new ones, thinking each better than
the last. By a perfect place I mean a tree which I could lean
against comfortably and which was so situated that other trees

would not block the sun at those times when I would be sitting down. As I say, I found several, and shall remember them all my life because of the happiness I found there and the glory that shone round me. There was one outstanding tree at the foot of which I took up my position very often. I did not cut my way towards it for some time, but when I had discovered it I made it my headquarters for meditation. Trees are particularly conducive to meditation: no doubt that famous Bo-tree did much to prepare Gautama for his hour of enlightenment.

This particular tree was not an ash, it was a fine old oak. Its trunk had considerable girth – three men holding hands could hardly surround it. At about three feet up it leant out and forked into such large branches that it was a question which might claim to be the trunk. At this fork, and for some distance along one of the branches, a fern garden was flourishing. (This arboreal garden was very delightful to contemplate in the summer. A maple-tree, not far off, had a mistletoe growing on one of its branches, and on my way to Blandford I used to stop and look at another maple where to my amazement I saw a young silver birch growing healthily in a moist niche high up.) The arrangement of branches was such that no great limb immediately roofed me blocking out the sun, but at a suitable height the leafage was so plentiful that as a shelter from rain this was perhaps the best tree I have ever known. That leafage, combined with the trunk which gently sloped outwards over me, prevented a drop of water from falling on me for quite a long time even when it was raining heavily outside. I say outside because on such occasions I could sit as if I were indoors without the slightest necessity to put on a coat. It was curious to see the rain pouring down while I, though out-of-doors, was really in-doors. It would be half an hour before the roof would begin to leak a bit.

The situation was not altogether perfect with regard to the sunshine, for after ten o'clock in the morning a big tree intervened. But up till then it was the best place in the wood, and during really hot weather it was superb for thoughtful shade. If there was wind at other places there was no wind here, for I placed 'drifts' either of hazel or of branches cut from my ash-poles, at each side. And finally, it was easy to lean against: the earth was soft and no roots stuck out; instead there was a sort of alcove into which I could fit and lean back so as to be comfortably upright.

I mention all these particulars because the reader will then recognize that since I also got a long view, a long sloping-down view of the wood and further woods beyond, seeing nothing but trees, and having behind me and at each side nothing but trees, I was in a highly favourable position, indeed a position in which not only happy hours but inspired and fruitful hours might be spent.

During the late spring and summer the sun fell upon this spot between 8 a.m. and 10 a.m. And as this was between six and eight normal time, the temperature of the sunlight could not have been improved upon. Since my job was being done on the basis of piece-work I was in command of my own time. On beautiful mornings my ideal was to do early work on the wood and sit down here for breakfast at eight when the sun had reached the oak. I took up my position carefully; back upright; head against trunk; legs straight out, with half-empty haversack under the knees, and a dry coat or sack to sit on; arms folded or hands clasped between knees. *Then* I immediately forgot my body, abandoned it – and became all spirit or soul or mind or whatever it is that sits inside us looking out of our two windows.

And now, at this point – to justify the foregoing details – I would gladly tell you what then I knew, what then I grasped. Ah, could I but do so, then would I have the power to bless and to save, even as I was saved and blessed! But I did not quite grasp it, I did not understand the Knowledge that seemed mine. As I strove, and strove again to penetrate the meaning of the glory and the promise in the scene around, and to frame into a conception something that I seemed to *know* – it eluded me, it always just drew back. Sometimes it came very close, as if it were about three feet above my head, at times almost brushing my forehead – but not coming in, and soon fading far away again. This experience of the Undeclared Announcement trembling on the verge of utterance, was imaged by Thoreau in terms of an eagle – 'an eagle that suddenly comes into the field of view, suggesting great things and thrilling the beholder, as if it were bound hitherward with a message for me; but it comes no nearer, but circles and soars away growing dimmer, disappointing me, till it is lost behind a cliff or a cloud'.

Yet something was clear to me, and I will set down here one note which I took as the nearest I could get to my finding – I turn off the road, enter the wood, and sit down under the tree. The sun gleams upon everything, there is glittering and shining everywhere. A green caterpillar is lowered down by an invisible thread in front of me, and as it swings about, the sun shines through its transparency. A little distance off a spider mounts upwards on another unseen rope, as if slowly falling upwards by inverse gravitation or being drawn up by an invisible crane, while another calmly walks on the air, and yet another takes a seat upon nothing. A bush over there is glittering with raindrops, little white lanterns fastened to the lower side of twigs; but if I swing my head slightly to one side, some of those lights turn colour, becoming red and purple. A creature alights on the back of my hand: its body being in the shape of a tiny solid canoe, which has one high brown sail rather out of proportion to the boat; suddenly the sail opens into two sails using the body at the base as a hinge, and the whole thing flies away – a butterfly, like a flying flower. Then there is the ground I sit on, the tree behind me, and the trees around me, and the flowers, and the thing I can't see, the air, yet stronger as a substance than, say, an aeroplane or a liner. A general voice is given to the whole thing by the birds. Most of this is incomprehensible to me, and even if a learned man describes what is going on and how it is all done, he will not be explaining it for me. And the interesting thing about it is that it *works*. Here we have nothing but a series of the most curious kind of miraculous activities and queer appearances and extravagant shapes, but it all works in concert. One might suppose that it could possibly work for a month or so or even a year – but it does it every year, it goes on

307

working without mishap and without running down. This in itself fills me with a great deal of confidence and some comfort. Added to this there is the general look of the place and the spirit in the atmosphere. Indeed we have all been so struck with its aspect that we have invented a word for it – beauty. I am surrounded here with law, order, and beauty, and am myself absolutely happy here. There is nothing to make me unhappy. No evil thing meets my eye, there is nothing bad here. I begin to grasp the obvious fact that this place is – perfect. And suddenly I realize where I am! I am in the Garden of Eden. I had heard about it always as a definite place in the past. There was no error in speaking of the Garden as existing, but the mistake lay in tying it down in time and place. For it still exists – all we need is the key of the gate. The first two persons in history dwelt in the Garden, it is said. But they ate of the Tree of Knowledge and had to go. That must be the truth: at the birth of consciousness we became *onlookers* and were separated from Nature, and left the Garden to create a world of our own apart from Nature. Our next step is a further extension of consciousness when we shall realize the unity of life on a higher plane of understanding. Having tasted of *that* tree of knowledge we shall enter the Garden of Eden once more, and Paradise shall be regained.

11. Ode to the Sun and to Idleness

It is true that at times I sought to pierce the mystery and to grasp the truth that seemed within my reach. But very often I refrained from thinking as much as possible, wishing just to receive what was given and glory in it. I certainly set myself against irrelevant thoughts, and against evil thoughts and thoughts of bitterness or annoyance concerning the outside world, which often pursued me into the wood like loathsome hounds. To think such things here would be fearful waste of time, I felt – the precious moments must not be lost. Here there was no need to think evil or to do evil, just as there was no chance of seeing evil. It was enough merely to sit in the sun.

To sit in the sun. This is still one of the greatest experiences of life for us in the West. And it is free. No millionaire can buy up the sun and sell it to us. All the inventions through all the centuries have added nothing to this gladness, nor may any frantic folly take it away. The poor deluded multitude, dungeoned and depraved by lunatics and magnates, may prefer *artificial* sunshine, but the real thing is there all the same, and cannot be taken down.

Pardon me if on this theme I speak with some slight intemperance. I am not quite normal in my love of the sun. It has always been a passion with me, I cannot call it less. To this day I remember the feeling of outrage I experienced when, in the schoolroom, on the sun shining in, the schoolmaster would get up and *draw down the blind*. I remember thinking the man must be crazy. 'Already I began to love the sun; a boy I loved the sun, Not as I since have loved him, as a pledge And surety of our earthly life,' said Wordsworth, 'But for this cause, that I had seen him lay His beauty on the morning hills.' Thus also have I loved the sun: because of his pledge, and because of his light upon the hill; but also because he transforms me – within no less than without.

Especially in March. Then the air is still chilly, but the sun is warm again – February's feeble ray is suddenly doubled, and sometimes if we can shelter from the cold wind we can get really warm. We are cold, and when the black cloud passes across, we shiver. Then the sun emerges from the silvered margin, the glowing ball comes out and blazes down upon us. At this moment I *give myself* to the experience. I close my eyes, and it is as if a warm velvet glove were laid across my face, an invisible blanket wrapped around me. We call it heat. But what is that? Am I taken in the arms of God? Everything is transformed, this is holy ground, even I am holy, my heart is purged of sin, I forgive everything, I love all things, I am lifted up; and in understanding I pass beyond all theory, all system, resting

309

utterly content in this blessing and this sign – worshipping the sun as if it were God himself, or at least his regent chaired beside the throne.

I have said I sat in the sun, but more often I *lay* in it – sideways, head on haversack (I cannot lie on my back). As a matter of fact I often take up this position – lying sideways – when I'm intellectually stuck over something and want to concentrate. But here I often did it because I wanted to sleep. The thing was to get as tired as possible, either by going to bed late or through strenuous work, and then lie in the sun – again especially in March or April – and go to sleep. I chose some particular spot at the foot of an ash to which the sun came and at each side of which I had placed drifts. At the chosen moment I lay down, curled up, and closed my eyes while the sun shone on my face. Often a strong, chilly wind blew, but it didn't come near me, I received only the sun. Then I entered my own special, simple paradise. I was absolutely tucked away from the world – several miles in all directions from it – I was totally hidden from sight of mortal soul, and no one knew where I was nor would be coming anywhere near me. I was free from the entire turmoil of the world. I lay there, almost sinking into, melting into the earth, waiting for sleep to come and take me right down – wondering if death in reality is more than such a joyous sinking down as this. But truly now I indulged in no thoughts, no metaphysical speculations, I became little higher than an animal – and no lower. I laughed to think what a reprehensible sight I would have made to any *busy* man who came upon me there, a sloping slacker, an untoiling son of earth! But I felt no need to offer up apologies to the unreproving Beings around. Let the world outside carry on, I would say, let them dash hither and thither, let them kill one another wholesale, let them go to hell, I'm wrapped in the embrace of Nature and filled with peace and love! And like any dog, like any savage, I lay there enjoying myself, harming no man, selling nothing, competing not at all, thinking no evil, smiled on by the sun, bent over by the trees, and softly folded in the arms of the earth.

12. Birds and Animals in the Wood

On such occasions I became so much part of the general furniture of the wood that my presence was not noticed by bird or animal. One day I was disturbed by a loud hammering on the oak tree. It came from a very small bird with a large beak. Then it flew to an ash, took up a position on a dead-looking branch and began hammering again – real hard strokes of the beak, not pecking but hitting. Then up to another place, a junction of branches and out of sight, from where I heard more hammering, and then in sight again higher up – exactly as if the bird was on business as a carpenter come to test the tree and knock in a few nails where necessary. It sometimes flew up, but more often walked up. After having made a thorough examination it descended the trunk, walking down backwards the whole way, quite oblivious of Newton's law, and knocking as it went along just as if it considered the decorative lichen needed some nailing down.

I wondered why it pecked so hard, since it would surely be difficult to catch hold of an insect that way. But bird authorities say that the insect in question is well behind the rotten bark and the beak has to pierce its way there. But how then does it see the insect to be picked up? The bird was obviously a woodpecker, I thought. But no, it was a nuthatch, a near relation. For the method of descending the tree, *walking* down either backwards or head first, distinguishes it: this mode of descent is evidently reserved for the nuthatch alone. Moreover, the woodpecker is inclined to make less of a hammering noise than a rattling; once when I heard one doing its stuff it sounded like a tractor-driver changing gear badly.

I know very little about birds, and I do not attempt to sort them out at all extensively, being content to watch them fly. The centuries pass, but we are just as fascinated as ever by these creatures who don't know what it is to *fall*, but go from the top of one tree to another upon the roads of air. They must be happy up there, we feel, housed in nests on trees, and able to pass along not in an aeroplane but as an aeroplane. But no one should even superficially compare a bird with an aeroplane: to figure such a thing one would have to imagine a bird whose outspread wings have got permanently stuck, and whose beak is a propeller. Yet the aeroplane shares this with birds – that it is a lover of woods. It is strange how pilots cannot resist the temptation to swoop down low over the tree-tops. On one particular occasion, a truly enormous and dark aeroplane passed just touching the tops of the trees above me: first the sudden thundering roar, then the flashing past of the huge structure. It was so colossal, so extreme a case, that I was driven right back across the centuries and saw myself as an Early Man in the jungle startled by the miraculous appearance of a flying monster, and dashing off to join the amazed and affrighted tribe.

I have nothing new to impart about either the birds or the animals in the woods. The usual performances were gone through here in the usual way. An agonizing screech at intervals broke the sylvan utopianism as intimated by the gentle cooing of the dove: but I could never be sure whether the cry was of death or love, pain or pleasure. The sudden loud flapping of unseen wings within the shades often startled me. The cuckoo made its appearance in due course, uttering its throaty gurgle while on the wing, and its famous announcement when in the trce. Occasionally a crow flew across, not as the crow is supposed to fly, but with sudden slight turnings and sharp hesitations as if it had remembered something too late. Sometimes, though very seldom, a peewit appeared, lover not of the woods but of the field and the wide desolate place dedicated to history and slow time, into which that plaintive cry, those mournful numbers, flow and melt away.

The birds which most often – late in the year – provided me with entertainment were the starlings. An immense force had taken up residence quite close, and towards evening they carried out extensive manoeuvres. Suddenly I would hear a noise from above as if a gale were blowing up, and I would see a black cloud moving much faster than a cloud; and as it moved, this composition of birds closed to the size of a football, then opened in the shape of a fan, closed again and now became a snake a hundred yards long twirling about in the air, then a carpet being shaken by invisible hands – each transformation being carried out with great celerity. Every bird went perfectly in wing with all the rest, so that however much the gathering twisted and turned it looked more like a single strange creature than a company – the few stragglers like feathers that had been blown off the body owing to the violence of the movement. What the purpose of all these operations was, I don't know. It gave all the appearance of being without utilitarian motive, and is, ten to one, pure *joie de vivre*, play, art for art's sake.

As for animals, I very often heard a sudden nervous chortle followed by a scampering noise, and looking up saw a red or grey squirrel, the creature that always delights us by the beauty of its tail and the strength of those paws that turn the perpendicular into the flat. Immediately my dog would bark, and it would dash higher up. Yet its behaviour was curious. It was as safe as a church in those branches; but it didn't think so, and leapt frantically from tree to tree, accomplishing jumps which made me nervous, and then coming to a very wide jump, failed to make it, landed on the ground uninjured, and scuttled into the undergrowth. It could have remained at ease in the first tree it went up. The species to which it belongs has had centuries behind it of practising in thus escaping from the earthbound beasts. Why has it not learnt to stay put in the security of the lofty boughs? Why does it lose its head?

The deer had more sense in using their legs. There were quite a few of these wonderful animals in the Chase, and the barks of the trees had suffered accordingly, for deer have a partiality for the barks of young trees. I did not see very many. Occasionally when I was making no noise, one appeared and came quite close. If I remained silent and absolutely still it did not observe me. For animals do not see with their eyes. Not that they are blind; it is that objects are not individually separated by a governing intelligence. This extraordinary fact has saved many a man's life in the jungle, and made close observation of animals

possible for the naturalist. Then if I stepped on a breaking twig
or deliberately clapped my hands it would leap away through
the wood with that aristocracy of speed and grace that makes
these creatures the queens of the forest. On an early morning in
the half-light at a particularly lonely part of the Chase I saw a
whole drove of them, and on another occasion at the same hour
my dog gave chase to a solitary deer. It stopped and gave battle,
and to my astonishment it looked as if my dog was getting the
best of it. I called him off. Afterwards I was sorry that I had
done so, for I might have witnessed a truly jungle scene.

Some animals alarmed me rather than I them. The tiny
weasel pursuing a large rabbit mesmerized to a slow wobbling
gait, is a sight most monstrous and intimidating. Indeed, weasels
almost paralyse me. Once I sat at a place where three holes
abutted a few feet distance from each other. When I sat down
there a weasel looked out of one of the holes and spat at me as
if delivering a curse, then retired only to appear immediately at
the next hole to hiss me again, after which it drew back its head
and shot it out again at the third hole to curse me from that
angle. This performance went on for some time: I had to keep
turning my head first one way then another as each second the
ferocious face looked out of a hole to glare and spit and curse.
It seemed to be charged with such potency that I really wouldn't
be surprised if I saw a weasel pursuing an elephant paralysed
with fear.

Another creature that alarmed me was the adder. Now and
then I came upon the reptile, even two or three together. In grey
scales or in chequered green. Finding one of considerable size, I
toed it, and it rushed away through the privet's undergrowth at
extraordinary speed. It didn't crawl, squirm, or hunch its way
forward; but *glided* along – as astonishing as if you saw a boat
dash through the water without oars or screw. I caught it up in
my hand by its middle. It turned its visored head round, opened
its trap-door of a mouth, and stuck its barbed fang deep into
my thick leather glove (which I had carefully slipped on). Once,
twice, three times it struck, then gave up and simply kept dart-
ing in and out of its mouth that long terrible tongue, shaped at

the end like a tiny anchor or arrow-head. Now and then it gave great wrenches with its whole body to escape my grasp. But I held it firmly and gazed steadfastly into its primeval countenance. It is remarkable how utterly baffling such a creature is. One gazes, one tries to concentrate but somehow one cannot *take it in*. One can hold a conversation with a dog; one could almost shake a horse by the hoof; many a sow is as human to look at as a Victorian lady being amused; a cow often reminds us of some friends; a lamb might be a baby; the birds, like many of us, are vocalists; the monkey shares our secret. But the reptile – I'm afraid no communication is possible. However, I put this one down to pursue its destiny without further hindrance from me, as I felt it had the right to do.

I shall not add much more to my list, but I loved the owl because of its astonishing silence and lightness of touch; I admired the nightjar which was like an alarm-clock which couldn't stop; and it would be wrong to forget the pheasant, little pleasure as that poor lumbering bird gives us. Every time I approached the wood it startled me by suddenly springing out of some hidden place on my path with its appalling rattle of a screech and made its straight, blundering, joyless flight away through the wood. That jarring sound is the nearest thing in Nature to something mechanical – as if a machine had been made by mistake. Which reminds me that there is one more animal entitled to a place here. Opposite my wood there was another one belonging to another estate, and rising on a slope so that I commanded a clear view of it. At a given time of the year the partridge and pheasant sportsmen appeared. As they beat their way along through the wood they uttered noises which brought them into such close relation to the brute creation that it is proper to include them here in this short account of animal life found in the woods from time to time.

13. The Old Woodman

During some of the summer a woodman and his grandson came from an adjoining estate to make hurdles out of the hazel which I had cut down. And at last, at long last, I came upon the countryman of tradition, the countryman celebrated in books, but who can now only be found in odd corners. He was not a Hardy 'character', nor a Wordsworthian 'leech-gatherer'. Not an 'amusing' man, nor quaint, nor given to making 'wise' remarks culled from his years, nor in command of a picturesque phrase. Such men can be found in Ireland, and probably in Scotland and Wales. The English equivalent possesses no playboy characteristics, nor love of generalization, nor much sense of humour, nor desire to make an effect; but he is so completely sincere that any remark he does make has the advantage of being genuine.

He belonged to the generation that had started work sixty-odd years ago at the age of eleven, beginning then to make spar-gads and hurdles such as he is still making now. The passage of years might be written in financial terms: today spar-gads are thirty-five shillings a thousand as against eight shillings a thou-and in the old days. Today a man can make £1 per thousand spars while in the former era he got 2s. 6d. – his wages then in the ordinary way being 10s. a week as opposed to the £4 of today. Thus a man of that kind will have seen some material changes.

Though he was well into the seventies he did not show many signs of being an old man, age had not wearied him; the expression on his face had no sourness in it whatever; his manner of addressing his grandson was extremely pleasant; and he seemed to get on wholly without swearing. He was not a talker, but he enjoyed talking on general topics, and took your point at once (if you did not exaggerate).

He showed me how to make hurdles and spar-gads, and how to loop together the bundles – this last being almost as elaborate a process as hurdle-making itself. He himself had dealt with this wood eighteen years previously, and obliquely I tried to find out his opinion of my thinning and axe-work. He found no fault with it, in fact praised it. In another man I would probably have taken this for politeness; but I thought he really did mean it, and this gave me no small pleasure.

One day, after he had given me the figures regarding the spargads, I asked whether he thought the labourers were happier today. He replied firmly and without hesitation – 'No, they are not.' He said they were not satisfied, and were less happy. He went on to say how he used to do general farm-work during the summer months and then return to the wood. He emphasized what a good time haymaking was in those days. Everyone turned out, whole families, having great tea-parties in the field: it was something everyone' looked forward to, including the children. No one had to work at a desperate pace, for there were so many workers; and since there were so many workers the job was done quite as quickly as at the present day.

Such are the imponderables of progress. More wages, less jolliness, and the machines not making for less hard work but for fewer workers. The goal of life, judging by our actions, is efficiency. It is really happiness. And the great snag is that neither machines nor £ s. d. seem able to open that door.

In the old days if the agricultural labourer was not religious he was at any rate superstitious. The superstitious man is profounder than the blasé sceptic, for he is at least *aware* of the 'mystery', and it is one of the little ironies of life that the latter imagines himself superior. Today the attendance at a village church is often only three. For the most part people simply do what is 'done', regardless of conviction. In the old days it was not done not to go to church. Today it is hardly done to go. There is no superstition, and the attitude towards religion is one of indifference at best, and at worst, and more often, of undisguised derision. Hence – quite apart from *believing* this or that – the whole background of word-music from the Bible with its accompanying attitude of reverence and its santification of joy and sorrow, no longer informs the life of the people.

The old woodman did not belong to the generation that had

lost these good things, and I knew it was safe to make a remark to him concerning the anti-religious trend of workers in general today. It pleased him, for presently he came out with a generalization of his own without any prompting from me. He glanced round the wood, and slowly and haltingly choosing his words, said: 'If I do say to a farmer now, Look how they plants do grow; look at thik field or yourn and see how they do grow without help; there must be a wonderful God behind they plants – he would not understand I.'

'No,' I replied, 'he would probably say that his overhead charges had been very heavy this year, and that he was not going to make nothing out of it, not a penny.'

'That's just what he would say,' affirmed the old man.

And I told him how the foreman had looked over the wood and declared – 'It's only dead money.'

'Oo ah!' said the old man, 'that's the way it is now. That's the way it is.'

Not more than a month or two had passed before he and his grandson had constructed about £40 worth of hurdles. There was something extraordinarily satisfactory about the rows of them leaning neatly one against another, or staked flat ten or more feet high – all twisted by the finger of man out of the hazel-bushes, while those same bushes were engaged in sending forth new shoots for future hurdles.

It was interesting to notice how woodmen, working within a given radius for a fair length of time, generally build a comfortable shelter for themselves, against weather and as a dining-room. A few pieces of corrugated tin, two or three poles, and some straw sheaves make an excellent little room to retire into when it pours, and a cloak-room and bicycle-shed at all times. Outside the shelter, on raw winter days, a fire is lit and kept going – very pleasant at meal times. In this, as in some other respects, the woodman has the advantage over other workmen on the land. I have yet to meet the woodman willing to change his job for any other department or agricultural activity.

One day I asked the old man – 'Do you ever wish that you had done anything else in life, been anything else?' He did not need to pause and think over his answer, and then perhaps give a non-committal one. 'No,' he said firmly, 'I do not, and the longer I live the more sure I am of that.'

At last I stood beside a contented man, one with many years upon his back, who did not feel that others had got a fairer deal out of life; who was not greedy for position, nor envious of riches, nor indifferent to the beauty that is freely given to the poor in places such as this.

I had noticed that he sometimes lay down and took a nap after dinner, and I mentioned how delightful it was to lie down and sleep in the wood. He agreed with me. 'It's as if thik birds do watch e,' he said, 'and thik trees do bend over e.'

14. A Way of Living

One of the great advantages of a woodman's job is that in his old age if he wishes to retire on his pension, he can at the same time supplement it by peaceful and easy-going piece-work. Just such an old man came to the woods from time to time to make stakes and faggots out of my drifts. He took it easy, arriving sometime before ten and going home at about four. This filled in his day beautifully. If it came on wet he was none too pleased for 'it don't do' he said, 'to get back too early'. But he wasn't in the least anxious about the money element. His simple needs were perfectly well met by his pension and what he made in the wood, and his days were filled pleasantly. He had a very nice cottage down in the village, free. So had the other old woodman, a delightfully placed and good cottage – for there is no sense in supposing that the countryman is always or even usually badly off in this matter as against the townsman. (And the man who talks about 'the disgraceful housing conditions of rural England' should go and have a look at an Irish village!)

Anyway, in the sphere, I found happy and contented men. Modern life is a labyrinth in which most men are lost. To find a way, a path is not easy. They had found one. Nothing elaborate about it; not the way of the Cross; not the Eightfold Path; but the way of the peasant whose *wants* are few. This gets them through, and I often think of them, I shall always think of them, as men who having escaped from all the escapisms of the modern world, were at peace. I used to visualize them sometimes when, on visits to London, I found myself again in the bus or under the ground. And when I got back amongst the trees again I would feel the full force of the farce of modern civilization; I would see with the clear vision of hatred the foul torrent of respectable insanity that makes the majority of men inferior to monkeys, and their works in thousands and thousands of cases absurd beyond the conception of any savage.

There were times when, sitting under the oak-tree in the early morning, I felt that so much was here given that if all the millionaires of all the world came ready to do my bidding and answer my Go here or Go there, I would have nothing to say except Go away. I was in a position to use my body for a period and then my head and pen. Could I ask more than this? or seeking, find? The Rights of Man are all very well, but we shall save the social world only when we pay attention to the *needs* of men. To do hard agricultural work half the day and hard cultural work the other half – that for many would answer their psychological needs. But no effort is made to make that kind of thing possible. We imagine that everything will be all right if we all produce as many objects as possible and distribute them to everybody. We refuse to think of man's Needs and go on and on thinking only of his Rights and his Pay. Never about his psychological and physiological needs – nay, never!

I could satisfy this need here, but only on condition that the whole of Europe, the whole of North America and Canada, the British Empire, Russia, China, and Japan could be engaged in warfare instead of welfare – myself only having to attend Home Guard. But there it was, I was able to do it. And I shall not easily forget, even when the frost of age is on my head, how after a few hours' work in the morning, I had earned enough to pay my rent, and in the afternoon the grocery bill. That is something that I shall never forget! And so, for a moment adopting the role of the wise councillor, I would say to any young man, or young man and woman, ambitious only for peace and sanity – Learn the craft of Forestry, enter the woods, and happiness may yet be yours.

15. Different Moods in the Wood

I can offer the above small piece of advice to anyone likely to be glad of it with a clear conscience, because any woodmen I have known always seemed to be doing well and were satisfied. But, speaking very personally, given the choice between permanent agricultural work of a general nature and forestry, I would not choose forestry – though doubtless I would often long to get back to the woods again. In this account I celebrate the pleasures of working in the wood, indeed I sing its joys. But too much hangs on the weather and the time of year. Long hours in a wood during wet or dark or heavy days, can be most melancholy. One can be elated amongst trees, even inspired again and again, in conditions such as I have already rehearsed. It is also possible, and indeed a frequent experience, to be numbed by trees. On dreary, drizzly days I often became stupefied and paralysed in mind as well as weary and lifeless in body.

I have always loved to have a View. The mountains and the sea appeal to me so strongly that I do not dare to think about them nor to mark the absence in England, save in the north, of the glen, the real glen through which the river roars. Thus I'm afraid that I am quite capable of feeling too enclosed working for long periods in an English wood. I love a view, I say, even from the field on the highest part of a farm, and to plough such a field is better than any work in the wood. Sometimes when I walked through the Chase beyond my fence, wandering along, getting lost even and wondering where I had got to, and suddenly came upon a gate leading into a cornfield washing knee-deep against the cliff of trees, I felt a great nostalgia for open spaces and clear views and the turned furrow and the glorious plough.

Thus my moods would go up and down, and as I have no axe to grind save my steel one, but only truth to tell, I shall not pretend that as a woodman I could ever be wholly satisfied. My spirits were very much influenced by the weather. In the fields, the cold, the dark, the dreary, or even the wet days make much less difference, sometimes none at all, sometimes a pleasant change. But the change from sunlight to a drizzle in the wood is a very definite thing, and makes its full effect. The kingdom of heaven is within you, it is said. No doubt there is great truth in that. But an honest man must acknowledge how often his interior is dictated by the exterior scene. Sometimes I have almost felt my heart *contract* at the sudden coming on of a cold darkness, and expand at the smiling beams swiftly pervading the weary, dripping scene around.

During March, April, and May the wood is the place. The sleeping trees awake. At their feet the flowers rise up and we gaze at them with absurd surprise. The birds declaim rather than sing. We stand in the midst of rejoicing life. By June the more obvious flowers have completed their act, they have had *their* summer, their autumn, and now are in their winter of desolation. Others are taking their place – the rock-rose, the herb-willow, the garlic, the foxglove – but the abundance has gone, and the colour blue, so rich, so varied, is seen no more save in the sky. We have become accustomed to the green of the trees. The birds are reticent.

In July a hush falls upon everything. The silence is disquieting. The silence of a wood at all times is something to reckon with; it seems to pervade one's personality, and I seldom open my lips even to speak to my dog. In July it is a principality. In such an atmosphere ambition wilts, mental strife seems futile, the arts unreal. Filled with unease, one would gladly leave the silent and too solemn trees for a more human scene.

For a more deadly silence go to a pine wood. One day in June when I had wandered farther into the Chase I came to a pine plantation. I stepped out of the privet-choked pathway into its darkness. I walked there without making the slightest noise, for there is no floor, no man-made carpet so soft and yielding to the tread as these massed needles. There was not a speck of green on this ground. I felt awe in the silence. No bird sang, nor wing flapped, nor rabbit scuttled, nor stick cracked. I was enclosed and submerged in a silence like a substance. It was broken occasionally by a squall of wind heard above in the branches of the pines, that wild, watery, bare-beached, oceanic sound that even at the height of summer has no summer in it, and beats against the heart and calls to mind man's endless tale of tempest and of wrong.

Standing there in the darkness of this fir wood, I looked towards the edge and saw the greenery beyond. It had become a bright green light and I thought the sun must have come out. Yet the sun had not come out, the sky was very cloudy. But from in there that undergrowth immediately outside did shine strongly like a green light. Also in the middle of this plantation there was a pool of green – owing to a break in the trees. Where the light could penetrate, the green had formed – chiefly moss and dog's mercury, a little pool that stopped immediately at the end of the open space.

I was hardly wrong, I reflected, in imagining that I was looking out upon green lights. For that is what I was looking at. The light from heaven shone upon the ground and the plants received it, and – by virtue of chlorophyll, we say – turned it into green substance. That undergrowth is light made visible: it is light made tangible.

Cheered by the thought of this radiant miracle, I emerged from the shade of the sombre aisles and pushed my way home through the tangible pieces of sunshine that blocked my path.

16. The Scavengers of Corruption

One day in July I was cutting down a very large and thick-stemmed hazel-bush. It had been left alone for so many years that the stool was full of holes and cups and soft, dry-leaved hiding-places. I had cut away about a dozen of the branches and had lifted my axe to strike another, when my eye was caught by something in one of those recesses of the stool. Five small yellow flowers, fresh and strange, stood erect amidst a little bed of dry leaves. They quivered as if blown gently by a breeze. But there was no breeze: and looking closer I saw that they were not flowers; they were five wide open beaks of new-born birds.

Abandoning my axe I knelt down and peered into this nest thus placed so low. The beaks closed and I saw simply the creatures, sightless, no eyes yet opened, no feathers to cover them save here and there a patch of furry stuff on the red flesh. They could not see but they could hear, and when I made a noise all the beaks opened wide again, quivering and giving the impression that they were really shouting an appeal for food, though their voices could not reach me. Then their beaks closed and the pitiful, hideous little bodies sank down into the nest once more. Pathetic beyond measure. Fatally forced into Being. Trembling symbols of the sheer affliction of life, the pure burden of birth.

Those open beaks had looked like flowers for a moment. Yet how different is a flower from an animal in the matter of food. The beaks shouted in mute agonizing appeal for one thing only – the death of another that they might live. Here in this tiny nook in England, as in the roughest jungles of the world, the Law must be fulfilled – thy life or my life. No doubt this proves that death is nothing to worry about and that we are all members of one another in the completest sense; nevertheless man turns away from the animals and from himself and gazes with relief upon the trees and the flowers. They are alive. They multiply in numbers, they increase in strength. Yet, though they may struggle together for light, they never hunt, never prey upon others, never eat themselves. Alive, radiant, yet free from our Order and our Law – eating only the air, only the earth.

I left the stool of this hazel without cutting any more branches, so that the birds might rest in peace. When I went again I saw a robin feeding them with a worm – though I couldn't get close enough to see what her scheme of distribution was amongst five. So they were evidently young robins, born at this strange hour of late July. But next time I came the nest was empty. The chicks had gone and did not return. Their home had been opened by me to the dangers of the wood, and so no doubt, before their time, they had perished that some other creature might not perish.

On my way home I picked up a dead bird. Having just gazed into the cradle of life, I felt a desire to take home the dead body and watch with like attention the activities of this poor discarded garment that was now the cloth of death. I put it in a basin and left it in a shed. Returning after a week, I found it had come to life again. It was breathing heavily. Its tongue popped in and out of its beak, its eyes flashed, and it made a grinding noise. This surprised me; but I then saw that the tongue was really a white worm, the flashing eye a white worm, while the body heaved owing to the squirming activity of the pack of worms inside the corpse.

To find the explanation of this we need go no farther than the female bluebottle on the point of laying her eggs. She prefers to lay them in meat, in a hole in the meat, which will serve as cradle and as food. For this purpose she finds nothing so good as dead birds. The procedure is as follows. She approaches the corpse and makes straight for the beak. If it is tightly closed she will go to the eye-sockets, but if it is open she thrusts her egg-conducting tube, her oviduct, into the hole and proceeds to lay her eggs, an operation which, allowing for rests from labour, may take two hours – after which she goes away and dies. The bird's beak has now been packed pretty full, the tongue and throat being white with layers of eggs. Here they remain for two days, after which time they are transformed into maggots who then descend down the throat of the bird.

I made my examination several days after they had gone down there and had been composing themselves while decomposing the bird. Indeed they had so completely taken possession that the whole body heaved about, and some of these white, squirming maggots, like small spaghetti, had returned to the throat and also entered the eye-sockets. Already the body had lost much of its weight, for death is heavy and life is light.

I opened the flesh a bit more so that I might observe the main work of reconstruction. I gazed down at the living tubes as they squirmed and twisted and turned and turned them at their task, building up new life in the abominable ferment of corruption. The bluebottle is necessary. The bluebottle is good. All things in Nature have a meaning and a purpose. All are necessary. All are right. If it were not so, if any one thing were wrong, then nothing could be right; if a single error marred the scheme then we could count on nothing, all would be lost, we could hope for nothing, there would be nothing for it, as Edward Carpenter said, 'but to fold our hands and be damned everlastingly'. But since it is not so we can afford to face the facts. It is expedient, on occasion, to gaze down into the pit as well as up towards heaven, to look at the roots of Nature as well as at her flags, regarding the burden of the beginning and the dereliction of the end alike without flinching, so that from time to time the seeing eye, the accepting mind, may receive the vision of what some men call beauty and others truth.

17. The Growth of Trees

I carried out my work of thinning on the basis of 'cuts' measuring twenty feet. Each of these slices went from one end of the wood to the other – a question of several hundred yards. The portion done presented a great transformation: from the side you could easily see through it till the eye hit the dark wall of trees and undergrowth not yet touched. When I had finished one cut and then went back and started again at a new one, so much time had often elapsed that shoots had already begun to grow from the stumps of the trees I had cut down earlier. The rapidity of their growth almost reminded me of bracken.

Looking at such shoots one might think that a tree is only a kind of big flower. But the most striking thing about a tree is that it remains standing. It does not collapse after a season. The flowers fall down every year: their trunks (or stalks) give way, and a whole new plant must take the place of the old. The tree-trunk does not fall down and start again; it bequeaths one year's work in the form of a monument, and next year builds another story on top of it. It lays foundation-stones called buds that grow into branches. And as it builds its head out of the air of heaven, as it opens its leaves, as it spreads its branches, the prop upon which it rests, its trunk, increases in strength and girth. It increases thus because every leaf connects itself with the soil by sending down a cable. Trees have been called *collective beings*: and truly we may think of each leaf as an individual plant with a separate stem joining it with the earth. This connecting link is at the same time a tax which each leaf pays to the whole, it is a tribute levied for its upkeep. Every new leaf on the great tree in the forest lowers down this cable, this silken thread, this fibre, this cord, until reaching beneath the surface of the earth it becomes a root – and the sum of these connecting wires increases the girth of the tree every year. A tree-trunk is really a mass of wood-covered waterways linking leaf with root, ever widening as the building grows from above. We see here a wonderful natural example of two offices being performed by a single operation. The leaves require extra sustenance from the earth, and having received it they reach out ever higher and bulkier into the air; but this increase does not break down the spray, the branch, or the stem, because of the tribute, the wood-tax that has been paid, in virtue of which the spray, the branch, and the stem become proportionally larger and stronger. That is how every tree makes its trunk. Every leaf of every tree has sent down a tiny string, covering and clinging to the shoot beneath, and increasing its thickness. Singly it may seem a slender offering, but not in its hardened multiplicity. By itself it might not appear to be equal to its great task or certain of reaching its goal; but softness is often the sign of strength and determination. Just as granite rocks will be worn away under the washing of the softer substance of waves, and water itself fail to impress the greater softness of the flowering polyps that build up the coral reefs, so this law of humble power can be seen in the flowing downwards of the wooden threads. 'Each according to his size and strength, wove his little strand of cable, as a spider his thread,' wrote Ruskin in this connection 'and cast it down the side of the springing tower by a marvellous magic – irresistible! The fall of a granite pyramid from an Alp may perhaps be stayed; the descending force of that silver thread shall not be stayed. It will split the rocks themselves at its roots, if need be, rather than fail in its work.'

Two interesting things follow from this. The first is that though a tree may be said to reach maturity in the eye of the timber-merchant, there can never come a time when it ceases to grow. A tree is not like an animal which grows to a certain size, then stops growing and eats only to live instead of to live and to grow. An animal does not build itself by eating through its limbs any more than a man through the tips of his fingers; it does not continually create a head any more than a man grows his head with his hair – it starts with a head. A tree starts without a head. Since it advances upwards by means of a self-building crown, and since every leaf thereof drops an anchor down beneath the surface of the soil, then so long as new leaves appear a greater bulk of crown and width of trunk must follow. But in proportion to the size of the tree will be the rate of growth. I have just mentioned how here in my wood I see several feet of new stems spring up in a few months. The process must inevitably get slower and slower as the ground to be covered by the communicating wires of wood increases. Were I to sit beneath the melancholy boughs of a six-thousand-years-old tree and attempt to note a season's difference, I fear I should not succeed in convincing myself that it had changed at all.

Six thousand years old? Yes, for this brings me to the second thing that follows upon the construction of a tree. Theoretically it need never die. Consider what a tree is – or any plant for that matter. It is not a single being, not one person, as it were – (though it may have great personality). It is a group of beings. Looking at a hive, we should be tempted to say – Here are many units, yet they may really be one unit. Looking at a tree, we should be tempted to say – Here is a unit, yet it may really be a multiplicity of units. If we examine the little creature called the hydra, found in stagnant ponds, we find that its manner of giving birth to new hydras is by growing them upon its person like buds on a tree. All of them feed from the communal stomach; but after a certain period they break off from their parent to live a life of independence. When we examine a coral reef we find that it consists of polyps. A polyp has the same organization as a hydra, the same method of budding its offspring – with one difference. The hydra breaks off from the parent body, the polyp continues to remain attached. But it proceeds in the same way as the hydra, each polyp budding its children rather than lying or delivering them, and they all feed from the communal sac, the continual growth of which means the spreading out and up of their domicile, their polypary. This polyp, or 'coral insect', is a little hollow globule of gelatinous matter, a tiny sac whose mouth is bordered by eight leaf-shaped appendages, fringed at the edges: eight tentacles opening like the petals of a flower. No wonder a coral looks like a rock covered with brilliant flowers. What is that rock made of? How did these flower-like animals called polyps come to have this pedestal? Because it is made of their own exudations. They exude stone. With their own excrement they build up and rest upon a monument as hard as marble. The whole reef is made of polyp. The softest of all creatures has turned into the hardest of all rocks. These reefs continue to grow by means of the collective effort of millions upon milliards of polyps, so that an archipelago such as the Maldive in the Indian Ocean can comprise no less than twelve thousand reefs, and a reef can spread over an area of thirty-three thousand miles. No term needs to be set to the life of a polypary since it is a collection of beings continuously giving birth to others by process of budding, and continuously bequeathing their excrement to the magnificent ocean-dunghill upon which they stand.

All life is related by the work of the twin sisters Time and Motion – often called Evolution – and it is not hard to see how similar is the growth of a plant to the growth of a coral reef. We can see that a tree is a community of beings rather than an individual. You cannot cut limbs off an individual and expect it to live, or the limb itself to live. That is exactly what we can do with a tree. If we want a fresh tree it is sufficient to cut off a living branch and plant it. It will spread roots and grow, while the parent will not suffer. We can even plant the young branches of one tree on to another tree, which we call grafting, an operation which explains the justice of Dupont de Nemours's definition – 'A plant is a family, a republic, a sort of living hive, whose inhabitants are fed in the common refectory upon the common stock of food.' This communal stock of food, this sort of omnibus sac, called the trunk, is even ready to feed a species of tree not absolutely fraternal. Figs will not grow on thistles – (though under this ruling one would not be surprised if they did). But Fabre mentions a certain pear-tree 'on which, by means of grafting, the whole gamut of cultivated pears was represented. Sweet or sour, dry or juicy, large or small, green or brilliantly coloured, all these pears ripened on the same tree, year after year, always unchanged, faithful to the racial characteristics, not of the tree, their foster-mother, but of the various buds transferred to the common support'. Such an experiment might well have served as proof of the individuality of a bud as opposed to the free association of a tree.

Thus granted, the age of a tree could be very great. In fact if it lives in a spot unexposed to the violence of storm or earthquake and out of the reach of man's commercial activity, it may continue to live for an extraordinary period. A good place to find tree-veterans is in the sanctified area of graveyards where, companions of the dead, they are unmolested by the living. Thus in the cemetery of Allouville in Normandy there stands an oak-tree some nine hundred years old, whose trunk at ground level shows a circumference of thirty-three feet, while within the aerial forest of its upper branches the cell of an anchorite has been built, and the lower portion of its partly hollow trunk has been used since 1696 as a chapel dedicated to Our Lady of Peace. Many a yew-tree in an old churchyard vies in age with the most ancient church, while others look back to times long before any temple was built in the name of Christ. There was a yew-tree at Fortingal in Scotland whose concentric rings amounted to two thousand five hundred, and another at

Brabourne in Kent whose age was thirty centuries. Oak-trees often stand sturdily against the blasts of time. In 1824, a wood-cutter in the Ardennes, on felling a giant of this species, found fragments of sacrificial urns and ancient medals within its trunk, thus connecting it with the barbarian invasions of Europe. It showed no more signs of failing health than the walnut-tree noticed by the soldiers of Balaclava in the Crimea, which, though two thousand years old, yielded an annual crop of 100,000 walnuts, the harvesting of which was shared by five families.

The size of such trees can best be imagined when we learn that on the occasion of a giant conifer which once stood on the slopes of the Sierra Nevada in California, falling before the axe, the woodmen had to use a long ladder even to mount its pros-trate trunk, as if scaling the roof of a house. The bark of this tree was removed in a single piece from a length of twenty-two feet, which served to enclose a room in which one hundred and forty children could play hunt-the-slipper. This giant displayed three thousand concentric layers of wood, showing that it reached back to the time when, according to tradition, 'Samson released in the cornfields of the Philistines, foxes, to whose tails incendiary torches were attached.' These conifers of the Sierra Nevada had grown to three hundred feet or more. Other vet-erans have expressed themselves more in their crowns, like that yew-tree in the cemetery of Haie-de-Routot which in 1832 spread its foliage over the entire churchyard and part of the church itself. I have already mentioned the Chestnut Tree of the Hundred Horses at Etna, under the cover of which the Queen of Aragon found room for her whole retinue; but in Mexico there is a cypress contemporary with Noah, standing in the cemetery of Santa Maria de Fesla near Oaxaca, beneath whose boughs Cortez, the conqueror of Mexico, found room to shel-ter his army. The crown of the baobab-tree at Senegambia near Cape Verde, is even more remarkable. The diameter of the trunk is greater than the height of the tree, the latter being but fifteen feet and the former thirty! – a column fit to support the mighty dome which is two hundred feet in diameter. This baobab-tree is a worthy companion in distinction with the dragon-tree of Orotova in the Canary Islands whose trunk cannot be encircled by ten men holding hands. Both trees, older than the Pyramids, hold the memory of six thousand years, and show every promise of ignoring the terms of Time.

18. The Feeling Intellect

On sultry summer days it was interesting to observe the insectitude activity. Before the temperature rose the air would be moderately clear, but when the sun came out into the heavy, windless, sultry atmosphere then swarms of insects, especially a certain kind of fly, rising from nowhere particular, began to buzz round and round madly as if at that moment created, released, unloosened from a melting solid.

A massive, solid unity – that's the impression one often gets of the earth; almost motionless and asleep at the freezing Poles, partially melted into bits at these climes, and in the Tropics, under the equatorial rays, melted out into a seething flow and flood of fast-moving particles in every shape and size.

Why does life hang together so well, seeing that everything is at everything else's throat? Presumably because it is not really in parts. It is not a question of parts that make a whole but of a whole presenting itself in parts. If this were not so, the parts would certainly not hang together, they would hang separately as it were. The unity is so obvious that it would hardly seem worth mentioning; yet I cannot feel any confidence that the reader will regard it as a platitude. Certainly our *working-habit* of thought is not unity, not synthesis; it is almost always in terms of disunity, which, so far from being regretted has been conceived as excellent, as a triumph meriting the title of 'victorious analysis'. The results are not wholly good. We can do wonders with the inorganic – there we are victorious, able to create a thing like the gramophone no less than other mechanical constructions, not all of which are beautiful or of good report. But in the field of medicine (not surgery), of religion, of philosophy, of economics and politics, we are nearly lost – because we cannot yet think in terms of the unity. (We do better in the field of agriculture, because we have to act in terms of unity or perish.)

I enter thoughts of this kind in this account because they arise when I am confronted with Nature. If thoughts are simple experience arising from common sensation, they are sometimes worth putting down. I hope I have Reason on my page. But not ratiocination, not thinking before I experience. It is Wordsworth's '*feeling* intellect' that holds interest for me. The old adage 'I think, therefore I am' is less helpful than the other way round, 'I am', that is 'I experience, therefore I think.' Wordsworth held that ecstasy is the highest form of thought, since it is the nearest we get to *communication* with truth. And after a visitation of ecstasy caused in him by the earthly spectacle, he said – 'Thought was not, *in enjoyment it expired.*'

If it be complained that on this showing our systems simply follow our feelings I see no harm in it. Sensation is not so very eccentric. We back each other up. Anyway, to think without the thought springing from felt experience cannot but be as void as merely second-hand thinking – with which anyone could fill a book, and which is as valueless as second-hand observation. During the daily intercourse of life we need second-hand thinking all the time, but if we do not experience our own philosophy and religion we have none. And if we write it down we do not expect to be able to hand it to anyone else. This kind of knowledge 'cannot be handed from one person having it to another person not having it', as Whitman said. But we can support the findings of others, and stimulate experience-knowledge.

The love of Nature is deep in England. And I think that what is behind this love is the instinct that Nature has a secret for us, and answers our questions. Take that foxglove over there – for we have now reached August in this chronicle. It stands singly where there had been such a wonderful display of bluebells that it then looked as if a section of the sky had been established upon earth (though not really the same colour at all!). That foxglove with its series of petal-made thimbles held up for sale

333

to the bees, puts me at ease upon the subject of – progress. It is quite obvious that the foxglove cannot be *improved*. There is no progressing beyond that point for that particular Appearance. There is no room for improvement in the bluebell nor in any of the other exhibits. The fact is we get perfection in this form and in that form. Hence Shakespeare's 'ripeness is all', and Tennyson's 'God fulfils Himself in many ways', and Whitman's 'there can never be any more perfection than there is now', and Heraclitus' 'Life is a Fountain of Fire, an ever-living Flame, kindled in due measure, and in like measure extinguished'. Evolution is not something going up and up and up – but a series of perfect Forms. The goal of each Form is the fulfilment of its own unique perfection. There is no point in our gazing raptly into the future for paradise if it is at our feet.

But this is not true of Man, you say. That is the paradox. In a perfect world he is imperfect. But then he has attained a new thing of his own – consciousness. Complete consciousness will be his ripeness, his perfection. That will probably take time, say several million years. But why worry? there might be five million years after that of perfect humanity. Meanwhile our foxglove can keep us sane at least about subjects such as beauty and art. There is no steady evolutionary 'progress' in these things, only different expressions. Just as there will never be a better foxglove so there will never be a better Shakespeare.

Near the foxglove are the bluebells. They have now dried into seeds. Every stalk is hung with a rattling belfry of seed pouches. These once green stalks are now dry, yellow, and very light. Each bell is a hard, closed pouch of seed. I pluck a whole stalk and open one of the pouches. I find an average of fifty seeds in each, and on each stalk there is an average of eight pouches. $8 \times 50 = 400$. There are ten stalks in every area of, say, my boots' width and length – that is, room for 4,000 seeds. Looking round, one is impressed by the massive number of possible bluebells. It is impossible not to feel the sweep of Nature's vitality. What is plainly seen is not death, but everlasting creation and life. Such a scene is as much revelation as the early garment of blue, it is as truly a sign of goodwill, and has in

334

it as great a promise. There is no need to *reconcile* oneself to the scene. A very small porportion of those seeds will succeed in their struggle for birth, and after birth not all will succeed in getting up. But what of it? It's worth the candle, isn't it? It is better than a *void*, surely. But if the Beginner of life could do what He has done, why could He not have done better, it may be complained; why could He not have eliminated the seamy side? Evidently He couldn't.

19. Each Its Hour

In the woods, as elsewhere, it is generally wrong to suppose that we often get the beginning of autumn in September, either in terms of temperature or colouring. I noticed no marked difference in the wood from what it was in the earlier month except that nothing now was due to have its hour. I have often used that phrase to myself, 'have its hour', with regard to woodland scenes; for it is interesting the way in which nearly everything has its particular hour when it, and perhaps it alone, catches the eye of the careless passer-by, though before that time, and again after it, there is nothing strikingly noticeable in that quarter.

Take the elder, for example. There, surely, is a miserable affair; a hopelessly plebeian plant. A bush posing as a tree, a tree failing to be a bush. It is impossible to praise its bark even when healthy, and when in decay it is an inch-thick pole of dirt, the nearest thing to real dirt to be found in Nature. Yet during a few weeks in July the elder has its hour. You actually pause to admire it. For then it is in flower; and those flowers are handed to you on a plate, as it were, or rather they are plates, beautifully decorated with the finest lace, held up before you. The same is true of the hawthorn. During the winter you hardly look at it, not to mention the unfriendly aspect of all armoured trees; but in spring first come the little round white buttons, and then the open flower turning half the tree to white against the blue sky, and giving out that scent which pronounces the spring and comes across to us less like a scent than a memory and a promise of happiness. More spectacular, though less rich, is the hour of that other bush the blackthorn, which, being neglected through the months, as it were, seizes upon our attention in March by a special act – that of jumping the season of green and going straight to the flower, white first and green second: so that all eyes are drawn towards this one illumination. For at this time there is no green on bush or tree in all the countryside; only the fields are green – and then how lovely they look in their brown and almost black frames! Ah, then it is that the green fields of England shine. All else is dark but they are light. Then suddenly the darkest of all the hedges are lit by artificial snow, the blackthorn becomes the whitethorn, and the poor bush that was so humble is exalted, and its proud peers rebuked.

Speaking as a woodman, I am no friend of the privet; for not only is it very difficult to clean up, but it strays and straddles about without beauty to recommend it; but I am not blind to the fact that in July it also comes into its own and looks positively pretty. Still less do I care for the honeysuckle; but I cannot deny that when those pieces of 'twine' show the green leaf and then the flower, they become the opium of the woods.

Life being what it is, we cannot say that everything has its great hour, though all have their hours of youth, even the evergreens, which though green for ever, put up new leaves every year. And some have two hours: the most striking example being the larch which is seen, when you survey from a rise some stretch of woodland still unleafed, to be the exception – a deep rich meadow-green amidst all the surrounding unopened twigs: and again in autumn it is often so fantastically striking in its decay that that which was dead seems alive again. The imperious hours of the laburnum, lilac, and chestnut need no recommendation from me; but the whitebeam holds our attention almost more than any of the others in spring when the grey sheen of the underleaf shines out, and later when in flower the whole tree is one of the aristocrats of the forest.

Some trees prefer to take their hour in winter. I would put in a claim here for the oak, though possibly its real moment is in spring when in fresh leaf it out-greens everything else – even the beech. But there can be no two opinions that the plane-trees come into their own properly in winter when they hold up their little balls before the gaze of the Londoner. And the same is the tale of the elm. It is a question of tracery. The tracery of plane-trees and elms is scripture. Could we read that writing, we feel we would have our answer, we would solve our problem, and be shielded from the dark sorrows of our weakness.

It is the elm that knows how to take the sunset better than any other tree. I have been made to pause in my path many a time by elm-tree tracery hung across the dusky winter sky. As I write these words, I recall, so clearly, how having gone up the stairs to the top floor of a high building at Rugby School, I stopped in the passage leading to the classroom. From the window I could see a marvellous sunset behind a line of elm-trees. I stood there for some time fixed by the sight. I came in late to that lesson and may have been reprimanded, I don't remember. Nor do I remember the lesson that day, nor the master, though I think it was G. F. Bradby. But now recalling that hour, I venture to praise the boy, who must have been capable of learning something from the stolen tuition, otherwise he would not have paused to take it. The child is father to the man, we say. Let me then praise my father, even salute him: for he stood there without any ulterior motive, furtively gazing into heaven: he didn't make a song about it, didn't dream of writing it up as a poem to be praised and admired – just stood and gaped!

20. Planting; The Head Woodman; The Fable

During the autumn I did some planting. My thinning process left plenty of room for useful underplanting. There are certain trees which grow best in their early years under shade, and amongst these are beech. Rolf decided to underplant the section of the wood that had been thinned, with beech. There had been a good deal of rain in September and thus the ground was all right for planting in October.

I have just been looking through two forestry manuals to find out what they said regarding Season for Planting. They said nothing. They talked about everything else. So I turned to William Cobbett's manual, not thinking it likely that *he* would let me down. Nor did he. He says with his usual dogmatic clarity – 'If the weather be open and dry, you *may* plant at any time between September and April.' He then goes on to explain which are the very best times. I was interested to note that he says you should not plant in the rain, for I had often heard it so plausibly asserted that it was splendid to plant in the rain, since you are *watering* the roots as you plant. 'A grand day for planting,' said a forester to me one wet afternoon, adding how he had already planted five hundred trees that day. As he happened to be a particularly glib, plausible man, I was not a bit surprised to be faced with a totally opposite school of thought on the subject – 'Never plant in *wet* weather, nor when *the ground is wet*, if you can possibly avoid it,' says Cobbett again (as you see from the italics). 'The ground never *ought* to be either moved, or walked upon, when it is wet at the top. But we are frequently compelled to do both, or to leave our work wholly undone. It is a very great error to suppose that plants take root quicker for being planted in wet weather. The contrary is the fact. One great thing is, to make the earth that goes close to the roots *fine*; and this you cannot do in wet weather. For this reason it is that I prefer March and April for doing the work of planting: but, be it done at what season of the year it may, the ground ought *not to be wet*; for then it falls in about the roots in lumps, or in a sort of flakes, like mortar. It never gets close and compact about the roots; and if you tread it in it becomes, in dry weather, so hard as to actually pen up the roots of the tree as if they were in a vice.'

We did not plant in the rain, but we did plant in the autumn, for circumstances were such as to permit it, the head woodman being able to come along at that time with two boys and another woodman. This headman, whose name was Reggie Wyman, was not the same type as the woodman previously

alluded to. He was only thirty-five, thus belonging to this generation, though not the last lap of it. If the new generation were
composed of men like him (and there may be many such), then
we need not feel too gloomy about the future. He hadn't the
rather over-serious virtues of the older race, but he had his own
virtues, chief of which was – humanness. The great thing is to
find a human being; that is, a person capable of friendship and
affection, and not submerged beneath class-consciousness, or
envy, or disappointment, or frustration, or general grudgingness
– and possessing life and inner warmth. We are never markedly
successful in our search in any quarter. As the working man
emerged from his long helotism, his attitude towards the world
was inevitably often obstructively self-defensive. Now it
becomes unnecessary, while dignity and pride, unforced, are
often substituted. Reggie was in possession of inner warmth,
and he felt in no sense inferior to anyone anywhere (but *not* the
'I'm-as-good-as-you' attitude), nor his work of less value and
importance to society than the highest in the land. He was too
proud and too conscious of this; but in him even that was delightful. For one's attitude towards a man, and his own attitude
towards life for that matter, depends so much upon his personality – (history is governed nearly as much by this as by
economic factors). Reggie had considerable personality, and of
an attractive kind. Most working men look older than their
arithmetical age. He looked younger. The most striking attribute of his slight wiry figure with its good-looking bronzed face,
was his hair – a crop of apparently not-thinning, silky flaxen
hair. Always conscious of his appearance, he never wore a hat
or cap – again rare amongst working men. He fitted perfectly
into the woodland surroundings, as he stood leaning against a
tree – he was then the best-dressed man, in his 'shabby' workman's clothes, that I have seen in the course of my life. Realizing this, he frequently draped himself against a tree while
gossiping in his high-pitched voice.

He brought with him for this planting, three assistants – an
old man and two boys. Boys, as is well known, 'have no character', so one can just say boys and be done with it, recognizing

that the word boy denotes life as yet unquenched or tamed; and that the extraneous wrappings of our barbarian modernism, like any other garment, could be exchanged in a twinkling if and when there are leaders of the people ready to introduce new values. Over against these boys was the old man, small, faded, insignificant, and incredibly inoffensive and humble, with nothing to say and hardly ever saying anything – he just wanly smiled amiably.

The method of planting is straightforward enough. You take a spade and thrust it into the soil at a perpendicular angle, and then at right angles to the cut you strike across it: finally dig in again at the foot of the cross, and tilt the spade backwards – and there will be a hole in the centre into which you can place your plant. The main thing is to get it properly in, with its roots spread out and not bunched together – to which end it is good to pull it up a fraction at the last moment while you take away the spade and tread down the earth firmly around the little tree.

Taking a line each, we proceeded to underplant with beech-trees a given acreage of the thinned ash-wood. Reggie worked by fits and starts, urging the boys forward in his high voice for a period, after which he often paused for a gossip. Keen on music-hall, he would outline the merits of various comedians then get down to some more planting before pausing again, to admit, perhaps, that he couldn't do with B.B.C. talks or classical music – which latter he described as 'music which stops and then goes on again'. The Announcers also intrigued him, and he referred to a Yorkshire one who was at that time being tried out, as sounding 'rather common' – though this did not mean that he liked Stuart Hibberd, whom actually he couldn't under-stand, could not *follow*. Then some more planting followed by a further extension of gossip, this time on the characteristics of a certain foreman of the estate, who had once, but once only, attempted to interfere in the affairs of the wood, and of that man's 'ignorance' – i.e. manners – when he called at Reggie's house and looked his wife up and down. More planting, and then likely enough a brief outline of the moral life of the village owing to the influx of the military when too many girls became a soldier's relaxation. His tone on most matters was the normal one of cheerful scorn, but on this latter he was rather scandalized, for, though not in the least religious, he was very moral, and a great family man in love with his wife and daughter, proud of the way his daughter had him under her thumb and highly indignant with Beveridge for presuming to extend State Assistance towards her upkeep, for he could look after his own maid, thank you, he didn't want no state assistance for his little maid ... And thus between our spurts of planting we covered a good deal of ground in conversation. But I write these lines in sadness, for not then did I guess, nor he in any faint way glimpse, the tragedy close ahead that would shatter him.

I do not remember how many trees we planted per day. Not too many I hope – for I want to come and watch this wood from time to time. This is a job which, were I owner, I would not like to have had done in a hurry, and might even feel inclined to praise the man who had planted the least trees per day. Certainly it would be fatal to have it done by piece-workers.

It is said – is it not? – that some men have a special 'touch' when planting, and that the trees put in by them thrive better than others. Hardy represents Giles Winterborne as such. One enjoys that sort of statement and swallows it. But we may well doubt whether it is really ever actually true. It would be interesting to adopt a severe scientific scepticism towards it and put it to the proof over a given number of acres for a given period of years (that is the scientific method) and see at the end if the magic-touch man really did better than Tom, Dick, and Harry, when they planted properly. Actually I asked the older men whether there was anything in this, and they didn't see what I was getting at. That's always my difficulty – the meeting in real life an approximation to fictitious characters. Take another assertion from Thomas Hardy (no man loves re-reading him more than I), when he says of his woodlanders – 'From the light lashing of the twigs upon their faces when brushing through them in the dark, they could pronounce upon the species of the trees whence they stretched; from the quality of the wind's murmur through a bough, they could in like manner name its sort afar off.' I did not strike lucky in coming across woodmen here, old or young, who would answer to that, any more than to Giles's capacity to make a generalization such as 'She's been a bit of a charmer in her time, I believe, a body who has smiled where she has not loved, and loved where she has not married.'

Having planted our acreage, we fenced it in, since everything being food for something else, young barks are much appreciated by rabbits. But our fence was not high enough to keep out deer. I should add here that besides my thinning and planting I carried out systematic pruning over one portion of the wood. There are, of course, two schools of thought concerning the advisability of pruning trees – that is taking away all branches as high as you can reach in order to ensure a straight, thick pole. Since I did prune a portion I shall be able to compare results. Knocking away the rotten lower branches is not the same thing as pruning and is called 'brashing'. This is a very enjoyable job when dealing with the fir variety of tree, for then a single slash with the back of the bill-hook knocks off a number of branches with a loud bang, and you get a clear space. A few more whacks and you see the straight trunk hitherto completely hidden by the multitude of small branches.

Though I planted, thinned, pruned, and brashed I took no part in the final operation of felling. This takes place when the tree has reached 'maturity'. Sometimes, at this stage trees look so well that owners have felt constrained to leave them standing. This is deplorable. It betrays uncertainty as to the purpose of life, which is commerce. We should always bear in mind the noble words of Mr C. E. Curtis who in his *Practical Forestry* writes – 'If we visit the woods in any part of the country we see this – (trees which having attained maturity have not been touched) – and with regret, and attribute it either to ignorance or to love of the scenic rather than the commercial aspect of forestry on the part of the landowner.'

Joking apart, if a man does not cut down his trees at the proper time, it really means that he does not take the job seriously. That has been the case in England far too long.

People want quick returns, and nothing is less quick than the returns of forestry – though if the whole thing is planned systematically there is a splendid ultimate return and *continuous* takings the whole time on faggots, firewood, stakes, spars, poles, fencing material, shaws, and hurdles. Unfortunately the general attitude towards planting trees is a feeling that only after one is dead will the rewards be coming in. We are reminded of Dr Johnson's saying – 'Most men when exhorted to plant a tree begin *to think of dying.*' They are discouraged by the thought that they shall not live to see the pecuniary profit of their endeavour. A sad reflection, which only serves to make out a case for State Ownership in order to arrest the decay of British Forestry. Yet any man who is in a position to go in for it, is with absolute certainty carrying out noble work, supplying the material for countless things necessary to the life of mankind, work which also has a moral and beautiful aspect. Cobbett, who saw much profit in the business, proving it with facts and figures for his day at any rate, also reminds us of La Fontaine's fable of *The Old Man and the The Three Young Men* – 'the wise, the generous, the noble sentiments of which ought to be implanted in every human breast ... I beg those, who may happen not to understand French, to be pleased to receive, from my pen, the following statement of the mere prosaic meaning of these words, for this absolutely inimitable writer, who, in marks of simplicity the most pleasing that ever followed the movements of a pen, has, on numerous subjects, left, to ages unborn, philosophy the most profound and sentiments the most just and exalted.' After which inimitable introduction Cobbett gives the following translation of La Fontaine's fable.

A man of fourscore was planting trees. 'To *build* might pass; but to *plant* at such an age!' exclaimed THREE YOUNG MEN of the neighbourhood. 'Surely,' said they, 'you are doting; for in God's name, what *reward* can you receive for this, unless you are to live as long as one of the Patriarchs? What good can there be in loading your life with cares about a time you are never destined to see? Pray devote the rest of your life to thoughts on your past errors; give up distant and grand expectations: these become only us

343

YOUNG MEN.' 'They become not even you,' answered the OLD MAN. 'All we do comes late and is quickly gone. The pale hand of fate sports equally with your days and with mine. The shortness of our lives puts us all on a level. Who can say which of us shall last behold the light of heaven? Can any moment of your lives even secure you a second moment? My great-grandchildren will owe shady groves to me: And do you blame me for providing delight for others! Why, the thought of this is, itself, a *reward* which I *already* enjoy; I may enjoy it tomorrow and for some days after that; nay, I may more than once even see the sun rise on your graves.' The OLD MAN was right: one of the three, ambitious to see the New World, was drowned in the port; another pursuing fame in the service of Mars, was suddenly stopped by an unexpected shot; the third fell from a tree, on which he himself was putting a graff: and the OLD MAN, lamenting their sad end, engraved on their tomb the story here related.

21. *Experiments and Questions*

'Leaf by leaf crumbles the gorgeous year' wrote the poet. But sometimes the year really *falls*, comes crashing down. Thus here, in November when the leaves were ready to fall but had not done so owing to lack of wind, there suddenly came a tempest lasting a day and a night. Next morning I looked round in vain for leaves still at their stations and saw only one, the terminal leaf on the highest branch of a young hazel-bush: just that one, a battered flag that had not fallen. Immediately I stepped into winter.

There are not many beautiful autumn trees, when you come to think of it: not many, I mean, that amaze us like the terrific screens of beech leaves, the bright yellow of chestnut-trees, the workmanship put into the evening drapery of the larch and silver birch. These do amaze us however often we see the show; we never look on them with indifference: that the decay of the leaf should be the glory of the leaf, that its day of withering and downfall should rival the beauty of its first unfolding, is a perennial encouragement to all mankind. I do not make any great claim for the ash as a particularly good autumn tree, I think it

344

takes the winter best; but no tree at this time of year displays a more fascinating scheme of seeds – the famous 'bunch of keys', inaptly called.

At this point I must quote Cobbett again (it is always a job to refrain from quoting him if he has touched upon a matter in hand, but I do my best to refrain, recognizing that it is my business unfortunately to give you Collis and not Cobbett). 'If you be curious and have a mind to see a tree in embryo,' he writes, 'take an *ash* seed, put it into a little water lukewarm, and there let it remain for three or four days. Take it out: take a sharp knife, split the seed longways down the middle, and there you will see, standing as upright as a dart, an *ash* tree, with leaves, trunk, and stem; that is to say the head of the root: and all this you will see with the naked eye, as clearly as you ever saw an *ash* tree growing in a field or meadow.'

Being extremely eager to see this I tried the experiment carefully. But I did not see it. I often tried but I never saw the little tree. Using a razor blade I slit the casket that holds the kernel, according to instructions, and I did find something. I found a very neat miniature *spade*. It was exceedingly attractive and surprising to look at, but it was not a tree.

William Cobbett is one of the most convincing writers who ever lived; even when wholly wrong, even when making a prophecy such as that the locust-tree will, in fifty years, be the most common in England (owing to his advocacy), even then he is so unqualified in the certitude of his tone that we feel that we *ought* to see locust-trees everywhere. And it may be that he was not right in this claim about the embryo *ash* tree. But I am inclined to think that the fault lies with me. This sort of thing, curiously enough, is often a matter of psychology. Experiments *don't work* for me. For other men, or rather for a scientist (who is a special kind of person), the right thing happens at the right time. The great scientist – and of course we are not thinking of anyone like Cobbett – is a man to whom things *occur*. He is not only a man of great research and organization of particulars, he is a man for whom things occur. An example of how they do not occur for me might amuse a reader willing to wander for just a moment away from trees. When wishing to acquaint myself with the life and habits of earth-worms, I studied as my chief source of information Charles Darwin's book *The Formation of Vegetable Mould Through the Action of Worms*, published in 1881 by John Murray. Amongst other things, he established by careful experimental proof how the worms manage slowly to bury objects, from stones to cities, if left alone. One day, when strolling in a great Cathedral Cloister, I observed that the grass in the middle contained many flat-slabbed tombstones, some modern, some quite ancient. How interesting, I thought, here I shall be able to see the result of worm-burial before my eyes. I saw a modern stone, 1921, how it was level with the grass, and near it another stone, 1804, which had sunk a considerable distance below the surface. This was excellent. I walked round so that I might see the old tombstones well sunk while the newer ones were still on the surface. I came to Martha Hunt, of Beloved Memory, dated 1870, and then to Nathaniel Groves, Resting in the Lord, dated 1791. But Martha Hunt's tombstone had sunk lower than that of Nathaniel Groves! Trying not to notice this, I passed on and continued to conduct my researches. Some of the other stones conformed to the requirements of the theory, but not all. Coming upon Arthur Mackensie of Beloved Memory, dated 1801, and then upon Elizabeth Wakefield, in Loving Memory of, dated 1910, I was grieved to see that the latter was lower than the former.

I need not say that I do not at all dispute Darwin's findings. Apart from the fact that a hundred reasons could doubtless be given as to why these particular stones were as they were, I feel confident that no fault lay with the worms. It is merely psychologically impossible for things of this kind to turn out well for me. Had Darwin experimented here, we can be sure that the tombstones would have arranged themselves in the proper order. The poet is the man who sees. The philosopher is the man who thinks. The man-of-action is the man who knows what to do. The scientist is the man who discovers. These are special kinds of men, as is soon found by any Tom, Dick, or Harry who assuming the role of one, attempts to see or to think or to

346

lead or to experiment. I fear that I have nothing of the scientist in me, nothing of the naturalist or botanist; I shall never propose a theory supported by experimental proof, I shall never discover anything, never make new things known. I am content to make known things new.

Sometimes I am willing to ask a question. But not often, owing to the difficulty of getting a reply. For instance, I cannot understand why all woods are not found on the highest part of the land. Should not all woods be on hills? It is remarkable what colossal results follow upon minute and slow processes. We see this everywhere, not least in the famous case of the earth-worm; and we might well be pardoned if we failed to believe that the mighty rocks of the early world could ever, by any process however slow, have been changed into soil. Now trees are things which in winter are one size and in summer another size, for they put on clothes called leaves. In the winter a given tree may look quite small—and in the summer enormous. Just outside my window there is a particular example of this, a silver birch. In the winter its marvellous network of twigs gives it a frail look, but when it becomes enleafed the change is remarkable; by midsummer it is a towering substance, a mighty mammoth of a tree standing there in the dusk huge and monumental. In the autumn it does not retain this extra substance, it lets it all fall to the ground. And those leaves do not all evaporate, many of them become vegetable mould. How is it then that after a few years, let alone a few centuries, a forest will not have added enormously to the ground on which it stands? They say that the fungi feed on this decay; but surely not enough. And the amount in evaporation doesn't seem likely to be equivalent to the deposit, and we cannot say that as much has been taken from the earth in order to make the leaves as is given by their fall, since they take huge supplies also from the air. They weave the atmosphere into visible shape. On a single oak-tree seven million leaves have been counted. These leaves hang there throughout the country in perpetual slight motion in the ever-moving air, and by the conjured labours of millions of pores the substance of whole forests of solid wood is slowly extracted from the fleeting winds. Every year it rains heavily, it rains leaves, these leaves woven from the winds. Why is there not a mountainous result quite soon where there are woods? This question may be stupid, but I do not find that the answers I have ever received are very good.

Another thing. Why do we not notice a great change of air in the summer from what it was in the winter? There are those leaves extracting that vast amount of gas from the air, a process not active in winter, and yet we do not seem to suffer from it, do not notice any difference. Again, this question may seem too obviously the mark of an uninstructed mind; but I am relieved to find that Mr H. E. Bates says that this very thing does affect him personally. 'It is as though – perhaps actually because – the air has been sucked up by a million leaves.' And he goes on to say (in *Through The Wood*), 'W. H. Hudson himself noticed this and had some comments on it in relation to the New Forest, where he felt that the great expanse of trees seemed to suck up all life and leave the mind and body and spirit as flabby as a sponge. He pointed out how pale the Hampshire people of that district looked, as though they were literally robbed of air.'

But one does not raise such questions with much hope of replies from specialists. They are far better at naming things than in answering questions of interest. If they can name a problem they often think they have solved it. 'Perhaps nothing is more curious in the history of the human mind,' said Ruskin, 'than the way in which the science of botany has become oppressed with nomenclature.' Thus do they overcome the problems of reality by simply labelling reality, just as in other departments the significance of a man's point of view, his truth in which he passionately believes, is side-stepped by a label – his truth becoming merely an -ism. Still, I do not worry myself about getting answers to my question. I rather like not getting them. And I can truthfully say that the phenomenon itself is good enough for me. Gazing upon phenomena, I find that my problems are not solved; but they are dissolved.

And of all phenomena concerning trees, that which appeals to me most is – the trunk. For me the most beautiful sight in the woods is not the foliage, not the flowers, not the squirrel, not the deer – it is the trunks of trees of about thirty years old upwards. Especially the ash: the smooth grey bark; then a patch of dark moss; above it a patch of pale-green lichen in beatiful fili-gree pressed against the bark; then a number of white spots; then bark again; then moss again – no pattern, yet all pattern, no design yet all design, making a rounded tapestry beyond all the powers of art to render. No bright colours yet many colours – and in winter-time how often we see from the train window, tree-trunks almost as green as grass set in the gloom of the leafless boughs, taking the rain and the dusk in silent alertness. Once, having been given four freshly cut logs of silver birch, I did not burn them (in any case they wouldn't have been good as fire), but put them on a shelf as pictures. And I assure you they held my attention for many a day. Often I have been glad that I am not a painter; never more so than when confronted by some magnificent tree-trunk. Here is something that cannot be told, cannot be rendered. Here is the object, the thing itself, so stag-gering in its presence that we fall back from it, the intricacy of the totality cannot be copied, and it is the intricacy that is the picture; before it the art of suggestion is powerless, only the lower art of photograph can give the total sum of the minutiae. Look at that old silver-birch trunk: knuckled, notched, and dented with its ditches, ruts, and causeways, all subservient to the majesty of design; look at the splashes of smooth white irregularly placed, the bark itself, not lichen: if a house-painter did a post with dabs of white here and there like that we would think it a poor, strange piece of work: but here it is magnificent, the impression of the Whole is terrific – we must leave our pen, our brush in face of it, abandon art as a hopeless substitute. Look at that old Scotch pine-tree. It has no lichen, all the beauty is in the bark alone: rubbed, fluted, seamed, deeply chiselled, it is a personality, it is a Being. Perhaps that's what I'm after here in these fumbling words: the power and the glory here is in the *substance* of the thing, and art is without substance.

Truly trees are Beings. We feel that to be so. Hence their

silence, their indifference to us is almost exasperating. We would speak to them, we would ask their message; for they seem to hold some weighty truth, some special secret – and though sometimes we receive their blessing, they do not answer, they make no sign. When we look upon a man we find that he is not satisfied, he wishes he were something else, or had done something else. When we look upon a monkey we see that clearly it is a lost soul. When we look upon a sheep we see that it is unhappy in itself. When we look upon a cow we cannot be certain that underneath its apparent calm it is not concealing a great unease. Whitman said that he could turn and live with the animals. I would not join him. But many men have turned and lived with trees. They are much more companionable than cows. Thoreau would sometimes refuse to make an engagement with a friend on the ground that he had 'an appointment with a tree'. What then is their final appeal, their message to mankind? Isaac Rosenberg alone has told it.

> Then spake I to the tree,
> Were ye your own desire
> What is it ye would be?
> Answered the tree to me,
> I am my own desire;
> I am what I would be.

22. Firewood

While carrying out my business of thinning the wood I piled up the thick poles which I had cut down, in batches of a hundred – for, working by the piece, I made so much per lug and so much per hundred poles. These piles of poles made a very satisfactory sight for me, since they were carried away at intervals to be used as firewood in the neighbouring village, superb firewood at that. It gave me considerable pleasure to know that one result of my work up here was that I supplied wood for a whole village throughout the winter. At irregular periods it was carted away by Reggie and the boys. I would hear his high voice from a long way off, shouting at the horse, and about half an hour later they would arrive with the trailer which they used for loading up.

One of the reasons why I am especially attracted by ash is because it has so much fire in it. That may not be the proper way to put it; but it certainly seems as if flame resides inside the wood. When we have *put fire* to wood, what do we see? We do not see the fire *devouring* the wood as it goes along: we see the wood *becoming fire*, 'bursting into flames' as we say. Everything has fire in it, we are told, even stones – though it takes much extra heat to set a stone on fire. Of all the receptacles of fire in the world, wood is the most famous and our debt to it without measure. It is easy to understand how the ancient Aryans regarded trees as the *store-rooms* of heat and that the sun itself was periodically recruited from the fire which resided in the sacred oak.

And of all trees, Ash becomes fire best. It need not be seasoned first, it burns almost equally well whether dry or cut down yesterday. If you cut down a bundle of fresh, green ash-twigs they do perfectly for lighting your fire, they are ready-made crackers, they are children's fireworks. Try the same thing with hazel and you'll never get your fire lit at all. Whenever I go to any new place in the country I look round at once to see if there are any ash woods nearby, for if so I know that I need not depend upon dry twigs for lighting fires. To my amazement I found many woodmen ignorant of this, while one or two who were not ignorant of it gave me surprising examples of wasteful folly caused by such ignorance. Observing the old man who worked with Reggie and the boys, taking home some hazel-faggots for his fire when there were heaps of ash around, I asked him why. He simply said that he had always done so. The fact that he had always done so was advanced in terms of a scientific statement that hazel made as good faggots as ash.

I used to take home a pole every day from the wood, and thus I was always in command of a magnificent fire – costing me nothing save the labour of carriage. Then the bitter cold of a winter's evening was transformed by the white-hot wood and I was nearly as happy in front of this earthly flame as in the summer under the sun.

I need not say that this job stimulated my interest in the financial aspect of fire-logs. All of us here were paid as wood-men, so much a week, or so much the piece; but occasionally I became familiar with the other sort of woodmen who, working on their own, made a good deal more by simply extracting wood and selling it – without any interest in the plantation. They made more, but of course they had to work hard for it, and to take risks. The man who really makes big profits is the man at the far end who distributes it – the man who neither plants, thins, tends, or extracts the wood. When I learnt the surprising prices charged for a sack of logs in the neighbouring towns, I realized that if you want to get rich in modern society you should not aim at securing the Means of Production, but rather the Means of Distribution. For today it is written – Blessed is he who distributes.

23. Winter Scenes: The Calamity

I looked forward during the day to my superb evening fires in the winter months. It is not often very cold in a wood even when it is biting outside, in fact the difference in temperature on the same day in the wood as against the field, is sometimes phenomenal. Nevertheless there were spells when my hands were too cold to grip the axe and the wind so keen that no amount of work served to make me warm. At such times I wanted to get away from the wood – though not into any other agricultural job.

Often it was merely damp, windless, and dreary. At such times I felt curiously lonely amongst the trees, in a pleasantly sad sort of way. The silence was so melancholy, the mystery of the trees and the dark undergrowth so great, that I felt exiled from truth as well as from mankind. I used to grope my way in explorations into the deeper darknesses beyond my immediate position, peering round with something of the expectancy and the fear of a man in a haunted house.

I frequently came upon fresh examples of fallen trunks lying on the ground in various stages of decomposition: there were some great hulks whose outer crust was as soft as earth, and whose inner caverns, on being exposed by the bill-hook, revealed curious insects curled up here and there in holes evidently intended as dormitories for the winter. That was one type; but there was another I almost preferred – the long trunk, sunk low, covered with moss and leafage, becoming indistinguishable from the ground as it tapered to what was once its top. I had one favourite of this kind. It was considerably long: the thickest end was like a mound, and it gradually tapered on getting smaller and smaller until it became level with the ground, and only the freshness of the moss showed me where the 'wood' was. And if I walked along upon this strange rise, it was exactly as if I were walking upon something as soft as a mountain swamp.

The moss was deep and clear upon these barks. It was also

laid across the whole floor of the wood. In the winter one becomes conscious of this new glory. When the spring flowers are long forgotten and the new series is in hidden preparation out of sight and of thought; when the bracken that rose so high and green has browned and fallen down; when the herb-willow has posted its final envelope of seed; when the latest storm has removed the last leaves from tree and bush; when the long, low kingdom of dog's mercury has disappeared – then the ground is not bare, it is not desolate: it shines again with a new growth; we enter the reign of moss. This is one of the sweetest and dearest of all plants. We think of it in the mass and speak of winding mossy ways, as so we should; but if we look close we see that it is a network of the most delicate little fronds whose massed formations give us the soft, deep carpet. It is not seen during the summer, and where we do discern it, it is parched and poor; but in the chill of winter when all other life is in abeyance this is in the ascendant, the floor of the earth is cushioned and all the scars of mortality are bandaged and made blessed.

During the short winter days I sometimes arrived in the wood while the moon was still the only light, and day had not yet broken in. At this hour, before the particular beam of the sun had changed the scene, the atmosphere was expectant. Nature appeared to be listening carefully for something and was evidently awaiting some great event. I did not dare say a word, even to cough. Objects which in the light of day were animated only with the life of plants, became informed with the life of beasts, so that mere bushes looked like tigers about to spring. When the day broke in at last it did not do so slowly as it is supposed to do in these climes, there came a moment when the darkness began to lighten up quite steadily and swiftly. The moon started to go out as if someone were turning down a lamp rather gingerly, and the light of the hidden sun illuminated the scene almost at the rate of theatrical lights slowly bathing a stage that had been in darkness.

At other times, arriving on a misty morning, I found that the wood was of immense size, receding into the distance on all sides as if it were boundless in space and belonging to any Age. The boles of the trees, erect in the mist, were as thin and pale as the pencillings in a Chinese drawing. They had no strength or substance: it would have been easy to rub them all out of the picture. As the day advanced and the sun rose to cancel the morning mist, the scene shifted. The Present Day came back again, the wood occupied a given number of acres, the trees were hard and firm once more. Then the afternoon sun was turned upon them, and they held the light, they stopped it and took it upon themselves, each a shining post, while the wind blew and the strange, unhappy hours passed by – for even in a wood at this time of the day, more so in a wood than elsewhere when the wind blows unceasingly, all solitary men are perplexed and feel the motion of infelicity.

These were days when a hot drink was the very thing in the course of the morning, and I never forgot to bring out my thermos-flask. Its cap was broken, lacking which I generally brought a china cup with me. But sometimes I forgot this item. However, I had a remedy when this happened. At this time of the year many more varieties of fungi attracted my attention. There was one species which particularly appealed to me. It was pale yellow and shaped like a large wine-glass. On the occasions when I forgot to bring out my cup I simply plucked one of these stalked cups made of fungus, filled it from my thermos-flask, and thus had my drink in comfort.

It was not possible to do much work in the intense cold nor in heavy rain. When it rained slightly it was quite all right, and many a time when I should have had to seek shelter if in the fields, I could carry on in the wood without a raincoat. But a continuously wet day made it impossible (especially earlier in the year when the leaves were still on the trees, for then your stroke brought down a great deal of extra water upon you) for the axe then became too slippery to hold. When it snowed my work stopped immediately, of course. I have often referred here to the silences peculiar to the woodman's life; but is there any silence so deep and rare as that bestowed by snow? Whether in a wood, or outside, it is a wonderful thing in our machine age to find the world in the morning ankle-deep in snow. Then the unwonted silence that falls upon our life is truly magnificent; and when the snow has been really heavy making all lanes and many roads impassable, the sense of isolation in our silence carries us right back to the days when communication even between villages was scarce and chequered. One heavy fall of snow in the country, and modern civilization is *silenced*!

These winter scenes are related in my mind with another scene, more human and more sad. Reggie occasionally came across from his part of the estate to see me. I think of a certain Friday when I heard him call my name (he used my Christian name), and appeared coming through the trees with his dog and his gun, which he often carried. He had some agricultural extra clothing-coupons to give me, and brought a paper for me to sign. And then we fell into conversation about this and that, his early life in Devon, the present life here, the wages young boys got nowadays and what they did with the money, his rank of Corporal in the Home Guard, and so on. He draped himself against a tree as usual, his remarkable flaxen hair, his brown face, and workman's clothes fitting into the surroundings perfectly and, indeed, beautifully. Thus we stood and talked upon the general affairs of life, amongst the friendly trees, well cornered from the rough traffic of the world, far away from the great battles that were then being fought, insensible in this leafy harbour to the noise and rumour of the field, secure from calamity and the sudden dart of death, or so it seemed. Presently he went away. He called to his little genteel black dog, and disappeared through the trees out of my sight, and went across a field towards the scene of his death. For he was never to return along these ways nor would that voice be heard in the woods any more. Later in the afternoon there was a dreadful explosion, louder and more earth-shaking than others I had heard in the neighbourhood, due to the practising soldiery. This explosion was not made by the army. Reggie had picked up a bomb which he imagined was quite harmless. He had brought it back to his shed. He thought it was a smoke-bomb of some sort and decided to examine its interior. Finding it difficult to dismantle, he took a hammer and began to tap it. The boys, who were standing near, became frightened and tried to dissuade him; but he sat there bending over the bomb, tapping at it. It exploded, blowing his hands off and killing him – the boys escaping death, but not injury.

The whole village shuddered at this meaningless tragedy. The catastrophe of our time was focused upon the body of this one man, cut down suddenly in the midst of abounding life.

24. Farewell to the Wood

In the company of flowers we know happiness. In the company of trees we are able to *think*, they foster meditation. Trees are very intellectual. There is nowhere on earth we can think so well as in a thin wood resting against a tree. Such at least is my experience, and it is the ultimate memory that I shall carry away from this place. For in parting I know that the greatest wrench of all is in connection with the old oak-tree (under which or in the vicinity of which I have written this account). It is not easy to say farewell to it; not easy to pass from the best spot in the whole world between the hours of eight and ten in the morning during May and August. For, as I have said, that is the time when the sun rested upon my seat.

Sometimes I could wish that my love of the sun were less genuine. How often I have felt compelled to alter my plans for the day's work because the sun unexpectedly came out to shine against my special tree or on some other favourite spot! I have been about to do a portion of thinning marked out as the minimum for the morning, when, the sun coming out, I have abandoned my schedule in order to seize, if only for a few cloud-chequered intervals, the gift of the sun at that hour, in that blessed place. I have had to turn back for the same reason, while on my way into the neighbouring town to get some much-needed things. The sun deflects me from my courses. I mention this as the kind of psychological fact that holds a certain interest, since we scarcely allow enough for the part such things play in the destinies of men. I often wonder at anyone accepting the Materialistic Conception of History. Many people, after Marx, began to say that circumstances are the cause of any given life. But since circumstances can be inside one as well as outside, the dictum holds little absolute meaning. Put two men in front of me, equal in talent, similar in circumstance, one loving, the other indifferent to the sun, and I will roughly out-line their careers. The man who really loved the sun would miss vital appointments, fumble momentous opportunities: the other would forge ahead. No self-made rich industrialist has ever loved the sun. Such a man may well benefit mankind, it is not to be denied. But also, that other man, in receiving into himself that warmth and that light, may perchance give back something to his fellows, tell something of what he has felt, what he has *known*, illuminate the darkness of the exiled, even raise up the parched and withering hearts of men. Let me then take a knife and inscribe upon the ancient oak these words — INDECISIVE, FOOLISH, SELFISH, LAZY: A MAN MAY BE ALL THAT AND WORSE, AND YET BE A BENEFACTOR OF THE WORLD, IF HE BUT LOVE TO SIT IN THE SUN LEANING AGAINST A TREE!

Having inscribed those words, I must take my leave. I shall return to this spot. It will remain the same tomorrow as today. When I return I will step back in time. I will step out of time. For one of the things that has struck me most about this wood, or of any sequestered wood known to me, is that having turned off from your road and entered the wood, you have really gone through a *gate* which now is closed behind you, and your ordi-nary world is shut out with all its noise and sorrow and care. Once inside, you seem to have stepped out of the flow of civi-lized time and to have entered into the peace of the ever-juvenile eternities of earth. The road along which you have come may be in a lonely rural retreat; but it belongs to your century and as you go along it you are in the atmosphere of that century. You enter the wood — and you might just as well be in the Middle Ages. When I hear people speak of the Dark Ages,

I remind myself how in those days the sun shone in just the same way as it does now, and the flowers glittered in woods where there was no difference from what we see today. Outside we have to think our way back into the past, trying to picture the village then, the lie of the land, the agricultural equipment. Inside the wood we are in the past as well as in the present. Perhaps the time will come when people will speak of these days as the Black Ages or the Darker Ages; if so let them then turn and read my words here and remember that the sun shone upon us even as upon them, that the trees looked the same in the glory of his light, and that at this time also you could side-step into happiness and peace.

Thus I attempt to say farewell, as I look around at this secluded scene. I look across at my sun-dial, wondering if that will be still there when I come again. For in the actual prosaic matter of knowing the hour of day I had no watch and worked outside the whole clock-world and dwelt far from the frame of mind of the B.B.C. announcer who says 'It is just coming up to half a minute to eight'. But I did not quite dispense with a clock. I used the lofty, golden time-piece of the sun and a tree which cast a clear, clean shadow with its trunk. At exactly twelve o'clock I stuck a stick in the shadow-line. Thus I always knew when it was twelve so long as the clock was unclouded. I put in other sticks for other hours, and so could tell the time of day within half an hour.

I look across at the growing and maturing trees now free from all entanglements. I had come to a wild entanglement, and now, as far as I can see in any direction, a free plantation meets my eye, accomplished by the labour of my hands alone. Nothing that I have ever done has given me more satisfaction than this, nor shall I hope to find again so great a happiness. Realizing something of what the work meant to me, and perhaps truthfully saying that he was very pleased with the result, Rolf entered this area of about twelve acres, in the books of the Estate, as COLLIS PIECE, and by that name it is now known. Thus then do I achieve what had never occurred to me could conceivably happen, that a piece of English earth and forest would carry my name into the future. Nobody is ever likely to confer upon me Honours or Titles or City Freedoms, nor will any Monument be raised to perpetuate and repeat my name. But this plot of earth will do it, these trees will do it: in the summer they will glitter and shine for me, and in the winter, mourn.

INDEX

INDEX

MORE ABOUT PENGUINS, PELICANS
AND PUFFINS

For further information about books available from Penguins please write to Dept EP, Penguin Books Ltd, Harmondsworth, Middlesex UB7 0DA.

In the U.S.A.: For a complete list of books available from Penguins in the United States write to Dept DG, Penguin Books, 299 Murray Hill Parkway, East Rutherford, New Jersey 07073.

In Canada: For a complete list of books available from Penguins in Canada write to Penguin Books Canada Limited, 2801 John Street, Markham, Ontario L3R 1B4.

In Australia: For a complete list of books available from Penguins in Australia write to the Marketing Department, Penguin Books Australia Ltd, P.O. Box 257, Ringwood, Victoria 3134.

In New Zealand: For a complete list of books available from Penguins in New Zealand write to the Marketing Department, Penguin Books (N.Z.) Ltd, Private Bag, Takapuna, Auckland 9.

In India: For a complete list of books available from Penguins in India write to Penguin Overseas Ltd, 706 Eros Apartments, 56 Nehru Place, New Delhi 110019.

A choice of Penguins

ROBIN PAGE

WEATHER FORECASTING
THE COUNTRY WAY

Observation of animal behaviour, plant growth or the wind, clouds, stars
and moon is an ancient and well-tried method of weather forecasting. You
may, for example, know what happens if it rains on St Swithen's Day or if
there is a red sky at night, but what if it snows at Easter or if spiders spin
long webs?

In this delightful book, Robin Page demonstrates that, by applying common
sense to country lore, you need never have your holidays rained off again!

THE COUNTRY WAY
OF CURES AND REMEDIES

Many of the old reliable cures and remedies have existed unchanged
for generations. Some are unreliable, but many are soundly based – as
twentieth-century medicine has discovered. Robin Page has included the
well-tried and tested cures in his enchanting book. Simple, inexpensive and
effective, they offer new interest to being off-colour.

COOKERY AND GARDENING IN PENGUINS

☐ *The Complete Barbecue Book* **James Marks**   £4.95

Advice on all aspects of barbecuing, plus mouth-watering recipes (including stuffed aubergines, bananas Diana, tangy steak strips) make this the most useful and inspired book on 'al fresco' entertaining.

☐ *A History of British Gardening* **Miles Hadfield**   £5.95

From Tudor knot gardens to present fashions, and from arboriculture to kitchen gardens: 'an extraordinarily rich harvest of valuable and entertaining information . . . it is hard to see that it can ever be superseded' – *Journal of the Royal Horticultural Society*

☐ *Jane Grigson's Vegetable Book*   £4.50

From the cabbage to the Chinese leaf, a modern kitchen guide to the cooking of vegetables by 'the most engaging food writer to emerge during the last few years' – *The Times*

These books should be available at all good bookshops or newsagents, but if you live in the UK or the Republic of Ireland and have difficulty in getting to a bookshop, they can be ordered by post. Please indicate the titles required and fill in the form below.

NAME _____ BLOCK CAPITALS

ADDRESS _____

_____

_____

Enclose a cheque or postal order payable to The Penguin Bookshop to cover the total price of books ordered, plus 50p for postage. Readers in the Republic of Ireland should send £IR equivalent to the sterling prices, plus 67p for postage. Send to: The Penguin Bookshop, 54/56 Bridlesmith Gate, Nottingham, NG1 2GP.

You can also order by phoning (0602) 599295, and quoting your Barclaycard or Access number.

Every effort is made to ensure the accuracy of the price and availability of books at the time of going to press, but it is sometimes necessary to increase prices and in these circumstances retail prices may be shown on the covers of books which may differ from the prices shown in this list or elsewhere. This list is not an offer to supply any book.

This order service is only available to residents in the UK and the Republic of Ireland.

● ● ●